PUBLICATIONS ON ASIA OF THE INSTITUTE
FOR COMPARATIVE AND FOREIGN AREA STUDIES, NUMBER 27

POLITICAL LEADERSHIP IN KOREA

EDITED BY

Dae-Sook Suh and Chae-Jin Lee

UNIVERSITY OF WASHINGTON PRESS

SEATTLE AND LONDON

Published with the support of a grant from the Joint Committee on Korean Studies of the Social Science Research Council and the American Council of Learned Societies.

LIBRARY OF CONGRESS CATALOGING IN PUBLICATION DATA
Main entry under title:

Political leadership in Korea.

(Publications on Asia of the Institute for Comparative and Foreign Area Studies ; no. 27)
Selected papers presented at two symposia held in Seoul during the summers of 1971 and 1972 under the auspices of the University of Washington, Seattle.
Includes bibliographical references and index.
1. Korea—Politics and government—Addresses, essays, lectures. 2. Leadership—Addresses, essays, lectures.
3. Bureaucracy—Addresses, essays, lectures. I. Suh, Dae-sook, 1931- II. Lee, Chae-Jin, 1936-
III. Series: Washington (State). University. Institute for Comparative and Foreign Area Studies. Publications on Asia ; no. 27.
JQ1725.A1P65   1976   320.9'519   76-5480
ISBN 0-295-95437-X

Publications on Asia of the Institute for Comparative and Foreign Area Studies is a continuation of the series formerly entitled Far Eastern and Russian Institute Publications on Asia.

To the future leaders of Korea

Acknowledgments

This volume contains selected papers presented at two symposia on Korean leadership held in Seoul during the summers of 1971 and 1972. The symposia were held under the auspices of the University of Washington, Seattle, and were directed and organized by Dr. George M. Beckmann, Dean of the College of Arts and Sciences of that university. Dean Beckmann was assisted in his efforts by Professor Dong-Suh Bark of Seoul National University and Professor Chae-Jin Lee of the University of Kansas.

Grateful acknowledgment is also due to those scholars who engaged in thoughtful and critical discussion in the symposia and to those who gave valuable advice on the papers compiled in this volume. Their names are too numerous to mention here individually. The second symposium was held at the Asiatic Research Center of Korea University, and thanks are owing to the Center for the use of its facilities.

Our appreciation is also extended to the Institute for Comparative and Foreign Area Studies of the University of Washington for aid in preparing the manuscript for publication, particularly the able assistance of Ms. Margery Lang in the final editing of the papers. The two symposia and this volume were assisted by a substantial grant from the Ford Foundation and by a smaller grant from the Joint Committee on Korean Studies of the Social Science Research Council and the American Council of Learned Societies.

We also express our appreciation to the center for Korean Studies at the University of Hawaii for the initial editing and typing of the entire manuscript.

THE EDITORS

Contents

Introduction

The need to study political leadership can hardly be overstated, particularly in a country such as Korea, whose political order has been transformed from stagnant monarchy to subjugated colony and finally divided nation without the emergence of a national leader or group of leaders, charismatic or otherwise, who could command the respect of the entire people. Despite the importance of leadership studies, however, there is no definitive study of a monarch or political leader of the traditional Korean kingdom that delineates the unique elements of Korean leadership style, nor is there a comprehensive study of the leaders of the Korean independence movement. Likewise, there is an almost total lack of such studies for the postwar period, during which the division of the country has produced leaders with disparate ideologies alien to Korea's traditional heritage and culture.

Perhaps it is difficult to characterize the nation's political leaders because of the nature of the Korean struggle against foreign domination. Political assassins and extremists are often eulogized as leaders without due appraisal of the direction and effects of their activities. Much of the literature available on Korean leaders was written by sycophants and servile flatterers of those about whom they wrote. In order to understand modern Korea, it is imperative that objective examinations of the political leadership styles of Syngman Rhee, Kim Il-sŏng, and Pak Chŏng-hŭi be undertaken.

The efforts in this volume are not intended to meet the need for such a comprehensive study of Korean leadership, but they are a modest beginning. The magnitude of the task necessitates that they be only an introductory examination of the problem. And a long list of disclaimers might be added. This volume is not a biographical sketch of important leaders, traditional or contemporary, nor is it a systematic exposition of all major phases of political leadership. Some important groups with strong impact on political leadership, for example, military, economic, and cultural leadership groups, are not treated here. Rather than dwell upon the disclaimers, however, it is more appropriate to introduce the nature of the attempts and some of the findings of these preliminary investigations.

This book is a product of a two-year collaborative research project in which twelve scholars studied and analyzed selected aspects of political leadership in Korea. Along with a succinct analysis of traditional leaderhip of the Yi dynasty, it includes examinations of legislative leadership, party leadership, bureaucratic leadership, and popular perceptions of political leadership in South Korea. To these have been added two studies of Communist political leadership in North Korea, one analyzing the leadership group of the Central Committee of the Workers' Party of Korea and the other analyzing the adoption of a new constitution in the fifth Supreme People's Assembly in December 1972 and the reconstituted leadership of the North. The final chapter presents a summary of our studies. Admittedly, the volume concentrates more on modern Korea than traditional Korea and, understandably, contains more empirical research on South Korea than on North Korea.

The first essay by James Palais, on political leadership in the Yi dynasty, presents a good example of royal leadership style in King Sejong, probably the most outstanding ruler of the dynasty. It also deals with the Machiavellian leader Yŏnsan'gun, an archtyrant, and the Taewŏn'gun, who was not a king at all, but exercised assertive leadership as regent for his son. This essay shows that the Yi dynasty had its great monarchs at its beginning, later surviving without able men at the top. It also examines the roles played by bureaucratic leaders, aristocrats and the literati, and rebel leaders.

Korean royal leadership in general suffered from four major restraints. The king was relatively weak because he was a member of the Sinitic cosmological order. Second, his bureaucracy was controlled by the yangban, and the aristocracy and bureaucratic institutions were means to check royal authority. Third, the king was unable to cut into the wealth and privileges of the upper class, and, finally, the king was subject to the restraints of the universally accepted Confucian norms of regal conduct. Leadership style was constrained by the dynastic structure and institutions, the values of the society, and tradition. There was no room for the exercise of charismatic leadership in the Yi dynasty.

The next three essays deal with legislative, party, and bureaucratic leadership in South Korea. In an effort to assess the role of legislative leadership in democratic development, the performance of legislators in South Korea from 1948 to 1967 was studied to determine the extent of democratic commitment and the sources of democratic attitudes. Contrary to widespread ideas of a decline of legislative functions in South Korea, the study by Chong Lim Kim and Byung-Kyu Woo found no significant decline in the level of legislators' performances over time. There is, however, a remarkable correlation between legislative action and the degree of legislative autonomy. Another important finding in this study is the presence of a higher commitment to democratic principles among the legislators who were elected in urban districts and who were members of the opposition party. There was also found to be an inverse relationship between the level of formal education and the degree of democratic commitment among South Korean legislators.

Political parties are often claimed to play less than adequate roles in South Korea. The role of the opposition party in the political process is particularly said to be minimal. The study of party leadership by Bae-ho Hahn and Ha-ryong Kim attempts to ascertain the factors constraining South Korean party development. Its conclusion is that party leaders fail to play an influential role because of the strength of the administration, the reliance on nonparty organization, the aspect of Korean culture that stresses avoidance of interpersonal conflicts, and, finally, the lack of interest in organization. As a result, party leaders are prone to pursue personal interests at the expense of official party goals.

The study of administrative leadership is based on interviews with 176 senior bureaucrats whose values and attitudes are discussed within the broad context of their social background, administrative experience, and attitudes toward development. The dominance of the military in South Korea's government is given special attention by Dong-Suh Bark and Chae-Jin Lee in their comparison of the social, administrative, and developmental attributes of career civil servants with those of persons recruited from the military.

Interestingly, social and administrative variables such as educational level and administrative promotion in the South Korean bureaucratic elite were found to predict attitudes toward development better than such other variables as class origin, military professionalism, and administrative function. The study also shows that younger bureaucrats are not always more interested in development than their older colleagues, and that military service alone is insignificant as a determinant of commitment to national development. Another important finding of this study is that there is a propensity among South Korean bureaucrats to give lower priority to democratic political norms than to national security and

economic growth. The bureaucrats studied seem to be more authoritarian and unitarist than democratic and individualistic, and
they seem predisposed to constrain civil liberties and freedom of
the press for the sake of anti-Communist struggles, to demand individual sacrifices for the public interest, and to use whatever
methods necessary to achieve their tasks.

How do the people perceive their political leadership and what
do they expect from their leaders? The next study by Sung-chick
Hong and Young Ho Lee probes these questions by examining
three major criteria for democratic leadership: responsiveness,
legitimacy, and effectiveness. The study, which surveyed five segments of South Korean society—high school students, university
students, farmers, journalists, and legislative aids to national
assemblymen, assumes that repeated satisfaction with leaders leads
to citizen allegiance to the system and that disappointment leads
to alienation.

Hong and Lee's study suggests there is a strong undercurrent of
political alienation in South Korea. Leaders are often perceived to
be unresponsive to citizens' needs, illegitimate in their rule, self-
seeking, and inefficient in the performance of their duties. Such
negative reactions were more frequent among the urban and educated segments of the society than among the farmers. Among the
groups surveyed, the most negative were the university students
and journalists, while the farmers tended to be generally uncritical
of their leaders. The authors qualify their findings by stating that
South Korean leaders and government officials might indeed perform poorly, but the population's critical response may be the result of unrealistically high expectations. Whatever the case may be,
this empirical study indicates that South Koreans' perception of
their leaders and government officials is negative according to all
three criteria of democratic leadership.

Systematic analysis of North Korea is more difficult than a comparable study of the South because of the unavailability of source
materials and the inaccessibility of the leaders and the people to
researchers. The examination of North Korean leadership in this
volume is thus more confined in scope and method. The two
studies presented here attempt to assess North Korean leadership
by examining the structure of the leadership and the pattern of
change in the powerful Central Committee of the Workers' Party of
Korea. The first study by Dae-Sook Suh is a survey of change in
leadership from the first to the fifth party congresses; the second

study by Chong-Sik Lee is a discussion of the line-up of top leaders following the adoption of the new constitution in 1972.

Following the partition of Korea, the northern leaders induced change in their ranks by removing any and all who had ever collaborated with the Japanese. Thereafter, Kim Il-sŏng successfully eliminated all factional leaders and consolidated his position by recruiting younger leaders with proper education and "party spirit." By such weeding and recruiting, North Korean Communist leaders developed a unique system for accomplishing rapid change in leadership. Fewer than half the members of the Central Committee at any time have been re-elected to the succeeding Central Committee, and fewer than one-third of the candidate members have been promoted to full membership in the Central Committee. In most cases, this has limited members of the Central Committee to a single term. Excepted from this pattern are the old partisans from Kim's Manchurian guerrilla revolutionary days, his most significant group of supporters. The leadership of the Central Committee seems to have developed from a struggle among various factional groups into domination by a single group. Developments since 1966 indicate an intragroup struggle among partisans on policy issues. The North has effectively eliminated the old revolutionaries from the anti-Japanese revolutionary days and has successfully recruited new and younger leaders trained and educated under the North Korean system.

The leadership line-up following the adoption of the new constitution, the first overhaul in twenty-five years, is discussed in detail in the second study of Communist leadership. Close scrutiny of the leaders assigned to various new positions provides evidence that the North Korean political structure was vastly reorganized to conform to Kim's leadership style. Top leaders in the inner circle are those close to President Kim Il-sŏng, but a trend toward functional specialization among top leaders is also apparent. Various important government and party organs such as the presidency, the Central People's Committee, the State Administrative Council, the Supreme People's Assembly, the Secretariat, and the Political Committee of the Workers' Party of Korea are described to provide an up-to-date picture of North Korean leadership.

The final chapter is an effort to summarize impressions of the goals, needs, and methods of our investigation and to offer suggestions for subsequent exploration. Glenn Paige maintains that the goals of this type of undertaking should be to describe and explain, to compare, and to understand the behavior of political leaders. These kinds of studies may also assist leaders in executing their functions and increase citizen competence in assessing leadership performance. A few suggestions are made for improving future research on Korean political leadership and for conducting comparative analyses of North and South Korean political leaders. Of special importance for future efforts is a three-dimensional concept —more precise description and interpretation of leadership at the highest level, and engagement of scholars from various social sciences in the development of political leadership studies.

The need for methodological refinement is also pointed out, particularly the need for greater precision in definition of socioeconomic status variables, evaluation of ambiguous answers to questionnaires, development of a research design that will permit comparative analysis, and the need for making concepts more relevant and operational. Paige stresses the importance of studies that combine personality, role, organizational, task, value, and setting parameters of political leadership in future investigations.

The contributors to this volume hope this modest beginning will lead to many future inquiries into political leadership. In a country where an orderly constitutional transfer of power in the top leadership has yet to occur, the study of leadership style is important, to say the least. Whether applied to deciphering the political strategies of the leaders or as an aid to understanding their basic norms for the future of Korea, the study of political leadership is an important element in understanding the modern Korean political scene. In view of the authoritarian tendencies and general lack of democratic attitudes among top leaders in both North and South Korea, a basic inquiry into the culture that produces such leaders should also be undertaken as a prerequisite to the future study of political leadership. The emergence of a virtuous and benevolent leader, if not a fiery revolutionary, who can command the respect and popular support of all the people is sorely needed in a divided country such as Korea.

DAE-SOOK SUH
CHAE-JIN LEE

PART I

Traditional Perspectives

1. Political Leadership
in the Yi Dynasty

JAMES B. PALAIS

INTRODUCTION

Traditional Korean society during the Yi dynasty (1392–1910) was governed by a centralized bureaucratic monarchy. Its social structure was hierarchical and dominated by a powerful aristocracy, yangban, whose status was based, for the most part, on inheritance and reinforced by landholding, degree-holding, and office-holding. Since its economy was overwhelmingly agrarian, there was no significant bourgeoisie to challenge the political supremacy of the yangban bureaucrats. One of the major features of the Yi dynasty polity was the relative weakness of the monarchy and centralized authority because of the aristocratic, bureaucratic, and normative restraints on royal power.[1] For such a polity, therefore, it is possible to describe its elite groups and its leaders, but it is difficult to find examples of leadership if that term is interpreted in the narrow sense as the exercise of personal power and authority over and above the limits imposed by traditional structures and norms.[2]

Since legitimacy and supreme authority were vested in the king, only kings or those who controlled the throne could attempt to act independently or arbitrarily; but even royal power was hedged in with restraints. Authority was channeled into a single bureaucratic structure that served to restrict the potential for individual leadership. While there were certain bureaucrats who were more prominent than their peers and who made their mark on history by force of personality and political skill, very few had the opportunity to exert innovative leadership in the formulation of goals and policies. Bureaucratic organization produces great leaders only with the utmost difficulty, and the Yi dynasty bureaucracy was no exception. Work was ritualized, every functionary was the subordinate of some other functionary or of the king. Individual initiative was repressed because it constituted a challenge and threat to the career and

3

power of superiors. Abhorrence of excessive power was probably the main feature of the Yi dynasty polity.

Because authority and legitimacy were predominantly traditional-legal, as Max Weber has defined it, there was little opportunity for the exercise of charismatic leadership.[3] The legitimate leaders of traditional Korean society were kings, bureaucrats, local yangban gentry, and yangban literati. The only charismatic figures were rebels and leaders of heterodox religious movements, but all of these were suppressed by the state when they became a political threat to the established order. The opportunity for creative leadership only came with the weakening of the old order in the late nineteenth century, the nationalist and Communist movements of the early twentieth century, and the creation of new polities in North and South Korea after 1945.

ROYAL LEADERSHIP

The potential for leadership among the kings of the Yi dynasty was limited by the restraints on their authority. Korean kings suffered from four major types of problems. Their traditional legitimacy was relatively weak; they were engaged with the bureaucracy and the aristocracy in competition for political power; they had to compete with the landowning and privileged aristocracy for control over economic and man-power resources; and they were hamstrung by the normative restraints of Neo-Confucian thought.

The traditional authority of the Korean king was relatively weak as he was subordinate to the Chinese emperor in the Sinitic cosmological and political order—under the terms of the tributary system the king received investiture from the Chinese emperor. While this process of external legitimation never really interfered with the independent resolution of succession problems by the Koreans themselves (even in the case of usurpers), it did weaken the ideological basis for royal absolutism.

The second type of restraint on royal authority came from *de facto* control of the bureaucracy by the yangban. While the civil service examination system, which was the chief means of recruiting officials, was theoretically open to commoners as well as yangban, the yangban monopolized the system to the exclusion of other status groups. The yangban bureaucrats restricted the king's freedom to appoint and dismiss officials by their control of the Ministry of Personnel; they used the offices of the censorate[4] as a means of checking royal authority by constant and vigorous remonstrance; they used the Royal Secretariat to inhibit the flow of royal orders when it served their purpose; and they used the Royal Lectures to indoctrinate young kings in standards of Confucian morality of which they were the supreme arbiters. In short, the aristocracy used bureaucratic institutions as a means of checking royal authority instead of implementing royal commands.

One of the major symptoms of relative royal weakness and yangban bureaucratic strength was the appearance of bureaucratic factionalism, a phenomenon that colored Korean political life for over two centuries after 1575. Although individual kings were not always subordinated to the power of the factions, the existence of the factions meant that the kings had failed to keep individual bureaucrats isolated and therefore more susceptible to royal control.

Among the major reasons for the strength of the yangban bureaucrats vis-à-vis the throne was that they were not entirely dependent on the throne for their position in society. Because yangban status was in most instances inherited, the king could only try to control their access to the higher levels of society as represented by academic degrees and office-holding, but even in these instances his power was restricted. Although an individual official could lose favor and position at court, his family could maintain its status and recoup its fortunes in later generations.

Private ownership of land also provided an independent economic base for yangban families. One of the most difficult problems for Korean kings, particularly after 1600, was maintaining control over wealth and man power. The Korean ruler was dependent on relatively independent landowners and landlords for his exploitation of national resources, chiefly through the taxation of land, its product, and labor service requirements. Royal control over these resources was limited by the expansion of private control over unregistered and untaxed land, and the decrease in the size of the tax-paying population. As bureaucratic efficiency decreased and bureaucrats became more exploitative in their treatment of the peasantry, peasants found it advantageous to commend their lands to powerful local yangban in order to gain protection from rapacious bureaucrats. As a consequence, the king's control over taxes and labor service decreased still further. Throughout the seventeenth and eighteenth centuries, kings waged a struggle to increase their control over resources, and this brought them into conflict with the aristocratic and landowning class. One criterion of royal leadership, therefore, was the extent to which a king could increase his command of resources and cut into the wealth and privileges of the upper class.[5] The little success that most kings achieved in this effort testifies to the relative weakness of the kingship in the Yi dynasty polity.

The fourth restraint on royal power was a normative one deriving from certain aspects of Confucian thought. Yangban bureaucrats and literati insisted that kings subordinate themselves to universally accepted Confucian norms of regal conduct. They insisted that kings tolerate the remonstrance of the educated and "virtuous" scholar-officials, and that they defend the hierarchical social status system on the grounds that it represented the proper application of Confucian moral teaching to the organization of society. The yangban defense of social distinction on moral grounds was, in fact, merely a rationalization of their tax-exemption privileges, but it proved an effective weapon in their protracted struggle with the throne for the control of resources.

Among the twenty-seven kings of the Yi dynasty there were several who displayed distinct qualities of leadership, although hardly two were alike in their approach to political problems. Yi Sŏng-gye (posthumous title, T'aejo, r. 1392–98), the founder of the Yi dynasty, was an exceptional leader because of his ability to gather support from political, military, and intellectual sectors for the usurpation of power and the establishment of a new dynasty. He provided the dynasty with a foundation of support based on the establishment of tributary relations with the Chinese Ming dynasty, land reform that weakened the late Koryŏ landed aristocracy and provided a stable revenue base for the new regime, promotion of Neo-Confucianism as state-supported orthodoxy in opposition to the Buddhist establishment of Koryŏ, and creation of a revised structure of central administration.[6] Having successfully created a new dynasty, however, T'aejo was unable to maintain firm political control and abdicated the throne to one of his sons, Yi Pang-wŏn, in the midst of a violent struggle over succession. Yi Pang-wŏn, a skillful though unscrupulous politician, defeated his brothers in the contest for succession and took the throne as the dynasty's third king, T'aejong (r. 1400–1418).[7] He completed the task of providing political stability for the new dynasty.

It is, of course, not unusual that not all the succeeding kings of the Yi dynasty were charismatic leaders, since their right to rule was traditional and inherited, but even the founders of the dynasty—T'aejo and T'aejong—were not truly charismatic either. T'aejo was a military commander who turned his army against the capital and seized power with the support of a group of Confucian scholar-officials who sought political positions for themselves and the destruction of the old Koryŏ landed aristocracy. T'aejong was a prince who came to power with the support of private military forces prior to the centralization of military power under the new government. Force and politics, not charismatic leadership, were the keys to their success. Once the new system of centralized bureaucratic administration was established under T'aejong, succeeding kings had to deal with the major problem of aristocratic and bureaucratic restraints on their authority.

An excellent example of the Yi dynasty style of royal leadership is provided by King Sejong (r. 1418–50), probably the most outstanding ruler of the dynasty. Sejong's leadership was manifested in military affairs, institutional reform, and cultural achievements. He extended the system of garrison defense into the northern provinces and responded aggressively to Japanese pirate raids in the south. He introduced important modifications into the land tax and crop assessment systems with the objective of producing graded and equitable taxation. He was also largely responsible for the invention of the Korean alphabet, *han'gŭl*.[8]

For all his accomplishments, however, it would be difficult to call Sejong a true despot. He was continually subjected to the carping criticisms of bureaucrats and Neo-Confucian purists, but he was able to control them by besting them at their own game rather than by resorting to force and punishment. He surpassed some of his tutors in the Royal Lectures in knowledge and understanding, he gave guidance and leadership to the scholars in the Hall of Worthies, *Chiphyŏnjŏn*, and pushed through the invention of the alphabet despite serious opposition, and in general he refused to be cowed by his officials. In his later years, he even defied them with a mild but open display of Buddhist piety.[9] Though he chafed under the Korean system of restrained monarchy, he learned to live with it and to use it skillfully to accomplish his major goals. Of course, the dynasty was still young, and the yangban had probably not become as firmly entrenched in terms of its social status and tax-exemption privileges as in later centuries. Sejong also did not have to deal with the problem of a contracted revenue base. Nevertheless, Sejong was still subjected to criticism and restraint that in other monarchies would be regarded as lese majesty. The key to his success was that he knew the limits of his power and was able to operate efficiently within them.

There were two other kings in the late fifteenth century, however, who were not so willing to abide by the traditional system of weak monarchs. King Sejo (r. 1455–68), one of Sejong's sons who in

1455 usurped the throne from his nephew, King Tanjong, was faced with the difficult problem of repressing the political opposition to his usurpation. He also attempted to alter the institutional structure of the state for the purpose of creating a powerful monarchy. He weakened the State Council by establishing direct royal control over the Six Ministries. He abolished the Hall of Worthies, lessening the institutionalized influence of scholars loyal to the deposed king, although he continued support for scholarly work. He also strengthened the military defense and communications structures throughout the country, tightened the system of population registration, produced the first major law code of the dynasty, and reformed the system of land allotments and official stipends.[10] Had his policies been continued, it is conceivable that there would have been a growth in the degree of royal despotism in the Yi dynasty and a subordination of the bureaucracy to the monarch, but his policies and, in fact, his whole style of rule, were reversed by the next king, Sŏngjong (r. 1469–94).[11] Because of Sŏngjong's respect for Confucian norms of royal behavior, the power of the throne vis-à-vis the bureaucracy and the literati was weakened, and the censorate began to grow in strength, setting the stage for the rule of Yŏnsan'gun (r. 1494–1506), who represented the extreme of royal despotism in the Yi dynasty.

Yŏnsan'gun was determined to rule in grand style and to exert all the prerogatives of absolute monarchy. He felt constrained, restricted, and frustrated by the growth of bureaucratic power, particularly in the censorate. When he found that he could not gain proper submission to his authority, he sought to enforce his commands by the use of force. He purged and executed his bureaucratic tormentors in 1498 and 1504, abolished many of their rights and privileges, and even turned their beloved National Academy, *Sŏnggyun'gwan*, into a royal pleasure park.[12] To generations of Confucian historians who came after him, Yŏnsan'gun was the archtyrant. He appears to have been driven to psychotic excess by bureaucratic busybodies. Yet there was a method to his madness. He believed that a king's authority was absolute, and that he had the right of life or death over all his subjects. He sought to illustrate this power by the often whimsical execution of his officials. As a result, he carried royal authority further than it had ever been or would be carried in the Yi dynasty and, unwittingly, helped define its limits. His deposition in 1506 by a cabal of civil and military officials proved that his style of absolutism was unacceptable. Despotic monarchy was an anomaly in the Yi dynasty; it could not be tolerated for long.

King Chungjong (r. 1506–44) presided over the opposite swing of the pendulum as bureaucratic power built up once again in the reaction to Yŏnsan'gun's excesses. He was soon caught between conflicting forces within the bureaucracy—his high officials and Merit Subjects who had deposed Yŏnsan'gun and placed him on the throne on the one hand, and new younger officials led by Cho Kwang-jo in the censorate on the other. The censorate reached the height of its importance as a political institution and as a center of political power under Cho's leadership, until he was dismissed and executed in 1519. King Chungjong may not have been an outstanding leader, but he did win an important victory in the protracted struggle between kings and bureaucrats.[13]

For the rest of the sixteenth century there were no genuinely outstanding leaders among Korean monarchs. Court life was dominated more and more by disputes between powerful officials and their families—Kim Al-lo in the 1530s and the Yun brothers in the 1540s. In 1575, what might be called hereditary or institutionalized factionalism had its origin in the famous dispute between Easterners and Westerners. King Sŏnjo (r. 1567–1608), though not a powerful king, did manage to control the political fortunes of the disputing factions by shifting his favor from one group to another.[14] He set a precedent for royal behavior toward bureaucratic factions that was perfected by King Sukchong in the late seventeenth century. Sŏnjo, however, was unable to overcome the debilitating effects of factionalism that left Korea weak and unprepared for the Japanese invasions of 1592–98.

Kwanghaegun (r. 1608–23) was one of the few Yi dynasty kings who showed signs of skillful leadership in international relations. He sought to steer a middle path between the demands of the declining Ming dynasty and the rising Manchus, and he succeeded in preventing an invasion of the Korean peninsula by either of them. But in domestic politics he was the victim of factional strife. He came to power with the support of the Great Northern faction, and he was deposed in 1623 by the Westerners' faction. The Westerners were also Ming loyalists who reversed Kwanghaegun's foreign policy and adopted an anti-Manchu line, to the great detriment of the Korean people. The Manchus invaded Korea in 1627 and 1636 in order to secure their flank in their struggle with the Ming dynasty, and they placed the Korean people under a heavy burden of tribute. The Manchu invasions were thus in part a product of the subordination of royal to bureaucratic leadership in the milieu of factional politics.[15]

The deposition of Kwanghaegun did not mean, however, that kings had been reduced to mere puppets in the hands of their bureaucratic masters. The enthronement of King Injo in 1623 resulted in the restoration of a balance of power between king and bureaucracy, and for the next half century factional strife was kept within limits. Paradoxically, bureaucratic factionalism reached the height of intensity in the late seventeenth century under a strong king, not a weak one.

The reign of King Sukchong (r. 1674–1720) is famous for the purges and counterpurges of bureaucratic factions, but the internecine political strife of the period did not signify either monarchical weakness or anarchy. On the contrary, the purges were a product of Sukchong's leadership style and were orchestrated by him in a very controlled way. The factions themselves merely provided the raw material for his political game of control through manipulation. The purge of one faction was often instigated by another faction, but the king made the final decision in terms of his own interest.[16]

At the end of Sukchong's reign, it was hard to say whether king or bureaucrat had emerged victorious. King Yŏngjo (r. 1724–76) was able to maintain monarchic supremacy, but the Patriarch's faction, *Noron*, had obtained a markedly advantageous position in the competition for the best bureaucratic posts. Sukchong had been unable or unwilling to eliminate factionalism, but he preserved royal supremacy over the factions. His reign, therefore, illustrates one type of royal leadership in the context of the royal-bureaucratic struggle for power.

King Yŏngjo was partly responsible for turning Yi dynasty politics away from the kind of factionalism that plagued Sukchong's reign, but he was not able to eliminate clique politics altogether. He assumed the throne in the midst of court intrigue, and he helped to perpetuate it when he executed his own son, the crown prince.[17] Courtiers and bureaucrats took sides on the issue, and this new alignment affected political life until the first decade of the nineteenth century.

In the meantime, the kings of the seventeenth and eighteenth centuries were called upon to deal with substantive issues of increasing urgency, in particular the shrinking tax base that stemmed from inefficiency in land registration and the inequitable distribution of taxation caused by privileged tax exemption and bureaucratic corruption. The record of late Yi dynasty kings on these issues was relatively poor. None of them was able to exert leadership sufficient to reverse the trend toward private wealth, aristocratic power, central government impoverishment, and peasant suffering. The reform of the tribute tax system, which required most of the seventeenth century, was carried out in spite of royal Fabianism.[18] The long debate over equalization of the tax burden and the imposition of the military cloth tax on yangban households culminated in Yŏngjo's compromise Equal Service reform of 1750. By the terms of this reform, Yŏngjo retreated from a confrontation with the aristocracy and chose simply to cut both the military cloth tax rate and central government expenditures.[19] King Chŏngjo (r. 1776–1800), who has earned a reputation for evenhandedness in his treatment of bureaucrats and factions, was hardly more able or vigorous than Yŏngjo in his approach to substantive problems. His investigation of land and land tax problems in the 1790s produced no major reforms.[20]

From 1800 to 1864 kings were overshadowed by powerful relatives of queens and dowagers, in particular the Andong Kim and P'ungyang Cho lineages. But when Kojong (r. 1864–1907) ascended the throne, a decade of the most active and positive exercise of royal authority in the history of the dynasty began. It was not the king himself, however, who was responsible for this era of royal assertiveness, but his father, the Taewŏn'gun. The Taewŏn'gun occupied a unique position in Yi dynasty history: although he had never been king himself, his son, Kojong, was chosen to succeed to the throne in 1864 when the previous king died without an heir. The Taewŏn'gun thus initially had no basis for his authority other than the respect due him as the father of a king still in his minority. He dominated court affairs by the force of his personality, but when his son decided to rule for himself at the end of 1873, there was little that the Taewŏn'gun could do about it.

Nevertheless, the Taewŏn'gun staked out new ground on behalf of the throne in its contest with the aristocracy for power and resources. He weakened somewhat the restrictions on the opportunity for office-holding resulting from factional discrimination. He imposed a household cloth tax on yangban as well as on commoner families. He abolished all but forty-seven of the chartered private academies that were the bastions of literati strength in the countryside. And he raised the prestige of the royal house by the granting of special privileges to royal relatives and by construction of the Kyŏngbok palace.

In other domestic matters, the Taewŏn'gun took bold steps to solve the nation's problems. He revamped the rural credit and grain loan system. He minted new currency at inflated face value to help finance government expenses. And he authorized a thorough and cruel persecution of French Catholic missionaries and native Korean Catholics in order to eliminate the threat of internal political subversion. In foreign policy he was even bolder. He rejected all requests for trade and treaty relations by foreign powers; he fought the French and Americans who landed small expeditionary forces at Kanghwa Island in 1866 and 1871; and he resolutely refused, even at the risk of war, all Japanese attempts to restructure relations along more modern lines.

The Taewŏn'gun tried to raise royal authority to a higher level than it had ever been before, but his efforts were doomed to failure because of the shortcomings of his policies and the resistance of the traditional political system to excessive royal authority. He failed to introduce institutional checks against the emergence of another powerful consort clan (the Yŏhŭng Min, relatives of his son's queen), and he failed to train his son in the style of despotic kingship. As a result of this last mistake, Kojong began his rule in 1874 thoroughly indoctrinated in Confucian prescriptions for sage rule and he dogmatically applied copybook maxims to complicated real problems. When they failed, he was left floundering, and he soon abdicated real leadership to his high officials, his queen, and her relatives.[21]

The dynasty ended with royal authority and prestige at a low level, subject to foreign dominance as well as to domestic restraints. King Kojong could thank the Chinese for saving his throne for him on two occasions—in 1882 after the military uprising that returned the Taewŏn'gun to power, and in 1884 when Chinese troops under Yüan Shih-k'ai drove a small band of Korean conspirators and their Japanese accomplices out of the country. Kojong's salvation was, however, obtained at a price—intervention and interference in Korean foreign and domestic affairs by the Chinese. From 1885 to 1894, Yüan Shih-k'ai, the Chinese resident in Seoul, kept a close watch over all Korean activities. Kojong was unable to take any serious action that conflicted with Chinese objectives.

Even when Chinese influence was removed from Korea by China's defeat in the Sino-Japanese War in 1895, the problem of foreign dominance was not solved; on the contrary, it became worse. Kojong was placed under virtual house arrest by the Japanese, and Queen Min was murdered by Japanese assassins. After Japanese control was weakened as a result of the Triple Intervention against Japan in 1895, Kojong made his escape from his own palace and took refuge in, of all places, the Russian embassy, where he set up headquarters for a year. After the Japanese victory over Russia in 1904–5, the days of the Yi monarchy were numbered. Kojong was forced to abdicate in 1907, and Korea was annexed by Japan in 1910.[22]

Kojong was a weak and confused king who had no feeling for the prestige and dignity of his own office. When his country demanded leadership in a period of extreme distress and pressure, he was totally unable to provide it. It is a sad commentary on his life that the most significant event in it was probably his death in 1919, for he then became the nostalgic reminder and symbol of the independence that had been lost almost a decade before. His death helped trigger the largest nationalist protest movement of the Japanese colonial period.

In a more profound sense, Kojong's weakness transcended his personal ineptitude: such weakness was characteristic of the limited monarchy that was an integral feature of the political system of the Yi dynasty. Koreans in traditional times abhorred an excess of royal power. There were few examples of strong kings and assertive leadership from the throne. Only when this system was destroyed was the potential created for truly powerful and autocratic leadership. Except for the Taewŏn'gun, who was really not a king at all, the Yi dynasty had its greatest monarchs at its beginning. It survived without great men at the top.

To the end of the dynasty Korean kings were unable to overcome the four major obstacles to total absolutism: weak legitimacy, yangban bureaucratic political competition, limited control over resources, and normative restraints. No progress was made in strengthening the basis of royal legitimacy. Chinese suzerainty was maintained and, in fact, led to a weakening of the independence of the Korean throne, particularly after 1882 when the Chinese decided to intervene more directly in Korean affairs to protect their own interests against Russia and Japan. Direct Chinese intervention, though unprecedented and resented, was not resisted by King

Kojong because it was regarded as legitimate. When Chinese suzerainty was eliminated in 1894, the Korean king did not really become independent despite the subsequent change of his title to emperor. Having been liberated from Chinese suzerainty, Kojong was immediately subjected to Japanese control. When he escaped from his own palace in 1896, he did not repair to separate private quarters as an independent monarch, but moved directly to the Russian embassy to seek the protection of a new foreign suzerain. After 1904, when Japanese control over Korea was re-established, Kojong did not seek to lead a mass nationalist resistance against Japan. Instead he sent an envoy to the Hague Peace Conference in 1907 to appeal to Western powers for protection. The weak sense of legitimacy and independent authority characteristic of Korean kingship could not easily be sloughed off despite the destruction of China's formal suzerainty. The monarchy was, therefore, incapable of exerting leadership over the nascent nationalist movement and of adapting itself to the new needs of the Korean people.

Korean kings were also unsuccessful in their attempts to expand their power vis-à-vis the yangban aristocracy. The Taewŏn'gun was more successful than others during the 1860s; but this period of royal power was but a brief interlude—yangban bureaucratic dominance of the throne was quickly re-established after his retirement in late 1873. The Japanese-sponsored attempt at administrative reform in 1894, which aimed at the creation of a modern cabinet with independent decision-making power, only contributed to bureaucratic strength. The Japanese hoped that by weakening the throne they could eliminate conservative obstruction to modernization. At the same time, they weakened the potential for royal leadership.

Korean kings were also consistently unable to expand their control over human and material resources. This shortcoming led to a serious maldistribution of wealth prior to 1876, but it did not interfere with the monarchy's ability to sustain itself. Indeed, yangban control over resources gave them a stake in the maintenance of the dynasty. After 1876, however, the lack of centralized control over resources inhibited efforts toward the development of national wealth and power, an objective that was essential to the maintenance of political independence. Royal leadership in this instance was, therefore, inhibited by dependence on the yangban class for political support.

The normative restraints on royal authority were a function of the prevalence of Neo-Confucian thought during the Yi dynasty. The educated yangban elite used Neo-Confucianism to bolster their own social position and to check royal despotism. Some kings may have been pragmatic in their actions, but none of them sought to put an end to Neo-Confucian orthodoxy. In the late nineteenth century when new changes were introduced into Korean society, the intellectual monopoly of Neo-Confucianism was threatened. But many Confucians became the intellectual leaders of conservative antiforeign nationalism, and the king was in no position to repudiate this support for Korean independence, even if he had desired to do so. Therefore, while normative restraints on royal authority were probably the least formidable of the king's problems after 1894, there was no attempt by the throne to seek major changes in the intellectual underpinnings of Korean society.

BUREAUCRATIC LEADERSHIP

Although bureaucratic organization by its very nature limited the opportunities for individual leadership, the most readily identifiable leaders in Yi dynasty society were government functionaries. Officials displayed qualities of leadership in three areas: administrative performance, policy recommendation, and bureaucratic and court politics. Of the three categories, we have the least information about administrative performance. Certain officials were able to work their way up the bureaucratic ladder on the basis of merit in the performance of tasks in central government agencies or as local magistrates. Individual officials were judged and rated by their superiors and by the staffs of the ministries of personnel and war. The system of local administration permitted the individual magistrate a relatively wide scope of discretionary power at the same time that it made him responsible for everything that happened within his jurisdiction. The system was conducive to timeserving and the routine performance of minimal obligations by magistrates interested mainly in completing their terms of office unscathed by scandal. At the same time, it permitted men of initiative and talent to operate without excessive restraint from the center. Through the system of written reports and memorials it was also possible for some officials of courage to make recommendations for the solution of local problems. Unfortunately, the historical record yields little information on the activities of the lower and intermediate level government officials and local magistrates.

Leadership in policy recommendation depended on the ability of individual officials to devise and recommend policy on substantive issues, and then to carry through the fight for royal approval and implementation against the great weight of bureaucratic inertia and conservatism that prevailed at court. The potential for leadership was also obstructed by the involvement of certain issues in factional or clique politics and by the resistance of the yangban class as a whole to any reforms that interfered with their economic, political, and social privileges.

The decision-making process itself was also not conducive to individual leadership and initiative. Policy recommendation was usually collegial and based on consensus; kings were generally unwilling to adopt measures strongly opposed by a substantial number of high officials. The chief state councilor was not a prime minister in the modern sense of the term. He shared influence with other high officials, and his position was not exalted. Major problems were also usually decided by councils consisting of a relatively large number of officials. Elderly officials were normally given prestigious sinecures after their retirement and brought into high level councils where they usually exerted conservative influence over policy questions.

The history of the Yi dynasty, therefore, yields few cases of officials whose individual leadership on policy questions was crowned with success. A recent study of Kim Yuk (1580–1658), the one official most responsible for the reform of the tribute system in the seventeenth century, illustrates the difficulties involved in administrative reform.[23] The story of the protracted struggle for the reform of the military cloth tax from the late seventeenth century to 1750 is simply a record of frustrated initiatives.[24] The 1860s was, of course, a period of conservative reform, but affairs were dominated by the personality of the Taewŏn'gun; bureaucrats played a secondary role in government affairs. Kim Pyŏng-hak (1821–79), minister of taxation and chief state councilor during this period, was one of those officials who exerted leadership in policy making, but his name is hardly remembered today.

Officials were sometimes very influential on foreign policy matters. After the Taewŏn'gun retired in late 1873, for example, the government under King Kojong discarded the Taewŏn'gun's policy toward Japan and moved toward rapprochement. The person probably most responsible for paving the way for an agreement with Japan was Pak Kyu-su (1807–76). Pak argued cogently and forcefully for a reordering of attitudes and relations with Japan, and it was largely due to his efforts that Korea avoided war and invasion when the traditional seclusion policy was discarded in 1876.[25]

Politics is the one area of activity in the Yi dynasty that yields numerous examples of outstanding and powerful men, and yet we must be most cautious in equating political power with leadership. Prior to and even after the emergence of institutionalized factionalism in the late sixteenth century, political success often depended on constructing a network of personal ties and influence, and obtaining the favor of the throne. Sin Suk-chu (1417–75) attained prestige and power because of his accomplishments in cultural affairs and administration as well as his political skill. His flexibility in political matters allowed him not only to attain an important position under King Sejong (r. 1418–50), but also to survive the rigors of Sejo's usurpation (1455). He became chief state councilor under Sejo while friends like Sŏng Sam-mun suffered martyrdom, and he continued in power as interim chief of administration, *wŏnsang*, during Yejong's minority (r. 1468–69) and as chief state councilor again under Sŏngjong (r. 1469–94). He was a leading official in Sejong's Hall of Worthies with important responsibility for the invention of the alphabet, *han'gŭl*, and he participated in the compilation of the first major law code, the *Kyŏngguk taejŏn* (1469), during Sejo's reign. He was also a diplomat who performed ably on missions to Ming China and Japan, and he took part in military operations against "barbarian" tribesmen in northeastern Korea. Sin attained prestige and high office initially because of his reputation for scholarship, but he was able to advance up the bureaucratic ladder because of administrative, diplomatic, and military abilities. He stayed in power because of his skill in steering a steady course through the turbulent waters of court intrigue. In terms of the catholicity of his accomplishments, he was the Yi dynasty version of a Renaissance generalist, with a Machiavellian flair for politics.[26]

Cho Kwang-jo (1482–1519), one of the most famous officials of the sixteenth century, was more of a political leader than Sin Suk-chu. Like Sin, he attained prominence in bureaucratic life because of his scholarly abilities. He rose to influence through the prestigious Office of Special Counselors, *Hongmun'gwan*, and the censorate and used the censorate as a base of power to challenge both the throne and the entrenched high officials and merit subjects of the time. Through his sponsorship of a special examination for young candidates for office with reputations for scholarship, he was able to bring several dozen young officials into the government. No matter how idealistic Cho may have been in his proposals for the Confu-

cian rectification of government institutions, he was mainly a political leader who utilized the respect for Confucian norms and the
powerful office of the censorate to create a power base in the
bureaucracy. Because this kind of political leadership constituted a
threat to the throne and established high officials, he was eventually toppled from power. He and his followers were purged in 1519,
and he was given poison.[27]

Cho Kwang-jo was acknowledged as a great man, if not by his
contemporaries, then by men of later generations who canonized
him and ensconced his tablets in the shrine of Confucius. But other
men in the sixteenth century who were more successful politically
than Cho Kwang-jo have not been held in high repute. One of these
was Kim Al-lo (1481-1537), known to history as one of The Three
Evil Men of 1537, a reputation not entirely undeserved.

Kim Al-lo also obtained entree to the higher circles of power
initially because of success in scholarship; he placed first in the
munkwa examination in 1506. He then suffered exile at the hands
of Nam Kon and Sim Chŏng, the enemies of Cho Kwang-jo, but was
able to regain favor at court and wreak vengeance on his enemies.
He stayed in power until his execution in 1537, largely through his
skill in the intrigue of court politics, and through his ability to gain
the favor of the king. One after another of his enemies were either
exiled or given poison, but Kim himself died a victim of the internecine struggle he had helped to foment.[28]

Yun Wŏn-hyŏng (?-1565) resembled Kim Al-lo with respect to his
skill in political intrigue, but Yun was able to construct a firmer
political base than Kim. Yun also passed the highest civil service
examination and was partially responsible for eliminating Kim Al-
lo in 1537. He gambled his political future by supporting one of the
heirs to the throne, the Kyŏngwŏn grand prince, Kyŏngwŏn Taegun
(later King Myŏngjong r. 1545-67), against a rival claimant. When
Myŏngjong finally came to the throne in 1545, Yun Wŏn-hyŏng's
power was assured, and sustained by his ties to the queen mother
and by the purge of his political enemies in 1545; he maintained his
influence until the death of his protector, Queen Munjŏng, in 1565.
Yun's political success was obviously a combination of luck and
skill, but he succeeded where others failed by maintaining strong
connections with the inner court, by allying himself with other
officials in the regular bureaucracy, and by the ruthless elimination
of his opponents in a major purge.[29]

Throughout the sixteenth century the pattern of political leadership consisted of success in the examinations, attaining a high rank-

ing official post, winning the favor of a king, or maintaining strong ties with royal relatives. Individual officials were still relatively isolated, and for this reason they sought protection from above rather than attempting to organize political power from below. Cho Kwang-jo was one exception; he sought to use the censorate to construct a base of power—but he failed in the attempt.

The political situation in the seventeenth century, however, was quite different from that of the sixteenth; it was the age of bureaucratic factionalism and it produced a new type of political figure—the factional leader. Probably the most famous factional leader of the period was Song Si-yŏl (1607–89), a member of the Westerners' faction, *Sŏin*, and founder of the Patriarch's faction, *Noron*. Since Song was the tutor of King Hyojong (r. 1649–59) when the latter was crown prince, he gained influence at court after Hyojong ascended the throne in 1649. Song held his position at court until the reign of Sukchong (r. 1674–1720), when he became embroiled in doctrinal and political disputes with the Southerners' faction. His rise and fall in the political world traced a seesawlike pattern as he alternated between the highest civil posts and exile. When he finally ran afoul of King Sukchong in 1689, he was forced to drink poison.[30]

An examination of Song's political style reveals that the qualities of bureaucratic leaders and the ingredients for political success had not changed much since the sixteenth century. Song's construction of a political base in a bureaucratic faction was not sufficient to obtain permanent political victory: the favor of the throne was still the most important criterion of successful politics. It might easily be argued that Song was, in fact, a poor political leader because he exposed himself and his faction to the attacks of the Southerners' faction and risked the disfavor of King Sukchong, rigidly adhering to a position on a question of mourning etiquette that cast doubt on the legitimacy of the deceased King Hyojong. He was obviously a vain man who believed in the infallibility of his judgment on ritual matters, but his inflexibility had disastrous consequences for him and his followers.

Song Si-yŏl was probably the greatest of a special breed of factional leaders who were forced because of the times to lead a precarious existence, subject always to sudden loss of favor, if not of life itself. Moreover, men like Song were not just political animals, they were also renowned scholars whose reputations lived long after them. They spawned a host of shrines and academies where their political descendants and scholarly disciples kept the embers of factional resentment burning through the cold periods of political eclipse.

In the eighteenth century, there was a lessening of the intensity of factional politics. Under Yŏngjo's reign (r. 1724-76) in the 1730s, the center of political action shifted toward the inner palace. Members of the Kyŏngju Kim clan, relatives of Yŏngjo's second queen, became influential at court. The main political dispute was the product of Yŏngjo's execution of his own crown prince, the *Sado seja*, in 1762. As the locus of power shifted toward the throne with the stabilization of factional politics, a new type of bureaucratic leader with close ties to the crown could emerge. Hong Kug-yŏng (1748-80) was a leading example of the new phenomenon. His political future was assured by his support for the *Sado seja*'s son, who later came to the throne as King Chŏngjo (r. 1776-1800). Hong consolidated his position by sending one of his daughters to Chŏngjo's harem. His power at court became so great that Koreans later coined a new term for the phenomenon he represented, *sedo chŏngch'i*, "the politics of influence," indicating the virtual seizure of authority at court by a powerful official, usually with marital ties to the throne.[31]

The precedent established by Hong Kug-yŏng was institutionalized in the nineteenth century after the accession of King Sunjo in 1800. Members of the Andong Kim, P'ungyang Cho, and Namyang Hong lineages married their daughters into the royal line, became fathers-in-law and grandfathers of kings, gained special favors for the male members of their own families, and subordinated royal power to their hegemony. The nineteenth century was the age of nepotism.[32]

Kim Cho-sun (?-1831) was typical of the period. He was responsible for founding the fortunes of the Andong Kim lineage in the nineteenth century, the most powerful of the consort clans until the accession of Kojong in 1864. During Chŏngjo's reign (r. 1776-1800), Kim was tutor to the crown prince, and he formed ties with Yŏngjo's second queen, who became dowager-regent during Sunjo's minority, from 1800 to 1804. As Sunjo's father-in-law, his power was unassailable.[33] Although his descendants were at times overshadowed by the P'ungyang Cho, they came back into power during Ch'ŏlchong's reign (r. 1849-64) and remained in high office well into the 1860s.

During the 1860s the consort lineages were reduced in power along with the traditional factions, but by the mid-1870s the Yŏhŭng Min, relatives of Kojong's queen, re-established the political hegemony of the consort relatives. It should be remembered, of course, that consort relatives were not the only leading officials in the nineteenth century. There was still considerable opportunity for advancement for other aristocrats through the examination system and promotion within the bureaucracy.

BUREAUCRATIC LEADERS IN A PERIOD OF CHANGE, 1876-1910

The abandonment of seclusion and the opening of Korea to foreign contact shook the foundations of the old order. The beginning of foreign trade caused serious dislocations in the economy and society. Korea was dragged into a complex and dangerous game of international power politics; foreign interference in Korea's domestic affairs upset the old structure of power and introduced new rules and methods for political action. The dismantling of the walls of seclusion led to an outflow of students and travelers who were exposed to new experiences and ideas. Koreans who were active politically established contacts in foreign countries and were given some opportunity for escaping the smothering jurisdiction of the home government. They could use foreign countries as a base for subversive activities, moving in and out of Korea as the political situation changed. The circumstances spawned a new type of rebellion in the Tonghak movement with revolutionary social overtones.

One of the most significant developments was the further weakening of royal authority by foreign interference and by internal clique politics, in particular the rivalry between the Taewŏn'gun and Queen Min. But the destruction of royal legitimacy and of the traditional monarchy was by no means an easy task. The monarchy proved surprisingly hardy despite King Kojong's own ineptness. Bureaucratic politicans risked and lost their lives time and time again in the gamble that royal authority and legitimacy had been replaced by foreign power. When the soldiers of the old army rebelled in 1882, the rebels succeeded in installing the Taewŏn'gun as chief of administration. They sought to kill the queen and her relatives and supporters, but they made no attack on the king. When Kim Ok-kyun attempted his *coup d'état* in 1884, he directed his attack against the leading officials and the Min clan. He sought to capture (not kill or depose) the king to provide legitimacy for his new government. When he was driven out of the palace by Yüan Shih-k'ai and lost his control over the king, the political ball game was lost.

When the Tonghaks rebelled in 1894, they demanded reform, punishment of corrupt officials, and freedom of religion, but not the deposition of the king or the overthrow of the dynasty. When the Kim Hong-jip cabinets were formed in 1894–95 with the support of the Japanese, they continued just as long as the king remained captive. As soon as Kojong escaped to the Russian embassy, Kim and his cabinet members were either stoned to death by the mob or forced into exile abroad. It made no difference that the king was locked inside the Russian embassy—the bureaucrats were *locked out!* There was little talk of constitutional monarchy or republicanism for the traditional legitimacy of the monarch was still strong and respected. Even when the Independence Club was active in the period 1896–98, it called for reform by petitioning the throne and by demanding the king's attention through newspaper editorials and street demonstrations. It lasted as long as the king tolerated it.

To be sure, the survival of the monarchy was a function of the shifting international situation and the inability of any single foreign country to maintain exclusive control over Korea for long. China maintained its control the longest, from 1882 to 1894, the Japanese from 1894 to 1896, and the Russians from 1896 to 1898. It was not until the defeat of Russia by Japan in 1904 that the monarchy was weakened beyond repair. Then Kojong placed himself in a precarious position when he sent a secret emissary to The Hague in 1907 to publicize Korea's plight. Officials such as Yi Wan-yong and Yi Yong-gu demanded the king's abdication because they knew the Japanese would force it. Until this time, however, the resiliency of the crown had made any attempt by bureaucrats to seize power a very risky business.

The quest for political power and the ability to sustain that power was, of course, one criterion of leadership, but politics during this period required more skill than ever before—not just skill in court or clique politics, but the ability to assess and anticipate changes in the international situation. Some pinned their hopes on Queen Min; but they were left exposed after her assassination in 1895. Those who preferred to lean on the Chinese were undermined by China's defeat in the Sino-Japanese War. Some chose Japanese protection in varying degrees; but the times were not ripe for total Japanese control until 1904. Thus, Kim Ok-kyun, Pak Yŏng-hyo, Sŏ Kwang-bŏm, and Sŏ Chae-p'il lost out in 1884, and Kim Hong-jip, Kim Yun-sik, and Yu Kil-jun suffered eclipse or death in 1895. Those who sought Russian protection had even shorter periods of success.

The officials who remained on top at the end were the ones with greater flexibility, or possibly the weakest scruples and convictions. Yi Wan-yong served under the queen's hegemony in the 1880s, joined the pro-Russian group in 1896, was a member of the Independence Club for a while, and then switched his allegiance to Japan in 1901 and won Itō Hirobumi's favor.[34] Other examples of this type were Song Pyŏng-jun and Yi Yong-gu. Song began his career as a retainer of Min Yŏng-hwan and then switched allegiance to Kim Ok-kyun in 1884. He survived the defeat of 1884 because of his friendship with Min and saved himself from execution later by fleeing to Japan. He returned to Korea with the Japanese army during the Russo-Japanese War, helped organize the Restoration Society, *Yusinhoe* (named for the Meiji Restoration), and joined forces with Yi Yong-gu's pro-Japanese Unity and Progress Society, *Ilchinhoe*. He supported Kojong's abdication and joined the Yi Wan-yong cabinet in 1907.[35]

Yi Yong-gu joined the Tonghak movement in 1890 and survived the defeat to organize the Progressive Society, *Chinbohoe*. After the turn of the century he maintained ties with both Song Pyŏng-jun in the formation of the pro-Japanese societies and Son Pyŏng-hŭi's reorganization of the Tonghak movement as the religion of the Heavenly Way, *Ch'ŏndogyo*.[36]

Not all men found it so easy to shift political allegiances and discard loyalties or convictions about the kind of reform that Korea needed. Probably the most outstanding leaders of the period, bureaucrats or otherwise, were those who were least successful politically. Even members of the Min clan suffered the vicissitudes of political fortune in this difficult age. Min Yŏng-ik was the leading young light of the Min clan in the 1870s and early 1880s and one of the targets of Kim Ok-kyun's coup of 1884. But he was also responsible for leadership in some of the first modernization projects conducted under the old regime. When he opposed the court's shift away from China and toward Russia in 1886, he sacrificed his own political future and was forced several times thereafter to seek refuge in China.[37]

Min Yŏng-hwan was an even more tragic figure. His father was killed in the 1882 uprising, but he emerged from mourning in the late 1880s to hold a series of important posts. He suffered a temporary eclipse after the queen's assassination in 1895, but became prominent again after a trip through Europe in 1896–97 as an advocate of reform. This earned him the resentment of other members of his clan, and he was forced out of office. He re-entered official life after the turn of the century, but became an outspoken opponent of Japanese dominance and eventually committed suicide after the signing of the protectorate treaty with Japan in 1905.[38]

Min Yŏng-ik and Min Yŏng-hwan were at least members of the Min clan and relatives of the queen. As difficult as political life was for them, so much more difficult was it for those without the protection afforded by such powerful familial backing. Among other bureaucrats three types of leaders—based on criteria of political allegiance, reform objectives, and mode of activity—can be distinguished. The first included men who were affiliated with the Min-dominated government during the 1870s and 1880s and were usually committed to some reform or modernization. Kim Yun-sik led the first mission of overseas students to China in 1881 to study weapons manufacture. He and Ŏ Yun-jung were instrumental in inducing the Chinese to abduct the Taewŏn'gun in 1882, thus saving the queen and the Min clan from obliteration, and Kim aided Yüan Shih-k'ai in driving Kim Ok-kyun out of the country in 1884. When he joined with Min Yŏng-ik in opposition to Queen Min's attempted shift to the Russians in 1887, he was exiled and remained out of office until the queen's assassination in 1895. He was then recalled to take a post as foreign minister in a Kim Hong-jip cabinet, but suffered exile after Kojong fled to the Russian embassy. Kim's political loyalty to the queen's relatives kept him in office until his convictions led him into conflict with the queen. His early political affiliations did not mean that he was conservative. On the contrary, he worked for moderate reform and for this reason probably had no qualms of conscience in joining the reformist Kim Hong-jip cabinet.[39]

Kim Hong-jip's career was similar to Kim Yun-sik's. He was sent to Japan as special envoy, *susinsa*, in 1880 and quickly became embroiled in controversy when he returned home with proposals by a Chinese official of the Chinese embassy in Tokyo, Huang Tsun-hsien, advocating that Korea quickly sign treaties with Western powers as a defense against possible Russian or Japanese aggression. He was forced to resign, but soon returned to active diplomatic service. He attained prominence by forming the first of four cabinets in 1894, and it was his regime that was responsible for introducing the series of radical measures known as the Kabo Reforms. While Japanese initiative, and certainly Japanese protection, were responsible for the introduction of the reform measures, men like Kim and Yu Kil-jun exerted a large measure of leadership.

Some of the reforms introduced in 1894 and 1895 stirred up considerable resentment, especially the "topknot edict" of 1895. Kim and the members of his government have been roundly criticized by writers for their reliance on the Japanese and for the excessive rapidity with which they tried to transform revered traditions, but Japanese hegemony in 1894 gave reformers the opportunity to institute their plans that they never had had under the king's or queen's leadership. Kim paid the price for his radicalism by his murder at the hands of the mob, but it must be remembered that his reformism was not simply a product of political expediency. It stemmed from his convictions about Korea's needs gained after more than a decade of administrative experience.[40]

Both Kim Yun-sik and Kim Hong-jip obtained most of their political experience at home, not abroad, and they differed in their backgrounds from men like Yu Kil-jun, Sŏ Chae-p'il, and Kim Ok-kyun and his cohorts. This latter group had spent many years abroad in Japan, the United States, or Europe, and they returned to their country to provide differing brands of leadership. Yu Kil-jun and Sŏ Chae-p'il (Philip Jaisohn) may also be distinguished in part from Kim Ok-kyun in terms of their capacity to work within the established system, although not with great success.

Yu Kil-jun spent a year in Japan in 1881–82 at Fukuzawa Yukichi's *Keiō gijuku*, and then accompanied Min Yŏng-ik in 1883 on his mission to the United States. He remained behind in the United States for another year and then toured through Europe. When he returned to Korea in 1885, he barely escaped execution because he was identified with the Kim Ok-kyun group. He spent the rest of the 1880s under virtual house arrest and used the time to write an account of his experiences abroad, purposely introducing the use of mixed Korean-Chinese script instead of classical Chinese. He joined the Kim Hong-jip cabinet in 1894 because he saw a good opportunity for achieving reform, and he is credited with inspiring much of the reform program. With the fall of the Kim cabinet, he was forced into exile in Japan and returned only with Kojong's abdication in 1907. After that time, he devoted himself to education and the promotion of popular organizations. Yu eschewed the violence that usually accompanied radical reformism in this period. In the long run his contribution to cultural and intellectual reform was more important than his work as a member of the Kim Hong-jip cabinet. He remained an impressive figure whose leadership was lost to his country because of the complicated and difficult political times in which he lived.[41]

Sŏ Chae-p'il's life experience was similar to Yu's in several ways. Sŏ spent much time abroad, more than any other figure in Korean political life in the late nineteenth century, from 1884 to 1896; most of it was spent in the United States earning a medical degree. Sŏ took part in Kim Ok-kyun's attempted coup in 1884 and was forced into exile because of it, and as was the case with Yu, his country was deprived of his services except for a brief period of two years. When he returned to Korea in 1896 he was active mostly in an extraofficial capacity, as founder of the newspaper *Independence, Tongnip sinmun*, and as organizer of the Independence Club, *Tongnip hyŏphoe*. He was among the first to apply pressure to the government for reform and for the maintenance of Korean sovereignty against foreign exploitation by mobilizing opinion among the intellectuals of the capital. He was forced to return to the United States in 1898, but not before setting an important precedent for a new type of leadership. He tried to organize the intellectual elite. He used the press for purposes of political propaganda, appealed to the nationalist sentiment of the people, and sponsored mass demonstrations.[42]

A third type of leadership was exemplified by the activities of Kim Ok-kyun and his followers, most notably Pak Yŏng-hyo. These men were more prone to the use of conspiracy and violence in the accomplishment of their objectives. Kim was a member of the Andong Kim clan, the same lineage that produced some of the leading opponents of his own plans for radical reform. Kim, Pak, and their other colleagues were introduced to reformist ideas in the 1870s through their association with Pak Kyu-su and others. Kim went to Japan in 1881 and returned in 1882 with Pak Yŏng-hyo, who was on an assignment as special envoy, *susinsa*. There they became acquainted with Fukuzawa Yukichi and were exposed to the results of early Meiji reforms, and they became convinced that Korea was in urgent need of change. After they returned to Korea, however, they were frustrated by the opposition of the entrenched higher officials of the Min clan, the Andong Kim and others, and they eventually decided that reform would not be possible without a bloody purge of the present leadership. With the aid of the Japanese minister to Korea, Takezoe Shinichiro, they captured the palace and killed about a half-dozen high officials, but were driven out of Korea after only three days of rule.

It is difficult to judge whether Kim's objectives were as thoroughly goal-oriented as he later professed in his ex post facto apologia, his *Diary of 1884, Kapsin illok*. There is also little use in speculating on whether he would have been successful in modernization and reform had he attained power in 1884. What is certain, however, is that his abortive coup introduced a new measure of violence and bitterness into Korean politics, and the government responded with ferocity against the relatives of the conspirators and all those suspected of complicity. Kim Ok-kyun was himself finally killed by a government assassin in Shanghai in 1894.[43]

Pak Yŏng-hyo, however, was able to save himself and spent the next decade in Japan. During the Kabo Reforms of 1894 he was pardoned and returned to Korea to participate in the second Kim Hong-jip cabinet. However, he was forced to flee to Japan in 1895 because of his involvement in a new plot and after joining the Yi Wan-yong cabinet he was exiled in 1907 for participating in another conspiracy. He lived on until 1939, however, enjoying high title and position under the Japanese. Thus, one of the most violent radicals of the nineteenth century ended his days as a Japanese collaborator. Pak's reformism was not combined with strong feelings of nationalism, and in the expression of patriotic sentiment he came nowhere near the examples set by Min Yŏng-hwan of the old regime or Ch'oe Ik-hyŏn, one of the leading Confucian intellectuals of the day, who helped organize the resistance movement in the first decade of the twentieth century.[44]

The political circumstances of the period from 1876 to 1910 allowed for a much greater variety of political activity and leadership than had ever been possible in the tightly enclosed cocoon of pre-Kanghwa Korea. But for those who operated at the top of the political structure as officials loyal to the king or queen, or as appointees in regimes sponsored by foreign governments, or as instigators of coups, the inertia of the traditional system and the sudden shifts in the international situation made the attainment of either political power or reformist goals most difficult. Most of the leading political figures of the era who sought some kind of reform were frustrated by certain types of handicaps. Moderates like Kim Yun-sik, Min Yŏng-hwan, and Kim Hong-jip could not bring themselves to advocate an overthrow of the monarchy because of their respect for traditional legitimacy. Others like Yu Kil-jun and Sŏ Chae-p'il could only operate in certain periods when foreign interference provided some freedom for their activities. And radicals like Kim Ok-kyun had no hope of success in the use of force without support from Japan. The monarchy and the institutional structure were weakened and decrepit, but Japanese power was the only force that could topple it completely in the end. There was still not enough of a basis in Korean social and political organization to allow the emergence of extragovernmental political leadership until the monarchy was overthrown. But because the old order was destroyed by an imperialist power from the outside, the chance for the evolution of indigenous leadership was lost altogether.

ARISTOCRACY AND LITERATI

Because of its relatively great political and economic power, which was in competition with the powers of the king, the aristocracy served to restrict monarchical and centralized bureaucratic authority. It is, however, difficult to speak of aristocratic leadership as an independent phenomenon, because aristocrats gained power as officials or influence as literati. Their control over land and wealth served as a base for leadership only on the local scene.

The local literati had a certain measure of institutionalized power through their leadership in establishing private academies. These academies were first founded in the middle of the sixteenth century mainly as centers of study and contemplation, but by the seventeenth and eighteenth centuries, they gained control over land and peasant cultivators and exerted a certain degree of political power vis-à-vis local magistrates. The private academies were probably more powerful in Korean society than their Chinese counterparts at any time since the founding of the Sung dynasty, no doubt serving as an indication of the relative strength of the yangban class and the weaker authority of the Korean king and central government. But even in Korea they were still subject to the restrictions of the central government. These restrictions were imposed with greater force from the end of the eighteenth century, and it was one of the few indications of central power that the strength of the academies was ultimately curtailed. The Taewŏn'gun brought a rapid and sudden end to the private academies for all purposes in the 1860s, but they had already been weakened by over a century of growing restrictions on their autonomy.[45]

Literati performed leadership roles in the intellectual and political realms in other ways. From the late Koryŏ period through the middle of the sixteenth century, they engaged in the struggle to displace Buddhism and replace it with Confucianism, not only as state-supported and state-sanctioned orthodoxy, but also as the exclusive body of normative and religious values in society. They engaged also in a dispute over certain priorities in Confucian education, especially whether the main purpose of education and the examination system should be the recruitment of officials for state service or the inculcation of proper moral values in the minds of educated men. The debate over literary style and accomplishment as opposed to mastery of the content of the Chinese classics was one aspect of this struggle.[46]

Scholars also engaged in contests over certain emphases in the Confucian tradition. The establishment of Chu Hsi's interpretation of the classics as orthodoxy involved efforts to prevent a dilution of the faith by the tenets of Wang Yang-ming, and the victory of the Sung dynasty brand of Neo-Confucianism was largely a function of the influence of intellectual leaders like Yi Hwang (pen name, T'oegye), 1501–70.[47]

As intellectual matters became more and more involved with political disputation and schools of thought developed with some relations with bureaucratic factions, scholarly leadership took on a political tinge. The intellectual world was divided vertically into leader-follower groups of masters and disciples who struggled to gain acceptance for their particular views on metaphysical questions.[48] To be sure, Confucian values of respect for superiors, elders, and men of learning contributed to factional and schismatic splintering of scholarly groups. But there was certainly room for "leadership" among intellectuals, no matter what one thinks of the value of divisive infighting on doctrinal and ethical matters for Korean society as a whole. Disputes over questions of ethics or protocol had great importance for political matters, and the ability of certain leaders to command respect in the intellectual realm was of great moment in the outcome of political struggles at court. The career of Song Si-yŏl in the seventeenth century is a case in point, since his political rise and fall was hardly ever dissociated from disputes over doctrinal and ritual questions.

REBELS

Rebel leaders in Yi dynasty society were men who had to work outside the regular structure of power and authority and had to rely on their own talents for inducing others to follow their lead, taking command of a rebellion once underway, or organizing their men for military activities against government forces.

The types of rebel leaders were related to the types of rebellions and uprisings that occurred throughout the Yi dynasty. The fullfledged antidynastic rebellion with the clearly articulated objective of overthrowing the existing dynasty and replacing it with another was not a major feature of Yi dynasty rebellions. Most uprisings fall into two categories: movements led by frustrated officials or discontented office seekers against the court, or spontaneous and local popular uprisings directed mainly against corrupt officials or in reaction to excessive taxation and exploitation. The Yi Si-ae rebellion of 1467, the Yi Kwal rebellion of 1623, and the Hong Kyŏng-nae rebellion of 1811 were typical of the former category. So was the abortive uprising of Chŏng Yŏ-rip in 1589, even though it had antidynastic overtones.[49] Peasant uprisings occurred during the latter part of the dynasty, and with the exception of the Tonghak rebellion, which will be discussed later, the most serious of these occurred in 1862, the Chinju rebellion.[50]

The relatively short duration and small scope of most rebellions and the government's success in putting them down may have been due in part to the relatively small geographical area that Korea had to control, the relative effectiveness of centralized administration at least until the nineteenth century, and the monopoly over weapons by the central government in a country closed off from potentially subversive foreign contact and influence. Other more subtle factors may have been the strength of traditional legitimacy and social status barriers to large-scale rebel movements. The "discontented office seekers," who came from the bureaucratic elite, may have had trouble in making contact with lower strata in society. The one exception would be Hong Kyŏng-nae, whose rebellion seems to have been fueled by regional discontent in the north with discriminatory aspects of the central governments' recruitment policies. But because of its regional nature, Hong's rebellion probably could not have spread to the rest of the country.

The typical peasant uprising may also have been restricted by a failure to forge ties with discontented elements of the upper class. Local uprisings were spontaneous, directed against the local magistrates and clerks who were the chief agents of oppression, and usually took the form of an outburst of violence against these people; once a clerk's house had been burned or a magistrate's yamen attacked and the guilty parties driven out or killed, resentment was dissipated. Moreover, standard government policy was skillfully geared so as to prevent any long-term dissatisfaction with the central government. The government was usually quick to condemn corrupt officials for responsibility in causing an uprising, so that it would appear that the government was sympathetic to the rebels' cause. At the same time, it made sure that all rebel leaders were executed while the followers were pardoned.

Rebels may have provided an example of raw leadership, but none of them did more than focus attention on specific problems of corruption and injustice. To the end of the dynasty, even including the Tonghak movement, institutionalized power could not be overcome by any rebel leader through the mobilization of discontented elements of the population.

The traditional order in the late nineteenth century was so weakened by new forces that greater opportunities were provided for a new type of rebellion and new types of leadership. The Tonghak movement of the late nineteenth century differed from previous rebel movements because it began as a new religious movement, was based on a sophisticated organizational network, and was inspired by xenophobic nationalism and a revolutionary social doctrine. The founder of the faith, Ch'oe Che-u (1824–64), was a religious mystic similar in type to Hung Hsiu-ch'uan of the Taiping rebellion in nineteenth-century China. He founded his faith, Eastern Learning, *Tonghak*, as a counterpoise to the foreign and subversive teachings of Western Learning, *Sŏhak*, a term denoting Catholicism as well as Western learning in general. The new faith was purposely syncretic; it brought together the major teachings of the East—Confucianism, Buddhism, and Taoism—in a way that sacrificed doctrinal purity for a kind of regional-cultural chauvinism. It also borrowed from Christianity in its concept of the lord of heaven, its doctrine of the immanence of Heaven in man, and the presumption of the equality of all men before Heaven. It was in this last respect that the Eastern Learning movement was revolutionary, for it threatened the very foundation of the hierarchical social order. Thus, the movement may be seen as a response to social conditions in the nineteenth century, although it is still difficult to ascertain whether the movement was fueled by the discontents of the downtrodden in a still rigid order of social distinction, or stimulated by the breakdown of discrimination and the leveling of society as some more recent scholars would have us believe.[51]

The movement owed its success not only to the inspired mysticism and spiritual leadership of its charismatic founder, but also to his ability to create a powerful organizational hierarchy and his foresight in ensuring an uninterrupted transmission of leadership to his leading disciple, Ch'oe Si-hyŏng (1827–98), before his own execution in 1864.

Ch'oe Si-hyŏng was as great a leader as the founder of the faith. In addition to his religious piety and organizational talents, he created a body of scripture and provided leadership in a time of trouble and persecution. Circumspect and cautious, he avoided involvement in the 1871 movement to obtain posthumous pardon for Ch'oe Che-u and remained in hiding until the 1890s while the movement grew in strength.

The movement might have remained pacifistic had Ch'oe Si-hyŏng been its only major leader, but in the early 1890s politics was joined to religion as the effects of economic dislocation and bureaucratic corruption produced an upsurge of rebellious discontent throughout the country. Two new types of Tonghak leaders emerged in response to the times, as represented by Chŏn Pong-jun and Son Pyŏng-hŭi. Chŏn assumed leadership of the Tonghak rebellion in 1894, brought discontented peasants into the movement, and achieved a number of military successes in the field against government forces. When Chŏn's southern forces joined with Son's northern forces against Japanese troops, it is reported that they were able to muster over two hundred thousand men.

The rebellion was crushed, but the Tonghak movement was kept alive thanks largely to the flexibility of Son Pyŏng-hŭi. He went underground in the late 1890s, traveled to Japan and cooperated with Yi Yong-gu in the founding of the Progressive Society, *Chinbohoe*, and then returned to Korea in 1905. He broke with Yi Yong-gu when the latter moved into the pro-Japanese societies, and he continued his political activities along with religious proselytization. He changed the name of the movement in 1906 from Tonghak to The Religion of the Heavenly Way, *Ch'ŏndogyo*, and he led the March 1 nationalist movement in 1919 and was one of the thirty-three signers of the Declaration of Independence.[52]

The foundation and organization of a new religious movement, the fomenting of the greatest rebellion of the dynasty, and the preservation of the movement into the colonial period and after was achieved partly by the emergence of types of leaders that would not have been possible before the mid-nineteenth century. The success they achieved was due to the creation of a faith that appealed to the masses of the oppressed and spiritually starved, the weakness of a central government continually beleaguered by foreign powers, the discontents aroused by economic dislocation and social disruption, and the establishment of a mass-based organizational network. The Tonghak rebellion, however, was in part the victim of unbridgeable separations in traditional society, since it was basically a lower-class movement that established too few links with the upper class and educated elite. When the political dominance of the Japanese was imposed in 1910, the movement sustained itself on a religious basis into the colonial period.

OTHER TYPES OF LEADERSHIP: MILITARY AND ECONOMIC

Military and commercial-industrial leadership has not been included in the discussion of Yi dynasty leaders simply because neither was an important form. The dynasty was not devoid of military leaders, since on occasion they were needed to participate against foreign invasion and to check domestic rebellion. But, notwithstanding Yi Sun-sin (the famous naval commander during the Hideyoshi invasions), military leadership did not play a major role in the Yi dynasty. Military leaders were handicapped by their relatively low status and the vicissitudes of bureaucratic politics. The major invasions of Korea were of short duration and ended quickly in defeat for Korea, so that military forces did not have to be maintained at a high level of preparedness for long periods of time. After the last Manchu invasion of 1636, the government maintained an extensive military establishment on paper, but its functional utility atrophied and it became more important as a source of sinecures for civil officials and as a source of taxation rather than as a service system for the general population. Furthermore, because of the Confucian emphasis on civil authority and possibly because of the fear of a recrudescence of the type of military domination that occurred in the Koryŏ dynasty, the military was relegated to a subordinate position throughout the Yi dynasty.

In the realm of economic endeavor, despite some growth of commercial acitivity after 1600, there were too many restrictions on economic growth and too great a stigma on economic activity to permit the emergence of powerful commercial or industrial leaders in society. Even after the breakdown of the rather narrow monopoly system of retail and wholesale shops that characterized the commerce of the early part of the dynasty, merchant middlemen were still too dependent on the government for support to establish an independent base of power. There was no growth of a town bourgeoisie to challenge the power of the yangban aristocracy.

LEADERSHIP IN TRADITIONAL KOREA

The varieties of leadership style possible in traditional Korea were limited by the structures, institutions, and values of Yi dynasty society. Leadership was confined for the most part to the political sphere and to a lesser extent the intellectual sphere; the recruitment of leaders in both areas was limited by the ascriptive values associated with a hierarchical social structure. Since the main theater of political action was a centralized bureaucracy under the control of a hereditary monarchy, the possibilities for the exercise of leadership had to be played out within the hierarchical organizational structure of the polity.

As is well known, bureaucratic organization tends over time to breed conformity, lack of initiative, and subordination of individuals to superiors. The task-oriented bureaucratic leader was the one who overcame these obstacles to accomplish goals, either as a local magistrate or governor, as sponsor of legislation, or as high level decision maker. The politically oriented leader was the one who achieved promotion or attained power either through individual action or as leader of a factional group.

Except for rebels outside the regular order of society, there was no room for the exercise of charismatic leadership. This conclusion is undeniable if emphasis is placed on the innovative or revolutionary aspect of charismatic leadership. We, therefore, have been dealing with a society in which traditional, legal, and bureaucratic authority have been the dominant themes. With that as a framework, however, it has been obvious that there was much variety in the types of leaders in traditional Korea, the type of leader changing as a function of circumstances.

Just how closed the old order was is demonstrated by the emergence of new types of leaders once the traditional system began to break down in the late nineteenth century. The most powerful political leaders were still members of the older structure—the king, queen, members of the Min lineage, and high officials—but in addition to those there were now leaders of a millenial religious and social movement, new types of officials who came into government service because of their experience abroad, and founders and organizers of political associations and newspapers. It is obvious that the changing situation was providing opportunities for more creative individual action as the controls over the population were weakening.

For most of the Yi dynasty, however, the potential for leadership was restricted to a small elite. Royal despotism was hampered by aristocratic and bureaucratic restraints and the general abhorrence of excessive authority. Innovative leadership by bureaucrats was obstructed by centralized, hierarchical organization and political leadership was limited by personal and small-group loyalties, family ties, dependence on the throne for favor, and the debilitating intermingling of moral and political issues.

NOTES

1. I have explored this theme in more detail in *Policy and Politics in Traditional Korea, 1864–1876* (Cambridge, Mass.: Harvard University Press, forthcoming).

2. The problem of whether leaders or elite groups actually exert leadership was raised by Etzioni in his discussion of elites. See Amitai Etzioni, *Complex Organizations* (New York: Holt, Rinehart & Winston, 1961), p. 114. Kenneth Janda seems to have raised the same issue in his discussion of the contrast between headship and leadership in "Towards the Explication of the Concept of Leadership in Terms of the Concept of Power," in *Political Leadership: Readings for an Emerging Field*, ed. Glenn D. Paige (New York: Free Press, 1972), pp. 45–68. Nevertheless, in this survey of leaders and leadership in traditional Korea, I have generally followed the broad outlines laid down by Glenn D. Paige, in "Part Two: A Conceptual Framework," in Paige, *Political Leadership*, pp. 69–84. In other words, I will discuss in topical and chronological fashion the six concepts of leadership that Paige stresses: personality, role, organization, task, values, and setting.

3. Max Weber, *Economy and Society: An Outline of Interpretive Sociology*, ed. Guenther Roth and Claus Wittich (New York: Bedminster Press, 1968), *passim*; Ann Ruth Willner, *Charismatic Political Leadership: A Theory*, Center of International Studies, Research Monograph no. 32 (Princeton, N.J., 1968); Dankwart A. Rustow, "The Study of Leadership" in *Philosophers and Kings: Studies in Leadership*, ed. Dankwart A. Rustow (New York: George Braziller, 1970), pp. 14–20; Etzioni, *Complex Organizations*, pp. 201–62.

4. I use the term "censorate" to cover the censorial functions exercised by three offices—the Office of Inspector-General (*sahŏnbu*), the Office of Censor-General (*saganwŏn*), and the Office of Special Counselors (*hongmun'gwan*). Competition between the throne and the aristocracy for resources is another theme that I have pursued at length. See note 1 above. The inspiration for this approach was provided by S. N. Eisenstadt, *The Political Systems of Empires* (New York: Free Press of Glencoe, 1963).

6. Han Woo-keun, *The History of Korea*, trans. Lee Kyung-shik (Honolulu: East-West Center Press, 1970), pp. 185–91, 203–6; Edward W. Wagner, "The Literati Purges, Case Studies in Factionalism of the Early Yi Dynasty" (Ph.D. diss., Harvard University, 1959), pp. 1–7; Yi Sang-baek, *Han'guksa kŭnse chŏn'gip'yŏn* [History of Korea, Recent Times, Early Period] (Seoul, 1962), pp. 25–71; Sohn Pow-key, "Social History of the Early Yi Dynasty, 1392–1592; With Emphasis on the Functional Aspects of Governmental Structure" (Ph.D. diss., University of California, Berkeley, 1963), chap. 1.

7. Wagner, "Literati Purges," pp. 7–10; Han Woo-keun, *History of Korea*, pp. 206–8; Yi Sang-baek, *Chŏn'gip'yŏn*, pp. 72–81.

8. Wagner, "Literati Purges," pp. 10–12; Han Woo-keun, *History of Korea*, pp. 208–12; Yi Sang-baek, *Chŏn'gip'yŏn*, pp. 81–91.

9. Gari K. Ledyard, "The Korean Language Reform of 1446: The Origin, Background, and Early History of the Korean Alphabet" (Ph.D. diss., University of California, Berkeley, 1966), pp. 79–123.

10. Wagner, "Literati Purges," pp. 12–17; Han Woo-keun, *History of Korea*, pp. 213–17; Yi Sang-baek, *Chŏn'gip'yŏn*, pp. 91–106.

11. Wagner, "Literati Purges," pp. 17–18, 49–99.

12. Ibid., pp. 100–235.

13. Ibid., pp. 236–427; Edward W. Wagner, "The Recommendation Examination of 1951: Its Place in Early Yi Dynasty History," *Chōsen gakuhō*, no. 15 (April 1960), pp. 1–79.

14. Sŏng Nak-hun, "Han'guk tangjaengsa" [History of Factionalism in Korea], in *Han'guk munhwasa taegye* [Grand Outline of Korean Cultural History], 6 vols. (Seoul, 1965), 2:232–71; Yi Sang-baek, *Chŏn'gip'yŏn*, pp. 562–84: Han Woo-keun, *History of Korea*, pp. 266–68; William E. Henthorn, *A History of Korea* (New York: Free Press, 1971), pp. 190–95.

15. Han Woo-keun, *History of Korea*, pp. 275-76, 300-301; Yi Sang-baek, *Han'guksa kŭnse hugip'yŏn* [History of Korea, Recent Times, Late Period] (Seoul, 1965), pp. 2–10; Sŏng Nak-hun, *Tangjaengsa*, pp. 272–87; Kang Chu-jin, *Yijo tangjaengsa yŏn'gu* [A study of Yi Dynasty Factionalism] (Seoul, 1971), pp. 84–95. Kwanghaegun has been held in low repute because he committed a fratricide. Furthermore, his diplomatic skill was not matched by political acumen; he could not control his bureaucrats.

16. Sŏng Nak-hun, *Tangjaengsa*, pp. 288–358; Kang Chu-jin, *Yijo tangjaengsa*, pp. 229–341; Han Woo-keun, *History of Korea*, p. 302.

17. Han Woo-keun, *History of Korea*, pp. 336–37; Sŏng Nak-hun, *Tangjaengsa*, pp. 372–83; Yi Sang-baek, *Hugip'yon*, pp. 62–67.

18. Choe Ching-young, "Kim Yuk (1580–1658) and the Taedongbŏp Reform," *Journal of Asian Studies* 23, no. 1 (November 1963):21–36.

19. See note 1 above. For general background, see Ch'a Mun-sŏp, "Imnan ihu ŭi yangyŏk kwa kyunyŏkbŏp ŭi sŏngnip [The Commoner-Service System and the Establishment of the Equal-Service System after Hideyoshi's Invasions], pt. 1, *Sahak yŏn'gu 10* (April 1961):115–31; pt. 2, *Sahak yŏn'gu* 11 (July 1961):83–146.

20. Han Woo-keun, "Chŏngjo pyŏng'o sohoe tŭngnok ŭi punsŏkchŏk yŏn'gu" [An Analysis of the Record of Recommendations Presented to King Chŏngjo in 1786], *Seoul taehakkyo nonmunjip* 11 (November 1965):3–51; Kim Yong-sŏp, "Chosŏn hugi ŭi nong'ŏp munje: Chŏngjo mallyŏn ŭi ŭngji chinnongsŏ ŭi punsŏk" [Problems in Agriculture in the Late Yi Dynasty: An Analysis of Recommendations for the Promotion of Agriculture at Royal Request at the End of Chŏngjo's Reign], *Han'guksa yŏn'gu* 2 (December 1968):53–103.

21. See note 1 above. See also Choe Ching-young, *The Rule of the Taewŏn'gun, 1864–1873: Restoration in Yi Korea* (Cambridge, Mass.: East Asian Research Center, Harvard University, 1972), passim. The interpretation presented here of the Taewŏn'gun and Kojong is mine.

22. For a survey of the last half of the nineteenth century and the end of the Yi dynasty, see Han Woo-keun, *History of Korea;* Hilary Conroy, *The Japanese Seizure of Korea, 1868–1910* (Philadelphia: University of Pennsylvania Press, 1960); C. I. Eugene Kim and Han-Kyo Kim, *Korea and the Politics of Imperialism, 1876–1910* (Berkeley: University of California Press, 1967); Chong-Sik Lee, *The Politics of Korean Nationalism* (Berkeley: University of California Press, 1963), pp. 3–85.

23. See note 17 above.

24. See note 18 above.

25. James B. Palais, "Korea on the Eve of the Kanghwa Treaty, 1873–76," (Ph.D. diss., Harvard University, 1968), pp. 667–796.

26. Yi Hong-jik, ed., *Kuksa taesajŏn* [Grand Dictionary of Korean History], 2 vols. (Seoul, 1962), 1:839–40.

27. Wagner, "Literati Purges," pp. 236–427; Wagner, "The Recommendation Examination of 1519"; *Kuksa taesajŏn*, 2:1397–98.

28. *Kuksa taesajŏn*, 1:282.

29. Ibid., 2:1068–69, Yi Sang-baek, *Chŏn'gip'yŏn*, pp. 555–62.

30. *Kuksa taesajŏn*, 1:775; Sŏng Nak-hun, *Tangjaengsa*, pp. 295–339; Kang Chu-jin, *Yijo tangjaensa*, pp. 127–70, passim.

31. *Kuksa taesajŏn*, 2:1742; 1:749; Yi Sang-baek, *Hugip'yŏn*, pp. 302–6; Yi Sŏn-gŭn, Han'guksa ch'oegŭnsep'yŏn [History of Korea, Most Recent Times] (Seoul, 1961), pp. 1–20.

32. Yi Sŏn-gŭn, *Choegŭnsep'yŏn*, pp. 29–36; Han Woo-keun, *History of Korea*, pp. 337–38; Palais, *Korea*, pp. 1–54; Choe Chin-young, *Rule of the Taewŏn'gun*, pp. 52–69.

33. Yi Sŏn-gŭn, *Ch'oegŭnsep'yŏn*, pp. 29–36; *Kuksa taesajŏn*, 1:300.

34. *Kuksa taesajŏn*, 2:1187–88; Ch'a Mun-sŏp, "Yi Wan-yong: minjok ŭi p'asan" [Yi Wan-yong: Treason and National Bankruptcy] in *Han'guk ŭi in'gansang* [Portraits of Famous Koreans], 6 vols. (Seoul, 1965), 1:478–99; Yi Sŏn-gŭn, *Han'guksa hyŏndaep'yŏn* [History of Korea, Modern Times] (Seoul, 1963), passim.

35. *Kuksa taesajŏn*, 1:772.

36. Ibid., 2:1188; Yi Sŏn-gŭn, *Hyŏndaep'yŏn*, passim.

37. *Kuksa taesajŏn*, 1:511–12; Yi Sŏn-gŭn, *Ch'oegŭnsep'yŏn* and *Hyŏndaep'yŏn*, passim.

38. See note 36 above.

39. *Kuksa taesajŏn*, 1:291; Yi Sŏn-gŭn, *Ch'oegŭnsep'yŏn* and *Hyŏndaep'yŏn*, passim.

40. *Kuksa taesajŏn*, 1:313–14; Yi Sŏn-gŭn, *Ch'oegŭnsop'yŏn* and *Hyŏndaep'yŏn*, passim; Yi Sŏn-gŭn, "Kim Hong-jip: Kwanghwamun ŭi pigŭk" [Kim Hong-jip: The Tragedy at Kwanghwa Gate] in *Han'guk ŭi in'gansang*, 1:453–78. The Kabo Reforms, with which Kim Hong-jip was intimately involved, have been studied recently by Young Ick Lew ("The Kabo Reform Movement: Korean and Japanese Reform Efforts In Korea, 1894" [Ph.D. diss., Harvard University, 1972]); Han Woo-keun, *History of Korea*, pp. 416–27.

41. Han Woo-keun, *History of Korea*, pp. 283–340; *Kuksa taesajŏn*, 2:1024; Yi Hŭi-sŭng, "Yu Kil-jun: Kŭndaehwarŭl hyang han paltodŭm" [Yu Kil-jun: A Foundation for Modernization] in *Han'guk ŭi in'gansang*, 6:109-124.

42. *Kuksa taesajŏn*, 1:719; Han Woo-keun, *History of Korea*, pp. 439-44; Kim and Kim, *Politics of Imperialism*, pp. 103-13; Lee, *Politics of Korean Nationalism*, passim; Homer B. Hulbert, *The Passing of Korea* (Seoul, 1969), pp. 148-68.

43. Harold F. Cook, *Korea's 1884 Incident* (Seoul, 1972); Conroy, *Seizure of Korea*, passim; Kim and Kim, *Politics of Imperialism*, pp. 41-52.

44. Cook, *Korea's 1884 Incident*, passim; *Kuksa taesajŏn*, 1:532.

45. See Warren Smith, "The Rise of the Sŏwŏn: Literary Academies in Sixteenth-Century Korea" (Ph.D. diss., University of California, Berkeley, 1972). Chap. 6 of my own manuscript (see note 1) also deals with the academies and the Taewŏn-gun's policy toward them.

46. Yi Sŏng-mu, "Sŏnch'o ŭi Sŏnggyun'gwan yŏn'gu" [A Study of the National Academy in the Early Yi Dynasty], *Yŏksa hakbo*, nos. 35-36 (December 1967), pp. 219-68; Choe Yong-ho, "The Civil Examinations and the Social Structure in Early Yi

Dynasty Korea: 1392–1600" (Ph.D. diss., University of Chicago, 1971), pp. 22–32, 87-98.

47. Hyŏn Sang-yun, *Chosŏn yuhaksa* [The History of Korean Confucianism] (Seoul, 1949), pp. 276-80.

48. Key P. Yang and Gregory Henderson, "An Outline History of Korean Confucianism," pt. 1, *Journal of Asian Studies* 18, no. 1 (November 1958):81–101; pt. 2, *Journal of Asian Studies* 18, no. 2 (February 1959): 259–76.

49. Han Woo-keun, *History of Korea*, passim. See also Yi Sang-baek, *Chŏn'gip'yŏn* and *Hugip'yŏn*.

50. Han Woo-keun, *History of Korea*, pp. 344–45; Kim Chin-bong, "Imsul millan ŭi sahoe kyongjejŏk paegyong" [The Socio-economic Background of the 1862 Peasant Rebellion], *Sahak yŏn'gu* 19 (April 1967), pp. 89–127.

51. Yi Sŏn-gŭn, *Ch'oegŭnsep'yŏn*, passim; Han Woo-keun, *History of Korea*, pp. 354, 405.

52. For Ch'oe Si-hyong, Chŏn Pong-jun, and Son Pyŏng-hŭi. see Yi Sŏn-gŭn, *Hyŏndaep'yŏn*, passim, and the relevant entries in the *Kuksa taesajŏn*. For accounts in English, see Han Woo-keun, *History of Korea*, pp. 403-15; Benjamin B. Weems, *Reform, Rebellion, and the Heavenly Way* (Tucson: University of Arizona Press, 1964); Conroy, *Seizure of Korea*, pp. 229-40; Lee, *Politics of Korean Nationalism*, passim.

PART II

Institutional Context of Leadership

2. Legislative Leadership and Democratic Development

CHONG LIM KIM and BYUNG-KYU WOO

INTRODUCTION

Progressive social change in developing countries is often the direct result of the concerted effort of a relatively small group of elite. The developmental role of the elite is important because of the fundamental social gap that exists between the modernizing elite and the mass populace.[1] Characteristically, the elite are Western-educated, committed to secular values, and aspire to rapid socioeconomic development. By comparison, the masses in developing countries tend to remain attached to traditional values: they have predominantly sacral, parochial, and nonparticipant orientations.[2] Therefore, if social development is to take place, the initiative should come not from the mass population but from the modernizing elite who stand in the strategic center of developmental possibilities.

Legislators are an important part of the modernizing elite in many developing countries. It is also true that the power of the legislature is often circumscribed by the executive, the bureaucracy, the military, or the ruling party. Nonetheless, popularly elected legislators may often provide an important link between government and the masses. Indeed, among elite groups, legislators are probably the most sensitive to the needs and demands of the masses simply because they are subject to periodic approval by the voters. Moreover, other institutions of political representation are usually not fully developed in these countries. First, few effectively organized interest groups exist, and even those that do seldom operate as autonomous bodies because they are frequently

The original version of this article appeared under the title "The Role of Legislative Elites in Democratic Change: An Analysis of Democratic Commitment Among Korean National Legislators," by Chong Lim Kim and Byung-Kyu Woo published in *Comparative Political Studies* 6, no. 3 (Oct. 1973): 349-80 and is reprinted herewith by permission of the publisher, Sage Publications, Inc.

organized by the government or the ruling party.³ As a result, these groups cannot serve as effective channels of interest representation. Second, political parties tend to be inefficient vehicles for interest representation. As David Apter has suggested, the ideology and organization of political parties in developing countries tend to be monopolistic and directed.⁴ The main goal of parties is to mobilize the population for policy objectives set by the party leadership rather than to bring together the diverse interests of the masses. Third, along with interest groups and parties, the bureaucracy is another institution that can, in theory, process the demands of the citizenry. In developing countries, however, the bureaucrats still retain elitist attitudes, a heritage from the colonial or traditional political order. They have an excessive sense of self-importance, and they lack the notion that bureaucrats are public servants accountable to the citizenry. These attitudes make bureaucrats of developing countries less accessible to the public and less responsive to the sentiments of the masses.

In the absence of other institutions that can share the burden of mass representation, it is only natural that the pressure for representation in developing countries falls mainly upon the legislature and its members. From the point of view of democratic development, the role of the legislative elite is important, not only because it is a part of national leadership, but because it occupies the most strategic position in linking the relatively nonpoliticized public to the government. The extent to which the legislative elite is committed to democratic principles may help determine the prospect for democratic change. If the legislative elite holds antidemocratic attitudes and resists democratic change, the chance for democratic development in a country will obviously be reduced.

The purpose of this study is to assess the role of legislative leadership in democratic development. More specifically, the study is divided into three sections: (1) an examination of the performance of the South Korean National Assembly from 1948 to 1967; (2) an analysis of the democratic commitment manifested by members of the assembly; and (3) an exploration of sources of democratic orientations. This study is based on interviews with legislators and on an analysis of documentary data pertaining to legislative performance. The interview survey was conducted during the period from July 1968 to March 1969. Altogether, 112 members of the seventh National Assembly (1967–71) were interviewed. Among those who completed interviews, 81 were members of the ruling Democratic Republican party (DRP), 30 were members of the opposition New

Democratic party (NDP), and one member was not affiliated with any party.⁵ This distribution closely represents the relative strength of each party in the 175-member assembly. The interview data include information on the legislator's social background, career experiences, role perceptions, and commitment to democratic principles. The documentary data are derived from the official history of the National Assembly, *Kukhoesa*, a three-volume compilation of legislative records and statistics.⁶

LEGISLATIVE PERFORMANCE: 1948–1967

By the standards of developing countries, South Korea has a relatively long parliamentary tradition. The National Assembly, *kukhoe*, was established in 1948 and has functioned more or less continuously ever since. Therefore, Koreans have a parliamentary history that extends well over two decades. During this period, the assembly has faced and survived many political crises. The most disruptive event was the Korean War of 1950, which lasted three full years, leaving the country completely devastated; it also seriously affected the normal operation of the newly established legislature. The April 19 student revolution of 1960, which resulted in the fall of the Syngman Rhee regime, brought an abrupt dissolution of the fourth Assembly before its term expired. Shortly afterward, the legislature was once again dissolved for almost two years following the 1961 military revolution. However, despite many political crises and conditions adverse to the development of a viable legislature, the National Assembly has remained a remarkably vital force.

Legislative Output

The six assemblies elected between 1948 and 1967 discharged their official function with various types of legislative actions including legislation, policy endorsement, investigation, inquiry, policy recommendation, resolution, and petition. These different legislative actions are defined as follows:

1. *Legislation:* The constitution permits both the government and individual legislators to initiate and sponsor legislative bills. During the period examined, a total of 2,318 bills were submitted; only 999 were passed by the assembly.

2. *Legislative policy endorsement:* Certain government actions, largely in the area of financial matters and taxation, require legislative endorsement as does the appointment of a high ranking official. Through the exercise of the power of legislative endorsement, the

assembly can in effect veto some actions of the government.

3. *Legislative investigation:* The assembly conducts two types of investigations—annual and special. Annual investigations, normally conducted at the end of each fiscal year, enable the legislature to probe any part of the executive branch. Special investigations of any social or political problem may be organized by the assembly if necessary. The six assemblies made a total of 144 annual and special investigations.

4. *Legislative inquiry:* The assembly has power to make both oral and written inquiries to various executive branches regarding their decisions and actions. In the case of a written inquiry, the branch of government concerned is required by law to reply within a specified period of time.

5. *Policy recommendation:* Although this action is not legally binding, the assembly can recommend to the executive branch that the latter consider, formulate, or modify its policy. This is an important legislative power through which the legislature may initiate or influence governmental action. The assembly adopted 325 policy recommendations from 1948 to 1967.

6. *Resolution:* The assembly can express its opinion in the form of resolutions. The bulk of resolutions that the National Assembly has adopted in the past relate to rather incidental matters, such as a congratulatory note to a Korean marathon team that gave a good performance. However, resolutions can provide, if used properly, an important means by which the legislature expresses its collective view on a wide range of social and political issues.

7. *Petition:* The citizens have the constitutional right to submit petitions to the assembly. On receiving such a petition, the Secretariat of the Assembly schedules a hearing in an appropriate standing committee. If appropriate, the assembly deals with a petition through legislation. Or, if a petition requires an administrative action, the assembly may send it to the appropriate branch of government with its written opinion attached to it. Over the years, the assembly has accepted between 100 and 300 petitions annually.

This list covers virtually all official activities in which the assembly engages as a collective body.

By analyzing the amount of legislative activity, it is possible to assess the past performance of the assembly.[7] Table 1 presents performance data, computed on an annual basis, for each of the six assemblies. The National Assembly appears to be quite an active body. On the average, it stayed in session for 147 days each year, deliberated an average of 196 bills, and passed some 63 pieces of legislation. Although the number of legislative investigations and inquiries varied considerably from year to year, on the average the assembly made about 10 investigations and 29 inquiries annually. In addition, it considered 27 cases of government action for each year for which the executive branch requested legislative endorsements. The number of policy recommendations and resolutions that the assembly adopted was also sizable: it made, on the average, 20 policy recommendations to the government and produced 49 resolutions.

One important activity of the assembly of direct interest to its constituency is, of course, its deliberation of petitions. When a citizen or a group of citizens submits a petition, it is normally sent to one of the 13 standing committees for deliberation and decision. The assembly received an average of 163 petitions a year, and granted decisions on about 57 percent of them. In most cases petitions accepted by the assembly were of a corrective nature: one group of citizens might attempt to reroute some municipal bus lines or protest the construction of a factory in their community. At times, citizens submit petitions in order to obtain direct social or economic benefits—such as the request for a school building or the construction of a bridge.

Of the six assemblies, the short-lived fifth Assembly was by far the most active. It was very much a product of the 1960 student revolution. After a brief period of the interim government under Hŏ Chŏng, a free election took place to elect 233 members of the fifth Assembly, and the Democratic party, led by both Chang Myŏn and Yun Po-sŏn of the "new" and "old" factions, won a clear majority. After many years of autocratic rule under the Syngman Rhee regime, the national mood in 1960 was clearly one of optimism and bright hope for democratic change. Gregory Henderson described the mood during the early days of the Chang regime:

> A wave of popular, press, and legislative feeling, even among former Liberals, supported this sweeping democratic thrust against autocracy. The stage seemed set for successful democratic government, responsive to public opinion at home, applauded abroad. An atmosphere of hopefulness, even pride, prevailed.[8]

However, the Second Republic was abruptly ended by the 1961 military revolution. With it, also came the dissolution of the fifth Assembly. Thus, this assembly functioned for less than nine months, the shortest term ever in Korean legislative history.

Despite its relatively short period of operation, the fifth Assembly was the most productive legislature. It considered and passed the largest number of legislative bills (370 and 87.5, respectively). It also deliberated and granted the largest number of legislative endorsements requested by the government (42.5 and 32.5). Furthermore, the fifth Assembly was the most active in the areas of investigations and inquiries. It organized 16 such investigations, and submitted 48 oral and written inquiries to the government. Not only did the fifth Assembly enact the largest number of policy recommendations to the government, it also adopted the largest number of resolutions. In terms of the number of petitions received, the fifth Assembly again ranks first: it received a total of 268 petitions, which may reflect the increased sense of political competence among the citizens in the wake of many democratic reforms. If one may judge the performance of each assembly according to the *amount* of its legislative action alone, the fifth Assembly might be considered the most active in Korean legislative history.

The total amount of legislative activity fluctuated from year to year. The performance data found in table 1 do not indicate that the assembly became steadily more active over the years; nor do they indicate a pattern of steadily decreasing legislative activity. Numerous studies of participant citizenship in developing coun-

TABLE 1

LEVEL OF LEGISLATIVE PERFORMANCE IN THE ASSEMBLY: 1948–1967
(Annual Output)

Type of action	Assembly 1	2	3	4	5	6	Average
Days in session	199.5	157.7	152.2	106.0	177.5	91.2	147.4
Bills submitted	117.0	99.5	102.5	161.0	370.0	164.0	169.0
Bills passed	74.5	54.0	39.2	37.5	87.5	83.0	62.6
Endorsements requested by government	24.0	28.0	29.2	17.5	42.5	22.5	27.3
Endorsements granted	20.5	23.5	25.7	13.7	32.5	20.0	22.6
Legislative investigations	9.5	7.7	13.5	6.0	16.2	5.0	9.7
Legislative inquiries	40.5	31.5	22.5	12.0	47.5	19.7	29.0
Policy recommendations submitted	26.0	34.0	41.2	26.0	88.7	40.7	42.8
Policy recommendations adopted	17.0	22.2	25.7	13.5	28.7	12.2	19.9
Resolutions submitted	46.5	77.2	41.2	55.0	122.5	46.2	64.8
Resolutions adopted	33.5	64.5	33.2	41.0	92.5	28.5	48.9
Petitions submitted	113.0	56.2	136.2	153.5	268.0	249.5	162.7
Petitions acted upon	76.5	25.0	85.2	32.0	137.5	200.7	92.8

NOTE: For each category of legislative action, the most active assembly is indicated by an underline.

tries suggest that, as their social and economic conditions improve, the citizenry takes on an increasingly higher interest in politics, becomes more politically active, and develops a greater feeling of competence with respect to its ability to influence the governmental process.[9] Therefore, urbanization, industrialization, education, and communications development are considered inducements to participant orientations among the citizenry. Politically aware and active citizens will, as a consequence, make more effective demands on various parts of the government and, consequently, the legislature will face an increasing number of demands from the public.

The impressive record of socioeconomic development in South Korea needs little elaboration here.[10] Suffice it to say that urbanization has occurred with phenomenal speed, even raising a serious problem of overurbanization. Illiteracy has been successfully wiped out and industrialization has taken place at a rapid rate, largely due to the influx of foreign loans and investments. The most impressive advance may be the development of communications networks and more efficient transportation, as indicated by the number of radio and television sets and the new road system that links the remote parts of the country with urban centers. All of these changes might have politicized a large number of citizens. But though the improved social conditions in Korea could have been expected to make citizens more politically aware, participating, and competent, the amount of legislative activity has not increased correspondingly. Perhaps the socioeconomic development did not effect participant citizenship; or perhaps the National Assembly was incapable of responding to the increased demands made by the ever active citizens. Whatever the reasons, the level of legislative performance in Korea has shown no signs of being directly related to socioeconomic progress.

Legislative Autonomy

Some students of political development contend that the pressing need for a rapid improvement of socioeconomic conditions of life in developing countries tends to accelerate the growth of a centralized administrative structure—which outstrips the pace of development in other sectors of the political system—and that the emergence of a strong modern bureaucracy tends to weaken the role of representative institutions.[11] Sigelman has succinctly summarized this view:[12]

The chief components of the argument that bureaucratic development hinders the prospects of political development are the propositions that: (1) the relatively high development of bureaucratic system in new states fosters overparticipation by the bureaucracy in the governmental and political functions; and (2) such bureaucratic overparticipation stunts the growth of viable representative institutions.

The imbalance between administrative and representative institutions, some students argue, is a common feature of politics in developing systems. Moreover, the dominance of the administrative system in new states is said to be an inevitable result of its high functional capability and high relevance to economic development. What these observations suggest is simply that political power tends to be concentrated in the executive branch of government, where there is a strong desire for a rapid economic development, as is the case in Korea, and that the establishment of a powerful administrative structure inevitably results in the erosion of legislative independence.

In Korea, the decline of the legislature has been observed and made a central concern in both scholarly and journalistic discussions. The subservient role of the National Assembly, *kukhoe sinyŏhwa*, has often been lamented by many concerned scholars and columnists.[13] The belief that the power of the Korean legislature is declining seems to be based upon the observation that the power of the executive branch overshadows that of the legislature to such an extent that the assembly functions as a mere rubber stamp organization.

Is it true that the autonomy of the National Assembly has diminished over the years? Both students of political development and some observers of Korean politics would have us believe so. The degree of legislative autonomy may be measured in several ways. The simplest measure might be the relative strength of the government party in the assembly.[14] Another simple measure is the frequency with which individual legislators, as opposed to the government, submit bills. Because both the government and individual members of the assembly can propose legislation, the frequency with which individual legislators sponsor bills could indicate the degree of legislative autonomy. More direct measures are also available; for example, one can take the percentage of individually sponsored legislation that is rejected. As the autonomy of the assembly declines, the chances of an individual member's bill passing may also decrease. Similarly, one can use the percentage of government-proposed legislation that is to indicate legislative autonomy. It seems plausible to assume that the greater the percentage of government-proposed bills that fail to pass, the greater the autonomy of the legislative body. It was mentioned earlier that the assembly has veto power over certain actions and decisions of the government, a power exercised through granting or denying legislative endorsements requested by the executive branch. The frequency with which the assembly withholds its endorsement from the government requests may reflect the degree of legislative independence. Therefore, one can employ the percentage of legislative endorsements denied to the government as an indicator of autonomy.

The National Assembly has various types of constitutional power to check and balance the influence of the executive branch, the most important of which is the power to organize legislative investigations and to address inquiries to the government. The assembly can also exercise some control over the executive branch by the adoption of the policy recommendations or resolutions concerning social issues of importance, both of which are effective instruments to express its collective view on various issues. If used frequently and judiciously, all these powers can enhance the autonomy of the assembly. For this reason, the frequency with which the assembly conducts investigations or inquiries, adopts policy recommendations, or expresses its view through resolutions, may be taken as yet another indicator of legislative autonomy.

In figures 1 through 4 we present data for nine indicators of legislative autonomy, calculated on a per year basis. The over-all pattern shows that the degree of autonomy of the legislative branch has fluctuated. Contrary to the contention of some observers of Korean politics, the data show no clear evidence that the autonomy of the National Assembly has steadily declined over the years. For instance, the percentage of bills initiated by individual members as compared to those of the government were relatively high in the second, fifth, and sixth Assemblies, whereas members of the first and fourth Assemblies were the least active in proposing legislation. Thus, it is apparent that legislators did not become less active over the years in initiating legislation. Regarding the frequency with which the assembly denies the passage of government-sponsored legislation, perhaps the most sensitive measure of legislative autonomy, one observes no visible pattern that the government has become more effective in securing the passage of bills it sponsors (see fig. 2).

We can also assess the degree of autonomy of the National As-

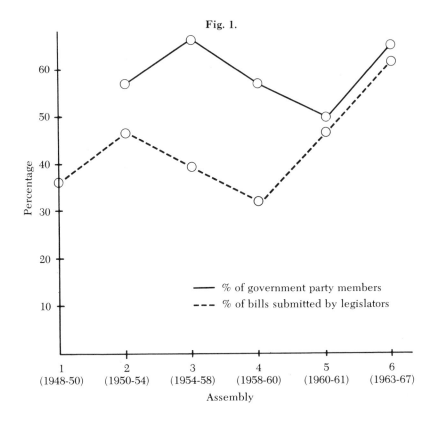

Fig. 1.

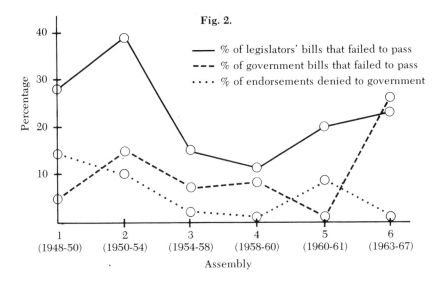

Fig. 2.

Fig. 3.

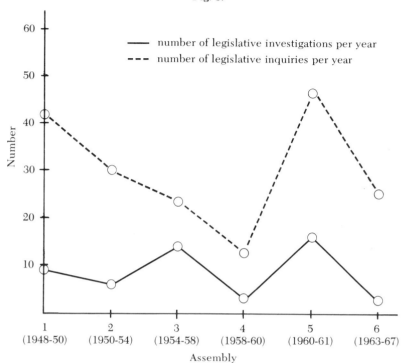

——— number of legislative investigations per year
– – – number of legislative inquiries per year

sembly in terms of its use of investigative and advisory powers. The extent to which the assembly exercises its investigative power, and the extent to which it makes policy suggestions and resolutions to the executive branch, indicate the relative power of the legislature vis-à-vis the administrative branch. If the autonomy of the assembly has declined over the years, one should observe a clear pattern of diminishing frequency with which the assembly exercises these powers. On the contrary, the data reported in figures 3 and 4 show no such pattern, suggesting that the National Assembly did not relinquish its power of influence over the executive branch.

Taken as a whole, our data show no evidence to substantiate the argument for *kukhoe sinyŏhwa*, the decline of the legislature. The autonomy of the National Assembly did not gradually decline during the period under examination, nor did it remain relatively stable over the period; the over-all trend was that of wide fluctuation from year to year. A close examination of our data also reveals that the degree of autonomy of any one assembly was generally coinci-

Fig. 4.

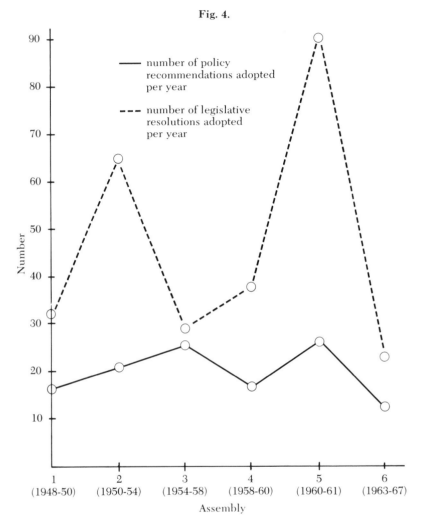

dent with its level of legislative activity. The more productive an assembly, the greater its degree of autonomy vis-à-vis the executive branch. The analysis of the past performance of the National Assembly therefore discloses neither a trend of declining legislative activity nor a trend of diminished autonomy.

DEMOCRATIC COMMITMENT AMONG MEMBERS OF THE SEVENTH ASSEMBLY

Although the term *political democracy* has many different meanings, normative and empirical theories of democracy suggest three central features.[15] One is the two-pronged principle of majority rule and minority rights. The former implies that once political preferences are registered, the views of the majority should prevail for the whole group. Institutionally, majority rule may be translated into universal adult suffrage and the one-man-one-vote principle. As a means of safeguarding against the potential tyranny of the majority, political democracy is also concerned with minority rights, the freedom of a minority to dissent from the majority opinion and to criticize the majority view.

Another feature of political democracy relates to accountable leadership. In complex modern societies direct participation by all citizens in political decision making is simply not feasible; thus, the rule by a few elite may inevitably result. Nonetheless, the governing elite can be made accountable to the governed by means of periodic elections. Schumpeter, Dahl, and other scholars have argued that political democracy should not be defined in terms of whether or not citizens participate directly in policy making, but in terms of whether or not citizens have institutional means to make leaders accountable.[16] The principle of leadership accountability is therefore another feature of democracy.

The third element of political democracy is flexibility in government; that is, the ability to adapt to the constantly changing environment. Dahl has argued that democracy is not a static system, but a dynamic one capable of altering with societal change.[17] As a society undergoes profound change, such as those changes now unfolding in many developing countries, the structure of political interests may also change. Since democracy is a system supposedly responsive to the needs and demands of citizens, it must reflect the restructured pattern of interests that come with societal change. In the Korean context, this principle has particular relevance, for until 1945, when Korea was liberated from Japanese rule, political democracy was an alien form of government.[18] Democratic change, in the Korean context, implies therefore an erosion of traditional political order. The less the commitment to traditional modes of politics, the better the opportunity for democratic development.[19] Favorable attitudes toward political changes, then, are prerequisites of democratic change.

The three central features of democracy—majority rule and minority rights, accountable leadership, and adaptability—served as our theoretical basis for ascertaining the degree of democratic commitment. Questions included in our interview survey were designed to measure a legislator's commitment to the three democratic principles. To assess a legislator's commitment to the principles of majority rule and minority rights, we asked him three Likert-type questions. Each of these questions pertained to a legislator's attitudes toward the right of the public to criticize majority views, the right to dissent, and the role of the population in politics.

With respect to the principle of accountable leadership, the legislators were asked to respond to four questions: are your constituents aware of your positions on key legislative issues; do your constituents have some knowledge of what is going on in the assembly; do your constituents know enough about politics; and how will your vote in the legislature affect your chance for re-election? The underlying assumption here is that a responsive legislator who understands the voters' competence is likely to anticipate the reactions of the voters, and therefore is likely to manifest accountable attitudes.

Commitment to the principle of adaptability was measured by three questions. We asked the legislators the extent to which they feel their primary duty is to preserve the existing political structure; the extent to which they are committed to accepted traditions and practices as the basis of political conduct; and the extent to which they are opposed to the adoption of Western institutions. With these three items, we attempted to assess the legislators' attitudes toward political change.

As shown in table 2, a clear majority of the legislators were committed to majority rule and minority rights. Approximately 82 percent of the legislators indicated that the minority should be allowed to speak publicly against the views of the majority (issue 1). Similarly, 84 percent of the legislators thought that the minority had the right to dissent (issue 2). With respect to the role of the masses, the legislators exhibited quite favorable attitudes: 59 percent of the legislators believed that they themselves should act in accordance with the will of the masses (issue 3). Although the commitment was not unanimous, a substantial majority of the legislators expressed a commitment to the democratic principle of majority rule and minority rights.

Table 3 contains data pertaining to the legislators' commitment to the democratic principle of accountability. More than one-half of the legislators asserted that their constituents were well informed about the activities of the assembly, and 42 percent of the legislators believed that the constituents knew what positions their representatives took on crucial issues. However, the responses to the remaining two accountability questions (issues 3 and

4) were not quite as favorable: only 29 percent of the legislators thought that the way they voted affected their chances for re-election, and only 26 percent of the legislators felt that their constituents knew enough about politics.

TABLE 2

DISTRIBUTION OF RESPONSE ON MAJORITY RULE AND
MINORITY RIGHTS ISSUES
(In Percentages)

Issues	*Strongly Agree*	*Agree*	*Dis-agree*	*Strongly Disagree*	*Not As-cer-tained*	*Total (N = 112)*
1. We should not allow people to say publicly that which is contradictory to the opinion of the majority.	8	8	22	60	2	100
2. When most of the people want to do something, the rest should not criticize	3	10	19	65	3	100
3. Politics must be guided by enlightened and experienced leaders rather than by the will of the masses.	6	27	27	32	8	100

TABLE 3

DISTRIBUTION OF RESPONSE ON ACCOUNTABILITY ISSUES
(In Percentages)

Issues	*Yes*	*No*	*Don't Know*	*Total (N = 112)*
1. Do you think most of your constituents are aware of the positions you take on key legislative issues?	42	28	30	100
2. Do you think most of the voters in your district know what is going on in the National Assembly?	57	20	23	100
3. Do you think the way you vote in the assembly will significantly affect your chances in the next election?	29	48	23	100
4. In general, do you think your constituents know enough about politics?	26	62	12	100

Compared to the level of commitment to majority rule and minority rights, the legislators indicated a considerably lower commitment to the principle of accountability. Speculatively, the low commitment to the principle of accountability may be explained in terms of the persistence of elitism inherited from Korea's past. The authority of public office traditionally originated from higher sources in the hierarchy of government, ultimately resting in the person of the king; public officials were accountable to their superiors. There was neither an institutional means nor an official ideology that made officials accountable to the governed. Protected by their status and the mandate from above, officials exercised an awesome authority over the people. This tradition might still encourage the belief that public officials are entitled to special privileges and power. Both the public and officials themselves still refer to the old adage, *kwanjon minbi* (officials revered, the people despised), which describes well the persisting elitism of officials. The low commitment to accountable leadership may be a result of the long tradition of such elitism.

The third dimension of democratic commitment is adaptability. The data in table 4 indicate that the legislators were evenly divided on the principle of adaptability. About 50 percent of them disagreed with the statement that their foremost duty was to preserve the existing political structure, which suggests that half of the legis-

TABLE 4

DISTRIBUTION OF RESPONSE ON ADAPTABILITY ISSUES
(In Percentages)

Issues	Strongly Agree	Agree	Dis- agree	Strongly Disagree	Not As- cer- tained	Total (N = 112)
1. The primary duty of a legislator is to work for the preservation of the present political structure.	23	17	31	19	10	100
2. Just like all other social institutions, political institutions function best when based on accepted traditions and practices.	41	19	13	20	7	100
3. We will be making a serious mistake if we adopt Western institutions uncritically, because our history and traditions are fundamentally different from those of the West.	15	20	30	30	5	100

lators were committed to some form of political change. On the issue of adopting Western institutions, almost 60 percent of the legislators indicated agreement with this practice. Thus, the legislators' attitudes toward political change were divided: half of them were willing to change and the other half were not. Many observers have characterized the ideology of the major Korean parties as conservative, arguing that Korean parties are "parliamentary parties" with weak or no visible organization outside the legislature, and that legislative members of these parties are not strongly committed to programs of social and political change. The indiscriminate accusation that the National Assembly is a bulwark of conservatism, a view often suggested both in scholarly and journalistic writings, needs to be challenged. Although the commitment to political change is not unanimous, a substantial number of legislators are in fact willing to effect political change. Therefore, the National Assembly can be seen as a political body representing both conservative and progressive viewpoints.

SOME CORRELATES OF DEMOCRATIC COMMITMENT

The members of the seventh Assembly manifested quite divergent attitudes toward the three democratic principles discussed above. To determine the possible sources for these differences we chose as variables five attributes of the legislators—birthplace, education, type of district, method of election, and party affiliation—with respect to which commitment to the three principles was scored as strong, moderate, or weak.

Table 5 shows the relationships between commitment to majority rule and minority rights and the five attributes of the legislators. Looking at birthplace first, the data indicate a pronounced tendency for rural-born legislators to be more strongly committed to this principle than urban-born legislators: approximately 32 percent of those born in rural areas were strongly committed to majority rule and minority rights, while only 19 percent of those born in urban communities were similiarly committed. The level of education gave a negative correlation with the level of commitment: the higher the level of education, the lower the commitment to majority rule and minority rights. However, previous studies of the public, conducted in South Korea and elsewhere, have shown that the highly educated stratum, as compared with less educated groups, tends to maintain attitudes more consistent with the democratic process, such as a higher sense of political efficacy, a higher political awareness, and a higher level of participation.[20] Among the legislative elite, however, the contrary was the case: the higher the education level, the lower the democratic commitment.

TABLE 5

RELATIONSHIPS BETWEEN SELECTED VARIABLES AND COMMITMENT
TO MAJORITY RULE AND MINORITY RIGHTS
(In Percentages)

| Variables | Level of Commitment | | | |
	Strong	Moderate	Weak	Total
Birthplace:				
Urban	19	38	43	100 (21)
Rural	32	34	34	100 (71)
Education:				
Advanced degree	24	42	34	100 (24)
College degree	34	31	35	100 (78)
High school or less	40	40	20	100 (10)
Type of district:				
Urban	52	26	22	100 (23)
Mixed	40	33	27	100 (15)
Rural	28	39	33	100 (46)
Method of election:				
Single-member district	37.	34	29	100 (85)
Nation-wide district	22	33	45	100 (27)
Party affiliation:				
Democratic-Republican	27	36	37	100 (81)
New Democratic	47	30	23	100 (30)

The level of democratic commitment was also associated with type of electoral districts from which the legislators were elected. Legislators elected from urban districts were more strongly committed to majority rule and minority rights than were those elected from mixed or rural districts.[21] This difference may reflect the varying degrees of political sophistication between urban and rural voters. The voters in urban communities are generally better informed about politics, and they are also more strongly committed to the democratic process than are rural voters. Consequently, the urban voters are likely to support candidates whose perspectives are more democratic.

The electoral system in Korea combined the elements of geographic and proportional representation. Two-thirds of the members of the National Assembly were elected from single-member districts; the remaining one-third were selected from prepared party lists.[22] Because both groups of legislators had drastically different constituencies, their democratic attitudes were also different. The data indicate that the legislators elected from single-member districts were more strongly committed to majority rule and minority rights than the legislators-at-large. While 37 percent of the regular members showed a strong commitment, only 22 percent of those with national constituencies exhibited similar attitudes.

There were two major political parties in the seventh National Assembly, the ruling Democratic Republican party (DRP) and the opposition New Democratic party (NDP). An earlier analysis of members of the two parties indicated that they held different views on a wide range of crucial political issues.[23] Do legislators of different parties have significantly different commitments to majority rule and minority rights? Among the members of the NDP 47 percent indicated a strong commitment, whereas only 27 of the members of the DRP reported similar commitments.

The evidence suggests that a higher commitment to majority rule and minority rights was found among those legislators who were born in rural areas, had relatively little formal education, were elected from the urban districts, had clearly defined geographic constituencies (such as those elected from single-member districts), and who were the members of the opposition party.

Another dimension of democratic commitment consists of the legislators' attitudes toward accountability of leadership. In table 6, the data indicate that those legislators born in rural areas were more strongly committed to accountability than were legislators born in large urban communities. Highly educated legislators were less committed to the principle of accountability than were those with less education. Along with our findings that the higher the level of education, the lower the commitment to majority rule and minority rights, the inverse correlation between education and commitment to accountability seems highly significant. Why is it that among the South Korean legislators a higher education tends to reduce one's commitment to democratic principles? The answer may lie in the elitist character of higher education in Korea. Democratic ideals have been emphasized in the textbooks and in classroom instruction at all levels of education since the liberation, and this might have instilled democratic perspectives among many students. Nevertheless, in higher education the success of this effort appears to have been considerably less. In advanced Western societies university students are not normally regarded as the ex officio elite, but in developing countries they enjoy a special social status[24] and a college education is often an exclusive avenue to privileged social positions. In a sense it is paradoxical that university students are taught in the tradition of liberal political philosophy—with great emphasis placed on such concepts as equality, responsible leadership, and mass participation—while they are constantly exalted as members of a privileged group. Evidently, university education in Korea tends to heighten one's sense of being a member of the elite and as a consequence, university graduates may feel that they stand above the ordinary citizen and are entitled to privileges and power without any obligation to account for how they use it.

TABLE 6

RELATIONSHIPS BETWEEN SELECTED VARIABLES AND COMMITMENT
TO THE PRINCIPLE OF ACCOUNTABILITY
(In Percentages)

Variable	*Strong*	*Moderate*	*Weak*	*Total (N)*
		Level of Commitment		
Birthplace:				
Urban	14	48	38	100 (21)
Rural	35	34	31	100 (71)
Education:				
Advanced degree	21	33	46	100 (24)
College degree	37	32	31	100 (78)
High school or less	30	50	20	100 (10)
Type of district:				
Urban	69	22	9	100 (23)
Mixed	40	40	20	100 (15)
Rural	32	37	31	100 (46)
Method of election:				
Single-member district	43	35	22	100 (85)
Nation-wide district	3	30	67	100 (27)
Party affiliation:				
Democratic-Republican	27	36	37	100 (81)
New Democratic	47	33	20	100 (30)

The level of commitment to accountability was strongly associated with the type of district and the method of election. The legislators from urban districts tended to be more strongly committed to accountability than were those elected from mixed or rural districts. The association between the level of commitment and methods of election was even more striking. Those elected from single-member districts were markedly more supportive of the principle of accountability than were the legislators selected from party lists. Note that 43 percent of the legislators with district constituencies as compared to only 3 percent of the legislators-at-large indicated a strong commitment. While legislators elected from single-member districts have clearly defined geographic constituencies, legislators-at-large represent a national constituency, a vaguely defined focus indeed. Therefore, legislators elected from regular single-member districts are more likely to show accountable attitudes.[25]

Party difference was also related to the level of commitment to accountability. Approximately 47 percent of the members of the NDP as compared to only 27 percent of the members of the DRP were strongly committed. With regard to the level of commitment to majority rule and minority rights, and accountability, it seems clear that the members of the NDP had more democratic attitudes.

Commitment to the principle of adaptability indicates the extent to which legislators are willing to effect political change. In table 7, one notes strong correlations between the level of commitment and the birthplace of the legislators, their level of education, and their

TABLE 7

RELATIONSHIPS BETWEEN SELECTED VARIABLES AND COMMITMENT
TO THE PRINCIPLE OF ADAPTABILITY
(In Percentages)

| *Variables* | *Level of Commitment* | | | |
	Strong	*Moderate*	*Weak*	*Total (N)*
Birthplace:				
Urban	14	24	62	100 (21)
Rural	35	38	27	100 (71)
Education:				
Advanced degree	62	21	17	100 (24)
College degree	27	37	36	100 (78)
High school or less	10	40	50	100 (10)
Type of district:				
Urban	40	30	30	100 (23)
Mixed	20	27	53	100 (15)
Rural	42	28	30	100 (46)
Method of election:				
Single-member district	36	29	35	100 (85)
Nation-wide district	26	48	26	100 (27)
Party affiliation:				
Democratic-Republican	36	34	30	100 (81)
New Democratic	21	36	43	100 (30)

party affiliation. Legislators born in rural communities tended to be more willing to effect change than were those born in urban centers. Of those born in rural villages, 35 percent showed highly adaptable attitudes, while only 14 percent of the legislators born in cities indicated similar attitudes. Those legislators with a high level of education tended to have more adaptable attitudes than those with a lower level of education. Among those who hold degrees from graduate or advanced professional colleges, almost 62 percent were willing to effect political change. By comparison, only 10 percent of those with a high school education or lower had similar inclinations. It is thus clear that the higher the level of education, the stronger the commitment to the democratic principle of adaptability.

The difference in party affiliation was associated with the level of commitment to the principle of adaptability. The members of the ruling DRP were more receptive to political change than were the members of the NDP. Approximately 36 percent of the DRP members indicated a strong commitment. Among the NDP members, only 21 percent showed a similar attitude, indicating that they were more cautious with respect to the question of political change. The DRP members clearly had a more progressive outlook than did members of the NDP. The greater inclination toward change manifested by the members of the DRP has been claimed ever since it was founded in 1963.

CONCLUSION

In spite of an impressive proliferation of literature on the subject of political development, the role of legislative leadership in political change has been largely ignored. The literature is replete with analyses of developmental roles of charismatic leaders, bureaucrats, military officers, and the intellectual elite in developing systems of Asia and Africa. Only in recent years have scholars begun to examine systematically the role of the legislative elite from a developmental perspective.[26] This paucity of research may reflect the common assumption that legislatures do not play a significant role in the political life of these developing systems. Some scholars even suggest that the decline of the legislature in developing countries is inevitable, given the high emphasis on rapid economic development in such countries. They argue that the development of a strong administrative structure is a common feature of new states in Asia and Africa; this phenomenon invariably diminishes the role of representative institutions. Concurrent views are expressed by many observers of South Korean legislative politics. They contend that the power of the National Assembly has steadily declined over the years to become a rubber stamp organization for the executive branch.

Our analysis has shown no such trend during the period examined. The level of the performance, measured by the amount of seven principal legislative activities, did not steadily decline in the six assemblies that we have examined; rather, it showed wide fluctuation from year to year. With respect to the degree of legislative autonomy vis-à-vis the administration, the analysis has disclosed no firm evidence to support the thesis of a gradual decline, but on the contrary, it, too, fluctuated widely over the years. What seems interesting, however, is that the total level of legislative action was closely associated with the degree of autonomy. We found that the assembly that was highly productive in legislation, in an investigative role, in making policy recommendations and resolutions, and in deliberating petitions tended to be the more autonomous.

We have argued that the role of legislative leadership in democratic change is important. The legislative elite operates within an institutional and ideological framework quite different from that of a charismatic leader, bureaucrat, or junta leader. In most developing systems legislators are popularly elected, and therefore their continued tenure depends on periodic approval by the voters. To legitimize the existence of the legislature, it is mandatory to employ one or another form of representative doctrine. Therefore, legislators are in effect the most important elite group linking the masses to politics. Because of this connecting role, legislators stand in the strategic center of democratic change in developing systems.

The extent to which the legislative elite can contribute to democratic development depends, in the final analysis, on the level of their commitment to democratic principles. Among the members of the seventh Assembly, a majority manifested a commitment to the three democratic principles. Roughly two-thirds of them indicated a strong or moderate support for the principle of majority rule and minority rights. The democratic principle of accountable leadership received a somewhat lower degree of support. About one-third of the legislators expressed commitment to this principle. When their attitudes toward political change were examined, the legislators were more or less evenly divided: half of them exhibited adaptable attitudes, indicating that they were willing to effect institutional changes. Although democratic commitments were not overwhelmingly pervasive among the Korean legislators, a considerable number did have such commitments.

The legislators showed varying degrees of commitment to democratic principles. What factors account for such differences? We have indicated five such factors: birthplace (urban-rural), formal education, type of electoral district (urban-rural), method of election (national constituency versus single-member constituency), and party affiliation. Generally speaking, a higher commitment to democratic principles was to be found among those legislators who were elected from single-member districts, among those elected from urban districts, among those who were born in rural communities, and finally, among those who were members of the opposition New Democratic party. The most striking finding was, however, the inverse correlation between the level of formal education and the degree of democratic commitment: the higher the education, the lower the democratic commitment. We speculated that this was probably caused by the education system in South Korea, which tends to confer elite status on those privileged to participate in it.

In conclusion, the performance of the South Korean National Assembly, measured by both its total volume of activity and its degree of autonomy, has not declined visibly over the years. Although there were fluctuations, the assembly has remained fairly active in a number of areas in which it is supposed to engage as a collective body. While the relative power of the National Assembly has not declined, neither has it shown a significant improvement over the years. The democratic performance of the assembly depends in large measure on the degree to which its individual members are committed to democratic principles. For this reason, legislative leadership can play a vital role in democratic change. The prospect for democratic development in South Korea may therefore depend upon the development of such democratic commitments among the members of the National Assembly.

NOTES

1. The literature on the nature and implications of a social gap is too extensive to list all contributions. A few representative examples might include: Daniel Lerner, *The Passing of Traditional Society* (New York: Free Press of Glencoe, 1962), p. 17; Edward Shils, *Political Development in the New States* (The Hague: Mouton & Co., 1962), p. 87; S. N. Eisenstadt, *Essays on Sociological Aspects of Political and Economic Development* (The Hague: Mouton & Co., 1961), p. 12; William J. Foltz,

"Building the Newest Nations: Short-Run Strategies and Long-Run Problems," in *Nation-Building*, ed. Karl W. Deutsch and William J. Foltz (New York: Atherton Press, 1966), pp. 117–23; and Myron Weiner, "Political Integration and Political Development," in *Political Development & Social Change*, ed. Jason L. Finkle and Richard W. Gable (New York: John Wiley & Sons, 1971), pp. 650–52.

2. Shils, *Political Development*, pp. 86–88.

3. Lucian W. Pye, *Politics, Personality, and Nation Building* (New Haven: Yale University Press, 1962), pp. 15–31; and Gabriel A. Almond and G. Bingham Powell, Jr., *Comparative Politics* (Boston: Little, Brown & Co., 1966), pp. 73–97.

4. David E. Apter, *The Politics of Modernization* (Chicago: University of Chicago Press, 1965), pp. 199–212.

5. The seventh South Korean National Assembly had 175 members. Of these 129 were of the ruling Democratic Republican party, 45 were members of the New Democratic party, and 1 was an independent at the time of the interviews.

6. The History of the National Assembly, *Kukhoesa*, was published in 1971. It consists of three volumes, totaling 4,428 pages. The first volume covers in great detail the period from 1948 to 1958, which includes the first three assembly sessions. The second volume covers the next three sessions, the fourth, fifth, and sixth. The last volume is a compilation of many useful legislative statistics. Although published by the National Assembly as its official record, they provide rich and useful information.

7. Few political scientists have so far utilized output data to assess the performance of representative institutions. Two exceptions are: J. Blondel et al., "Legislative Behaviour: Some Steps toward a Cross-National Measurement," *Government and Opposition*, Winter 1969–70, pp. 67–85, and Chong Lim Kim, "Legislation, Public Policy, and the Korean National Assembly" (*Journal of Comparative Administration*, in press).

8. Gregory Henderson, *Korea: The Politics of the Vortex* (Cambridge, Mass.: Harvard University Press, 1968), p. 177.

9. See, for example, Alex Inkeles, "Participant Citizenship in Six Developing Countries," *American Political Science Review*, December 1969, pp. 1120–41; S. M. Lipset, "Some Social Requisites of Democracy," *American Political Science Review*, March 1959, pp. 69–105; and Philips Cutright, "National Political Development: Its Measurement and Social Correlates," in *Politics and Social Life*, ed. Nelson W. Polsby, Robert A. Dentler and Paul A. Smith (Boston: Houghton Mifflin Co., 1963), pp. 582–92.

10. For a discussion of economic performance in the postwar period, see David C. Cole and Princeton N. Lyman, *Korean Development: The Interplay of Politics and Economics* (Cambridge, Mass.: Harvard University Press, 1971).

11. The advocates of this view include: Ferrel Heady, *Public Administration: A Comparative Perspective* (Englewood Cliffs, N.J.: Prentice-Hall, 1966), pp. 64–65; Michael F. Lofchie, "Representative Government, Bureaucracy, and Political Development: The African Case," *Journal of Developing Areas*, October 1967, pp. 39–40; and Fred W. Riggs, "Bureaucrats and Political Development: A Paradoxical View," in *Bureaucracy and Political Development*, ed. Joseph LaPalombara (Princeton: Princeton University Press, 1963), pp. 120–67.

12. Lee Sigelman, "Do Modern Bureaucracies Dominate Underdeveloped Politics?" *American Political Science Review*, June 1972, p. 525.

13. *Sinyŏ* literally means maidservant in Korean. For the reference, see among others: Byung-kyu Woo, *Han'guk ibbŏp kwajŏng ŭi chŏmunje* [Problems of Legislative Processes in Korea] (Seoul: Kukhoe tosŏgwan ibbŏp chŏsaguk, 1970), pp.

142–48; Kwak Chi-yong, "Ŭihoe nŭn wae chŏngbu e apto doenŭn'ga?" [Why the Legislature is Overpowered by the Government?], Sasanggye 16, no. 7 (July 1968):26–30.

14. For the first National Assembly (1948–50), this measure does not apply because the political parties were extremely amorphous in form and the partisan alignment along government and opposition lines was not yet fully developed.

15. Arne Naess has examined three hundred different definitions of the term democracy in his book Democracy, Ideology and Objectivity (Oslo: Oslo University Press, 1956). For recent analyses of the concept of democracy, see Giovanni Sartori, Democratic Theory (New York: Praeger, 1965), and Robert A. Dahl, A Preface to Democratic Theory (Chicago: University of Chicago Press, 1963).

16. Dahl, Preface to Democratic Theory, pp. 63–68; Joseph Schumpeter, Capitalism, Socialism and Democracy (New York: Harper & Row, 1947), pp. 242–302; and S. M. Lipset, Political Man (New York: Doubleday, 1960), pp. 45–76.

17. Dahl, Preface to Democratic Theory, pp. 124–51, and also see his Who Governs? (New Haven: Yale University Press, 1961), pp. 211–325.

18. For a discussion of traditional political structure in Korea, see Henderson, Korea, and Takashi Hatada, A History of Korea (Santa Barbara: Clio Press, 1969).

19. We do not argue that all political changes are by definition democratic changes but that they do involve necessarily the breakdown of traditional political relations in the Korean context. Therefore, some form of political change is a necessary condition, if not a sufficient condition, for democratic change in Korea.

20. See Young Ho Lee, "Social Change and Political Participation in Korea" (Paper presented at the Conference on Tradition and Change in Korea, Seoul, Korea, September 1–6, 1970), Sun-ch'ang Hong, "Chŏngch'imyŏn e nat'anan han'guk sahoe ŭi chŏn kundaejŏk chŏyoin e taehayŏ" [A Survey on Pre-modern Factors Prevailing in Korean Politics], Han'guk chŏngch'ihak hoebo [Korean Political Science Review], no. 4 (1971), pp. 105–25.

21. A mixed district is normally located toward the outer limits of a large urban area thus consisting of both urban and rural parts.

22. Each political party could elect roughly one-third of the total legislative seats won in single-member districts from its party list. See Pak Il-kyŏng, Sin hŏnbŏp haeŭi (Seoul: Chimyŏng munhwa-sa, 1963), pp. 195–202.

23. Byung-kyu Woo and Chong Lim Kim, "Intra-Elite Cleavages in the Korean National Assembly," Asian Survey, June 1971, pp. 54–61.

24. Edward Shils, "The Intellectuals in the Political Development of the New States," in Political Development and Social Change, ed. Finkle and Gable, pp. 254-55.

25. In this connection, it is also worth noting that legislators-at-large differed significantly from legislators elected from single-member districts in terms of their representative role perceptions and behavior. See Byung-kyu Woo and Chong Lim Kim, "Taeŭi chŏngch'i wa kukhoe ŭiwŏn" [Representative Behavior of the National Assemblymen], Chŏnggyŏng Yŏn'gu [Political and Economic Review], September 1970, pp. 23–32.

26. See Allan Kornberg and Lloyd D. Musolf, eds., Legislatures in Developmental Perspective (New York: David McKay Co., 1972); and G. R. Boynton and Chong Lim Kim, eds., Legislative Systems in Developing Countries (Beverly Hills: Sage Publications, forthcoming).

3. Party Bureaucrats and Party Development

BAE-HO HAHN and HA-RYONG KIM

INTRODUCTION

The problems of party building in new nations have drawn the attention of scholars who study the process of political development. A few studies have been devoted entirely to the question of the potential role of parties and party systems for initiating, managing, and consolidating dynamic political change and development in newly developing societies.[1]

Historically, parties and party systems in Europe grew out of a setting in which the parliamentary combinations of representative oligarchies, under the pressure of democratization, developed extraparliamentary machinery to provide themselves with new sources of power. Until late in the nineteenth century, parties were amorphous, loosely organized, and in flux. They were no more than associations among parliamentarians and nobles. Because of the substantial consensus among the ruling elite in the European setting, the restricted franchise, and the limited activities of government, political parties were not important and thus the stakes involved in partisan competition were low.

All of these factors changed by the early part of the twentieth century as a result of an increase in cleavages created by the diversifying social structure and because of the rapid expansion of the electorate, which, to a great extent, shifted the focus of political machinations to the level of the general electorate. Increasingly, the men interested in realizing their political aspirations took the recruitment, articulation, and aggregation functions of political parties seriously.

Political parties are organizations created by various processes of political competition, which pursue a goal of placing their avowed representatives in government positions. As such, a party must be viewed in relation to the offices that it seeks to capture. In other words, basic to the understanding of political parties is the "awareness of the structure of political opportunities within a given political system; the public offices available; the rules, formal and informal, for their attainment and the attitudes of politicians and voters toward these offices."[2]

Inasmuch as political parties operate both within an institutional framework that probably determines their chances of winning an office, and within a social and attitudinal milieu that shapes the attitudes of politicians and the masses, attempts at developing a competitive party system have met with limited success in most of those developing societies where the political systems are largely dominated by oligarchical groups intent upon monopolizing political power. The level of social mobilization remains low and the tradition of popular involvement in politics is either weak or nonexistent. Party systems in these nations have been characterized by a high degree of fluidity involving the constant appearance and disappearance of parties and the constant ebb and flow of partisan consolidation and fragmentation. They have also been characterized by a highly "personalistic" style of party leadership.

Despite the frequently asserted importance of political parties as the "source of legitimacy and authority" and as an effective means for coping with the "breakdown" of traditional political institutions or the "crises" of political development in developing nations,[3] what little evidence there is indicates no general trend toward greater emphasis on the development of an institutionalized party system in these countries. On the contrary, the leaders in the developing countries, who now confront a highly telescoped modernization process, tend to react to the "breakdown" or the "crises" with a strong proclivity to rule with the tidy simplicity of coercion, avoiding the ambiguities of consensus.[4]

Generally, party systems are closely associated with a particular kind of political process, which is in turn closely tied to certain political structures and functions. The structures are representative governments. The functions are those that elections perform in representative systems, namely, political recruitment and interest aggregation. To the extent that parties are linked structurally to these political processes, the significance of the party system relative to other structures involved in the political process would be increased, and the prospect for the development of a competitive party system would be enhanced.

The purpose of this study is to make a preliminary examination of the major problems that affect the actual operation of political parties in Korea and that work as constraining factors in the development of political parties in Korea. We have tried to identify these problems by interviewing a selected number of party cadre members from the ruling and opposition parties. We solicited their views and opinions about the nature of "party environment" in Korea; the level of party performance; the degree of organization and coherence in their own party; and the future of Korean political parties.

THE CONTEXT OF THE SOUTH KOREAN PARTY SYSTEM

Even a cursory review of the history of party politics in post-liberation South Korea reveals that political parties have not established a durable relationship with the political process that has prevailed in the Korean political system. Even the ruling Democratic Republican party (DRP), which set out in 1962 with an ambitious goal of creating a mass-based modern political party, fell short of its avowed goal, and now seems to be grappling with a problem of maintaining its image as a mass-based party when in reality it bears many striking resemblances to the ruling party of the previous regime, the Liberal party. The opposition New Democratic party (NDP) has never fully overcome its built-in weaknesses and has been plagued by its inability to establish contact with the masses and to recruit new forces into the party and its leadership.

Consequently, parties seem to perform only limited functions within the over-all political processes in contemporary Korean society. They remain dormant during off-election years, and only become somewhat active during the period of election campaigns. They operate merely as a procedural device in the formalization of candidates for the presidency and the National Assembly. In the case of the opposition, the party seems to exist primarily for the sake of a few old-line politicians who depend upon it as a major vehicle for obtaining seats in the legislature. To a certain extent, the opposition party also works as the safety valve for many "explosive" social elements that could seriously undermine the operation of the entire political system. Given the limited functional significance attached to political parties within the over-all political process in South Korea, party salience is very low.

There are several factors that account for the low level of party salience in the Korean political process. One, particularly after the military coup in 1961, is the constitutional amendment of December 26, 1962, that gave extensive powers to the president, making him constitutionally independent of the National Assembly. Because of these powers, the constitutional role of the National

Assembly has inevitably been reduced to secondary and corrective actions. But even the corrective role of the legislature is substantially circumscribed by restrictive policies imposed by the executive on ruling party members of the legislature.

Also contributing to the relative insignificance of the party system in Korean political process is the relationship between the ruling party and the administration. Despite the emphasis placed by the founders of the DRP upon the development of a modern political party, and their aspirations to play a substantial role in the governmental decision-making process, the ruling party has actually been accorded a minor role in formulating the major policies of government, acting simply as an administrative hierarchy or a handmaiden to a few leading individuals within the executive and the legislature. Furthermore, while executive power, in the process of implementing economic plans, has steadily increased with the rapid expansion of governmental functions, the importance of the ruling party as a basis of power and legitimacy has been eroded.

Not least in contributing to the low level of party salience in Korea is the increasingly dominant political role being assumed by the South Korean Central Intelligence Agency (CIA), which serves the administration as a major instrument of power and control, and which obstructs the cooperative relationship between the ruling party and the administration. Executive reliance on the CIA became more conspicuous as the ruling party failed to prove itself as an instrument capable of coping with the opposition party and was shown to contain disunity within its own ranks.

Consequently, the general Korean political process manifests the following characteristics: an accessory role for the legislature compared with executive authority, which strives for greater centralization of power in the hands of the very few men occupying top administrative offices, or more precisely in the hands of the leader at the apex of the political structure; a heavy reliance on the intelligence agencies for social control and for curbing disunity within the ruling party leadership; the development of political tension, which is largely confined to the competition among subordinate leaders who occupy top positions in the governing apparatus; and the relegation of the opposition party to the status of a "permanent opposition" or a "vocal opposition," impoverished by years of fruitless struggle against the overwhelming superiority of the party in power.

Conspicuous in this trend has been the emergence of a supreme leader with increasing personal authority. In the early 1960s, the

South Korean president acted primarily through the party and the administration and was able to consolidate his position by creating a closely knit power nexus of party and government leaders who coexisted in a state of tension, a tension that stemmed largely from the desire of the party leaders to have a greater degree of control over the governmental decision-making process. It should be recalled that one of the aims of the founders of the DRP was to develop a party that could expand its authority to a broader sector of the Korean political system and could monopolize the process by which top leadership for the political system would be chosen. It was expected that this would be achieved by strengthening the authority of the party and by achieving a high level of institutionalization of the party's administrative secretariat. The party bureaucrats or cadre members were to assume the major responsibility for formulating and recommending major policies for the government to pursue, and to set the direction for the executive leaders.[5]

Government leaders reacted to these party aims with suspicion and contempt. For the leaders, the development of a highly institutionalized political party implied that the administration, as well as the authority of the president, could easily be restrained. The strengthening of a ruling party capable of selecting the top leader for the political system also implied a virtual exclusion from the process of the nonparty organizations, particularly the CIA and the military, which had come to play a crucial role in Korean politics since the coup. It could also threaten those whose status was inseparably linked to existing administrative leadership and who were adamantly opposed to any disruption of that leadership.

The tension within the power nexus developed gradually into an open conflict as the various groups became embroiled in the issue of presidential succession. Some outspoken party leaders openly opposed any attempt to remove the constitutional restriction that limited a president to two consecutive terms. The party leadership was split between those who favored removal of the constitutional restriction to allow the incumbent to run in the 1971 presidential election, and those who rallied around the chairman of the DRP, Kim Chong-p'il, in support of his move to succeed Pak Chŏng-hŭi. As a result of this split, the institutional basis of the party authority was hopelessly weakened, while the personal authority of the paramount leader remained not only intact but strengthened after the constitutional revision bill was approved by a national referendum, clearing the way for his election to a third term of office.

It seems clear, therefore, that Korean political parties assume very little functional significance in the actual operation of the Korean political system and that nonparty organizations command the political processes by taking over the functions of political recruitment and interest aggregation normally ascribed to parties in a competitive political system. Given the highly personalistic authority of the top leader, who appears to rely on an unswerving loyalty from the military elite and the executive bureaucracy and who aspires to have a direct access to the populace as the leader who alone can deliver them into modernization, there is little room in the Korean political system for political parties to develop into viable political institutions. They will remain peripheral organizations until they succeed in broadening their political base and securing autonomy from the overwhelming dominance of the nonparty organizations attached to the executive, as well as achieving a greater degree of organizational coherence to increase their functional effectiveness.

In an effort to examine the actual operations of political parties in Korea, we asked forty cadre members—twenty each from the ruling and opposition parties who now occupy middle positions in the hierarchy of the two parties—the following questions:[6] Is there any regular contact and exchange of personnel and information between organizations at the center and local levels? What functions do Korean political parties actually perform? What functions do Korean political parties tend to neglect or avoid? If they neglect or avoid functions, why? What are the major sources of cleavage and conflict in the parties? Is there any conflict between formal and informal channels as they affect the party decision-making processes? What kind of impact will current social changes in Korea have on the future of party politics in Korea? If political parties are to achieve a higher degree of institutionalization, what needs to be done by the parties themselves?

After completing the interviews and analyzing responses, we arranged several meetings with four selected respondents in order to aid us in interpreting the results, which are presented in the following sections.

PARTY CADRE MEMBERS' ORIENTATIONS TOWARD PARTY POLITICS

Internally a political party is a vast network of personal ties, authority relationships, and incentives for activity. Basic to these relationships are the rewards and sanctions that a political party commands. If the party is to continue functioning as an organization, it

must have at its disposal an adequate supply of incentives in order
to induce into the party men with the skills required for its operation. In general, three factors seem to be related to the pattern of
recruitment of party cadre members: the availability within the
party of incentives; the demand for those incentives by the politically active; and the needs of the party. The ruling and opposition
parties have at their disposal different capacities for making "pay-
ments" to party cadre members and they operate with a different
set of incentives in stimulating party activities. It is assumed that
these differences are reflected in the attitudes of the cadre members that the two parties are able to attract.

Although many categories have been used by various studies of
the effects of incentives on party recruitment, we have selected the
following four to examine the motives of party cadre members in
joining their respective parties: (1) job opportunities, (2) material
rewards, (3) ideological reasons, and (4) power and status. These
overlap somewhat, but seem relevant for the examination of the
general orientations of party cadre members in Korea. The cadre
members were asked to rank each of the four items in the order of
importance they attached to them. The results of their responses
were analyzed with Kendall's coefficient of concordance (W) to
check the degree of over-all agreement. This test provides a way of
measuring the degree of association between variables measured in
ranks and is useful in studying the reliability of responses.

The one attitude widely shared among party cadre members from
both ruling and opposition parties is their idealistic orientation toward politics. When asked about their reasons for joining political
parties, the majority of them ranked "political ideology and convictions" as most important (table 1). In the case of the opposition
party cadre members (table 2), there is nearly perfect agreement on
this point, which is understandable in view of the limited capacity
the opposition has in dispensing the incentives of patronage, political office, material rewards, and job opportunities. However, the
DRP, as the governing party, has greater access to policy makers
and administrators and would be expected to have more influence
over the distribution of patronage in the government. Yet, only four
of the twenty DRP cadre members rated power and status as their
main motivating factor, and none ranked material incentives as an
important motivating factor. The responses of the ruling party cadre
members may be interpreted from the perspective of the political
culture in Korea where Confucian ethics still carry a considerable
weight in shaping the expectations, goals, and mores with which

the people appraise the political system. Inasmuch as the Korean political culture rejects the ethic of patronage, power, and material gains in politics—all of which violate the traditional values of austerity and harmonious interpersonal relations—the majority of the DRP cadre members might have shunned items other than political ideology and conviction.

TABLE 1

RULING PARTY CADRE'S MOTIVES

	Material Reward	Power & Status	Political Ideology	Job Seeking	Ti
A	3	3	1	3	2
B	3	3	3	1	2
C	3	2	1	4	0
D	3	3	1	3	2
E	3	1	2	4	0
F	3	3	3	1	2
G	3	1	2	4	0
H	3.5	3.5	1	2	0.5
I	3	3	3	1	2
J	3.5	3.5	1	2	0.5
K	3.5	3.5	1	2	0.5
L	3	3	1	3	2
M	3	1	3	3	2
N	3	3	3	1	2
O	3	3	1	3	2
P	3	2	1	4	0
Q	4	1	2	3	0
R	3.5	3.5	1	2	0.5
S	3	3	3	1	2
T	3	2	1	4	0
Xi	63	51	35	51	ΣTi = 22
$Xi - \dfrac{\Sigma Xi}{N}$	13	1	-15	1	$\dfrac{\Sigma Xi}{N} = 50$
$(Xi - \dfrac{\Sigma Xi}{N})^2$	169	1	225	1	396

NOTE: N = 20; s = 396 > 258 significant at 0.05 level

To compute W (the coefficient of concordance), the following formula was used:

$$W = \frac{s}{\frac{1}{12}k^2(N^3 - N) - k\Sigma T} = 0.2538$$

Where the s = sum of squares of the observed deviations from mean of xi

k = number of sets of rankings, e.g., the number of judges

N = number of entities (objects) ranked

$\dfrac{1}{12}k^2(N^3 - N)$ = maximum possible sum of the squared deviations, i.e., the sum s, which would occur with perfect agreement among k rankings

T = number of observations in a group tied for a given rank

TABLE 2

Opposition Party Cadre's Motives

	Material Reward	Power & Status	Political Ideology	Job Seeking	Ti
A	3	3	1	3	2
B	3	3	1	3	2
C	3	2	1	4	0
D	4	3	1	2	0
E	3.5	2	1	3.5	0.5
F	3.5	2	1	3.5	0.5
G	3	1	2	4	0
H	4	2	1	3	0
I	3	2	1	4	0
J	3	2	1	4	0
K	3	3	1	3	2
L	3	3	1	3	2
M	3.5	2	1	3.5	0.5
N	3.5	1.5	1.5	3.5	1
0	3	3	1	3	2
P	3	3	1	3	2
Q	3.5	2	1	3.5	0.5
R	4	2	1	3	0
S	3.5	2	1	3.5	0.5
Xi	63	43.5	20.5	63	ΣTi = 15.5
$Xi - \dfrac{\Sigma Xi}{N}$	15.5	−4	−27	15.5	
$(Xi - \dfrac{\Sigma Xi}{N})^2$	240.25	16	729	240.25	

Note: s = 1225.5 > 258 and therefore significant at .05 level.

$$W = \frac{1225.5}{\frac{1}{12} \cdot 19^2(4^3 - 4) - 19 \cdot 15.5} = 0.8113$$

The high idealism among the opposition party cadre members can be appreciated in terms of the peculiarities of Korean political culture, which invariably shape the attitudes, norms, and goals of these members of the cadre. In a political system where a tradition of a peaceful transfer of power between political parties is nonexistent, the opposition party tends to lapse into a cynical political resignation with a greater concern for doctrinism. Many young men, after feverish efforts to secure respectable jobs, find in the opposition party an outlet for the expression of their discontent with the society since the opposition offers a psychological substitute for those in search of some abstract values and a body of doctrine. For them, the opposition symbolizes a crusade against social and political ills in Korean society, a struggle against "dictatorship," and a crusade for democracy.

However, the highly idealistic orientation of party cadre members toward party politics and their own parties may breed a serious cynicism when the parties fail to accommodate their demands and to live up to their expectations. Thus, the higher the expectation of one of the cadre toward his political party on an ideological level, the greater the sense of frustration he would be expected to experience when exposed to the realities within that party. This appears to be the case with the respondents from both parties. Asked whether they had experienced any serious discrepancy between expectations they had had of their parties before they joined it and the reality that existed within the parties, the cadre members responded as shown in table 3.

TABLE 3

DEGREE OF DISCREPANCY BETWEEN EXPECTATIONS AND REALITY

	DRP	NDP
Very wide	10	14
Fairly wide	10	6

As expected, there is a far greater degree of cynicism and even bitterness among the members of the opposition cadre. The question, what are the situations in your party organization that disappointed you most? elicited the following: an absence of the sense of right and wrong among party leaders; wavering of party leaders' resolve to win political power; inability to act as an effective restraint upon the party in power; an absence of mutual trust among leaders as well as between leaders and their followers; the prevalence of factionalism; the tendency of leaders to pursue self-interest at the expense of party goals; the inability of the party to build broad mass support and recruit new political aspirants. One member of the cadre described his party as a collection of men with no firm opinions and principles, who easily submitted themselves to injustice in pursuit of their own realistic interests.

A negative feeling toward their own party is equally strong among the cadre members of the ruling party. To the same question, the DRP cadre members gave the following responses: inability to perform coordinating functions for various social groups; inability to lead public opinion; the primitive nature of the party decision-making process; conflict between the interests of the party and those of the party leaders; domination of the party by executive authority; lack of concern for recruiting competent leaders; an absence of a permanent channel for contact with the masses; degrading of the party by using it as a tool for serving some personal interest of party leaders.

Frustrations stemming from a wide discrepancy between expectations and actual conditions prevailing within party organization are further exacerbated by the ambiguous nature of the individual rules in a party system characterized by a low level of functional salience. In general, the higher the level of party system salience, the greater the sense of involvement of party cadre members in the performance of party functions, and the more articulate are their roles within the party organization. Conversely, the less effective parties are in the performance of these functions, the less involved are members of the cadre in party programs, and the more ambiguous are their roles.

In studying this problem, we have selected the following three major functions that are deemed essential if political parties are to fulfill their role in Korean society: mediating—involving political parties as an impartial mediator in the settlement of disputes and conflicts between social, economic, and other interest groups; expediting—helping citizens attract the attention of the administration and unravel the maze of governmental regulations; and finally service—promoting the social welfare of the populace and linking subsequent action to the party organization or to the political system. These functions have a limited scope and range, and they should be distinguished from more latent ones, such as the creation of a sense of national identity, and the awakening of participant attitudes among the masses, which are closely associated with the activities of mass-based, highly disciplined political parties.

The responses from the cadre members indicate that there is considerable divergence in their opinions of the extent to which their parties actually devote energies and attention to the fulfillment of these tasks. One-half of the cadre members in both political parties agree that their parties perform these functions to a very limited extent, while the rest are divided between those who think that their parties attend to these functions "very actively" and those who think that their parties pay virtually no attention to these functions. Judging from these responses, neither the ruling party nor the opposition seems actively engaged in the performance of these functions. It is conceivable that in Korea these functions are performed by nonparty organizations such as the Korean Central

Intelligence Agency or the bureaucracy so that parties are left only with some obscure roles directly related to the elections of president and the members of the National Assembly. Where the parties perform obscure functions and contribute little to the operation of a given political system as they do in Korea, the party cadre seems to have no reason for existence and consequently the concept of the roles of its members is likely to remain ambiguous.

LOW LEVEL OF ORGANIZATION AND COHERENCE

If a party is to function as a political institution, it requires a certain degree of organization and coherence. Organization is defined as the existence of regularized procedures for mobilizing and coordinating the efforts of party supporters in executing the party's strategy and tactics. Thus, a highly organized political party would operate with a structure, clearly defined lines of authority in the decision-making bodies, and intensive as well as extensive organizational units.

Political parties also require a certain degree of coherence in the attitude and behavior of party members. A highly coherent party exists when there is no sharp disagreement between party leaders and their followers on specific issues, when there is no serious internal disruption caused by personality conflicts between party leaders, and when there are no labeled factions that divide the party on matters of issues, personality conflicts, or ideology.

In our interviews, questions bearing on these important features of political parties were asked in order to gain insight into the structural dimensions of Korean political parties. The responses (table 4), indicated that Korean political parties are oriented mainly toward the central party organization, which maintains tenuous links with its local counterparts. When party members were asked how much exchange of personnel and information exists between central and local party organizations, three of the DRP members felt there was much, seventeen felt there was little. Asked the same

TABLE 4

AMOUNT OF EXCHANGE IN PARTY PERSONNEL AND INFORMATION
BETWEEN THE CENTER AND THE PERIPHERY

	DRP	*NDP*
Much	3	6
Little	17	14

question, the opposition party was a little more favorable—six of them felt there was much, fourteen felt there was little.

Korean political parties are not only devoid of permanent organizational bases in the countryside, they are also characterized by a low degree of structural articulation in the central organization. The decision-making patterns within these parties do not seem to conform to the formal lines of authority indicated by their organizational charts. Rather, as revealed by the responses of the cadre members, both parties tend to operate with dual structures consisting of formal and informal channels.

Reasons given by the cadre members for the prevalence of informal decision-making practice within their parties indicate that both parties are severely handicapped by a low level of institutionalization. Members of the DRP cadre attribute the prevalence of these practices among party leaders to the interference from such institutions as the intelligence agencies and the executive branch of government. For the ruling party, autonomy appears to be the major problem, and securing a structural independence from the sources of interference is considered essential for the development of the ruling party as a viable institution. Members of the opposition cadre are more prone to look within their own party to identify the sources of the high degree of reliance on informal decision making in the NDP. They stress the predispositions of some party leaders to give primacy to their own factional interests over the interests of the party, and to rely on informal channels in the settlement of conflicts regarding party affairs.

Because of the limited nature of the data, it is beyond the scope of our study to examine in detail the level of coherence in both parties and to assess the consequences of varying degrees of coherence upon the parties' effectiveness. We realize, however, the importance of assessing the degree of congruence in the political orientations of the established party leaders and the party cadre members, as expressed in intraparty politics. In view of the flourishing factionalism in Korean political parties, which deeply divides them internally, it may be assumed that cadre members, both in the ruling and opposition parties, might be tempted or pressed to develop links with factions in their respective parties. This seems particularly true for the opposition, where cadre members tend to join not the party, but one of the many factions that the opposition party contains.

To gain insight into this question, we asked how serious cleavages within the party were. Five DRP and ten NDP cadre members thought them very serious. Twelve DRP and eight NDP cadre members thought that the problem of cleavage was fairly serious, while three DRP and two NDP cadre members denied the existence of any cleavage within their parties.

We also asked whether or not there had been occasions on which cadre members had disagreed with their leaders and, if so, on what matters did they disagree. Twelve DRP and eleven NDP cadre members indicated that they had had disagreements with their leaders on policy or ideological grounds, whereas five DRP and six NDP cadre members replied that their disagreements were based on different tactical or strategic considerations.

It is generally assumed that Korean parties are not ideologically oriented. Divisions and internal disruptions have tended to center on specific issues, and on conflicts of personality and individual ambition, especially relevant to the choice of party candidates for public office or nominees for party posts. As conservative political parties, both the ruling and opposition parties share a strong suspicion of and resistance to the emergence of any political force that makes an appeal to the masses with platforms couched in progressive ideological terms.

It seems, therefore, more justifiable to analyze the source of the disagreements of the cadre members with their established leaders in terms of the "idealistic" orientation toward politics that we have already alluded to, rather than regarding these disagreements as a fundamental, ideological cleavage between the established and aspiring leaders. In other words, the cleavage existing in both parties is likely to be caused by differences in values between the established and aspiring party leaders, by age or generational differences, and by what is known in Korea as "localism."

Another aspect of the intraelite relationship that has a close bearing on party coherence is the degree of openness of the established leaders toward the aspiring leaders. The capacity of the two parties to absorb aspiring leaders is rather limited and the willingness of established leaders to share power with them is not strong. This is particularly true of the opposition party, which is severely hampered by its inability to reward its members and to accommodate the demands for power by an aspiring elite, such as the party cadre under examination. To some extent, the ruling party encountered the same problem when the party excluded those cadre members who had played a crucial role in the 1963 elections from the choice of party candidates for seats in the National Assembly. Intraparty conflicts ensued with the DRP between cadre members and those party leaders who chose to run, but who had not come up through the party ranks.

Because of the highly closed elite system within Korean political parties, a serious threat to party leaders would be posed if cadre members were to form a united force of their own and take concerted action against established party leaders. However, party cadre members are divided and are in competition with one another. This is recognized by the established leaders (table 5) and allows the leaders to remain unafraid of being displaced by an aspiring elite.

TABLE 5
COHESIVENESS AMONG CADRES

	DRP	*NDP*
Cohesive	7	4
Not cohesive	13	16

Aspiring party leaders seem to rely on their personal connections and resources as a means of achieving an elite position or of being co-opted into the party leadership position. The tension created by the closed nature of the dominant party hierarchy toward the aspiring leaders may be ameliorated to some extent, in the case of the ruling party, by using the system of legislators-at-large[7] for co-opting some of the disgruntled cadre members into the legislature. However, the same device was not employed by the opposition party, which exchanged it for an acutely needed campaign fund. This was tantamount to blatant sales of public offices, and also meant the total exclusion from the choice of party candidates for the National Assembly of the poorer cadre members who had remained loyal to the opposition party for many years and had waited to be co-opted into the party leadership position. The serious internal disruptions that have frequently plagued the opposition party, even leading to the brink of a party split, seem closely related to the closed nature of the opposition party hierarchy.

LOW EMPHASIS ON ADAPTIVE AND INNOVATIVE ROLE OF PARTY

Many studies of the political development process stress that a party as a political organization is essential for those political systems actively engaged in a comprehensive transformation of the social and economic systems of which they are a part. The more successful they are in accelerating economic growth and social change, the more tensions they create within their systems. For such political systems, one of the most serious problems is the creation of organizations with the ability to cushion the tensions created by the changes, and at the same time accelerate innovations essential to any kind of modernization. Historically, political parties have performed this role more effectively than other types of organizations, and it is difficult to see how a modernizing political system can cope with the problem without a party system capable of creating concerted effort among diverse, complex organizations within the system.

We have, therefore, asked cadre members of both parties a set of questions designed to tap their perceptions of party role with respect to the increasing problems created by social and economic changes in Korea, the direction in which Korean political parties are likely to develop, the conditions conducive to the achievement of more institutionalized political parties in Korea, and the time required for developing such party organizations in Korea.

Asked whether the kinds of changes that Korean society is presently undergoing would work favorably for Korean political parties, cadre members from both parties were split evenly in their responses. Furthermore, five DRP cadre members and an equal number from the opposition thought that the changes would have rather adverse effects on the future of their respective parties.

We asked those who responded positively to rank each of the following four items on the basis of their importance to the relationship between social change in Korea and party development: (1) absorb the demands of social groups and other interest groups to expand the supporting basis of their parties; (2) provide more channels of participation to the intellectual strata in Korea; (3) increase "autonomy" of the party; and (4) win the greater confidence of the populace. Their responses show no clear consensus as to which of these factors is the most important.

It is interesting to note (see table 6) that the majority of the respondents share the view that Korean political parties will remain

TABLE 6

FUTURE DIRECTION OF PARTIES

	DRP	NDP
Conservative	13	11
Ideological	5	8
Do not know	2	1

as they are now—conservative, pragmatically oriented parties—rather than change into ideologically oriented parties.

Apparently, the majority of the members of the DRP cadre we interviewed do not share the common notion of an ideological party system that some intellectual and political leaders in Korea view as a desirable vehicle for solving many great political and social ills of Korean society. Moreover, cadre members from both parties seem to mistrust such prospects for their own parties. Even those opposition cadre members who stressed ideology in projecting the future of their party answered, when we inquired further, that they were thinking of a party system in which parties would compete with a set of articulated policies and party programs designed to implement democratic reforms in the society.

A feeling of uncertainty is also manifest in the opinions of the party cadre members as to what the most important conditions are that must be met in order to develop a stable and durable party system in Korea. Of the four items ranked, improvement of political consciousness and the level of formal education was given the highest ranking by cadre members from both the ruling and opposition parties. But, for the other responses, each group gave a different set of rankings: members of the DRP cadre ranked improvement of economic conditions, role of party leadership, and local autonomous system, in that order; members of the opposition cadre rated the same items in the order of local autonomous system, improvement of economic conditions, and finally role of party leadership.

What these responses seem to imply is that the development of a stable, institutionalized party system in Korea will depend largely on changes in the environment of the Korean political system; and until changes conducive to the operation of party politics are brought about, Korean political parties are bound to assume a passive role. And yet, without adequate channels through which individuals are brought to work together in an organized fashion for common purposes, and without institutional mechanisms by which individuals may effect a significant change in the environment, the discontinuities brought about by modernization in Korea (the increasing gaps between urban and rural areas and between rich and poor), may seriously undermine the legitimacy of the Korean political system and may lead to perpetual political instability. This problem may not be overcome unless political parties in Korea succeed in functioning as adaptive and innovative agencies through which individuals may acquire new political orientations more suitable to the functioning of the present Korean political structure.

In this regard, the alienation of the intellectuals from party politics in Korea takes on a special meaning since it is the intellectual stratum that normally produces the organizational talents as well as ideological substance that the parties must have. Party leadership needs the talents of the intellectuals to run political parties as highly innovative and adaptive organizations in the changing political environment. We have, therefore, asked cadre members what they thought the single, major cause of the alienation of the intellectuals in Korean party politics was.

Interestingly enough, members of the DRP cadre blamed the intellectuals themselves for their alienation, whereas the opposition cadre members held their own party largely responsible. The DRP cadre members were of the opinion that Korean intellectuals ought to change their attitude and orientation first if they are to make any useful contributions to Korean party politics. The opposition cadre members blamed their own party leaders for lacking the capacity to assimilate the intellectuals into their party organization.

The problem is much more complex than the cadre members conceive it to be. First, Korean political culture tends to associate contemporary party politics with the traditional factional squabblings of the Yi dynasty period. The legacy of "monopolistic" politics inherent in the traditional imperial system has had a lingering effect throughout postindependence Korean politics. Furthermore, legal constraints severely inhibit the participation of the intellectuals in party politics. Whatever the major causes of the alienation of intellectuals from party politics, the low capacity of Korean parties to act as innovative and adaptive agencies for organizing the masses and creating a new network of human associations will not be significantly improved until the parties succeed in the "intellectualization" of their party apparatus and program.

Throughout this paper, we have placed our central focus of inquiry on the problems related to the development of an institutionalized party system in contemporary Korean political context. As suggested by Huntington and others, institutionalization of the party system can be assessed in terms of the four criteria of adaptability, complexity, autonomy, and coherence. A party system that acquired the features of structural articulation in the party's decision-making process, permanent party organizations both at the center and periphery, a basic congruence in attitudes and behavior among party members who identify with it, and sufficient freedom from nonparty organizations and institutions may be considered "developed" in contrast to one in which party units undergo a constant ebb and flow of consolidation and fragmentation, and where the party leadership style seems to rest largely on "personalism."

We realize that more detailed empirical research on Korean party organizations and functions will be required to throw light on the present level of institutionalization of the Korean party system in terms of these criteria. We have made an attempt to elicit the views of party cadre members as to the minimum period required for Korean parties to achieve the level of institutionalization with those features characteristic of developed party systems.

The majority of the cadre members from both parties were not optimistic about the development of a highly institutionalized party in the near future. The DRP cadre members' time perspective is more long-range: eleven of them thought that Korean parties would be well established by the 1980s; four were thinking in terms of the 1970s; three in terms of the 1990s. The opposition cadre members were divided into those who thought that their party would achieve a sufficient level of institutionalization in the 1970s and those who look into the next decade as the propitious time for their party to take firm roots within Korean politics.

SUMMARY AND CONCLUSION

In spite of the very limited scope and nature of this preliminary study, it seems worthwhile to make some generalizations in the hope of shedding some light on the present level of institutionalization achieved by Korean political parties, those factors seemingly related to the low level of party system salience, the determinants of the interparty dynamics in Korea, and the outlook for the development of Korean political parties.

One obvious conclusion to be drawn from this study is that Korean political parties are likely to remain ephemeral organizations with very limited functions to perform within the Korean political system. This is due to the overwhelming strength of the administration, the reliance of the top-level leadership in power on nonparty organizations as expedient instruments of control and suppression, the tendency of the Korean political culture to stress the avoidance of conflicts in interpersonal relations (a factor identified by the Korean populace with membership in political parties), and finally a general lack of interest in organizations tied closely to political parties. These factors may be regarded as independent variables that have affected the nature and dynamics of party politics in Korea.

In addition, it seems reasonable to regard the following intervening variables as having had a significant impact on Korean political parties: factional proliferations within parties, which have adversely affected the level of party coherence; limited opportunity and a limited supply of incentives within parties, which condition the level of party organization and its effectiveness; and a lack of detachment from coercive organizations that undermine the independence of political parties.

As the views expressed by party cadre members from both the ruling and opposition parties suggest, Korean political parties are political organizations that perform only in a very limited manner those functions that parties are required to perform in order to increase their effectiveness as organizations capable of assimilating social forces into the political system. They have failed to create sufficient internal cohesion, partly due to a perennial disunity among the established leaders who pursue their own personal interests at the expense of party goals. Korean political parties have also failed to gain enough external support to achieve their purposes. The absence of interest organizations that would support the causes of these parties is crucial in determining their character. Further, there is a deep-rooted suspicion, and even antipathy, toward parties among the general populace, who are inclined to associate parties with corruption and disorder in Korean politics. The high level of political frustration that can easily be detected in the responses of party cadre members stems largely from their awareness of these factors inimical to the development of party politics in Korea.

While the appraisal by cadre members of the realities of the party environment and of party organization is generally accurate, these men show no clear idea of how they could overcome the difficulties and problems that condition the nature and hamper the development of party politics in Korea. They seem vaguely committed to the passage of time as a way of escaping from the gloomy reality of the present, and they anticipate a better future when a more enlightened electorate makes its appearance on the Korean political scene.

Underlying this anticipation among cadre members is a hidden assumption that a modern, institutionalized political party can emerge only as a consequence of an increased level of modernization in South Korea, which is usually defined in terms of economic growth and technological change. Yet, the difficulty of viewing party development in such a sequential fashion is obvious when there is no empirical basis for such an assumption in the history of political change. Nevertheless, the party cadres in Korea are firm in their view of the future of Korean party politics. In a fundamental sense, party building in Korea requires a highly innovative and adaptive effort to assimilate the masses at the grass-roots or the constituency level, an effort that must be made by the established and aspiring leaders. When the parties fail in these ventures, there exist only factions, cliques, or cabals, but not political parties.

NOTES

1. The following works represent a growing interest among Western political scientists in the problem of party development in the developing countries: Myron Weiner, *Party Politics in India* (Princeton: Princeton University Press, 1957); Myron Weiner, *Party Building in a New Nation* (Chicago: University of Chicago Press, 1967); Samuel P. Huntington and Clement H. Moore, eds. *Authoritarian Politics in Modern Society: The Dynamics of Established One-Party Systems* (New York: Basic Books, 1970); Samuel P. Huntington, *Political Order in Changing Societies* (New Haven: Yale University Press, 1968); Aristide R. Zolberg, *Creating Political Order* (Chicago: Rand McNally & Co., 1966).

2. Joseph A. Schlesinger, "Political Party Organization" in *Handbook of Organization,* ed. James G. March (Chicago: Rand McNally & Co., 1965), pp. 764-801.

3. Huntington and others have stressed the important role of political parties for the developing political systems as "strategic" organizations best suited for coping with the breakdown of the pre-existing institutions in these systems.

4. For an analysis of the nature of political conflicts in the non-Western political systems, particularly in Africa, see Aristide R. Zolberg, "The Structure of Political Conflicts in the New States," *American Political Science Review,* March 1968, pp. 70–87.

5. A detailed account of the history of party politics during the sixties, subsequent to the military takeover in 1961, appears in a number of articles written in Korean, as well as newspaper reportings. For example, Yu Hyŏk-in and Yi Chin-ŭi, "Minju konghwadang" [Democratic-Republican Party], *Sindonga,* August 1968, pp. 89-119.

6. A majority of them have held or now hold senior administrative posts within the party bureaucracy. Nine of the twenty members of the DRP cadre have held or now hold the rank of bureau chief; five, deputy bureau chief; and the rest are divided among three senior staff in the office of the policy planning board and two junior members of the party bureaucracy. Members of the opposition cadre also are of senior administrative ranks. Approximately half of them have held or now hold the rank of bureau chief and the rest have membership in the policy planning committees in the central party bureaucracy.

7. Instituted in 1963, the system may more accurately be called a "bonus system" rather than a quasi-proportional representation system. Each party prepares before the election a list containing the names of that party's candidates for this

system. Of forty-four seats reserved for this purpose, half go to the majority party in the legislature and the rest are divided proportionately among other parties on the basis of the percentages of seats held by each party in the National Assembly.

PART III

Bureaucratic Elite and Popular Perceptions

4. Bureaucratic Elite and Development Orientations

DONG-SUH BARK and CHAE-JIN LEE

INTRODUCTION

It is widely assumed that public administration or bureaucracy is a crucial variable in determining a nation's capacity to manage its environmental conditions and to implement its developmental goals. For this reason, Esman concludes that "the administrative system, civil and military, is the minimum universal and indispensable instrument through which modern governing elites achieve active (i.e., developmental) relationships with the community."[1] Many other scholars emphasize the substantive strategic role of the bureaucracy as a key institutional framework for development strategy.[2]

The instrumental and 'unifunctional view of the role of senior bureaucrats has been seriously questioned in recent years. La Palombara argues that a conception of senior bureaucrats as essentially an instrument available to those who make political policy is empirically untenable in any political system.[3] Weaver advances the thesis that they even assume an independent role in advancing political change in developing countries;[4] not merely being limited to the implementation and execution of developmental policies, but often becoming actively engaged in formulating priorities and programs for national development.

Viewed from the multifunctional perspective, Almond and Powell state: "Bureaucracies dominate the output end of the political conversion process; they are indispensable in the rule-making and adjudication processes as well as influential in the political processes of interest articulation, aggregation, and communication."[5] Likewise, Harris suggests that the multifunctional content of the role of senior bureaucrats is significantly affected by changes in the personnel, structures, and goals of a political system.[6] This multifunctionality, according to him, embraces a wide range of roles—namely, policy maker, policy adviser, program formulator, program manager, program implementor, interest aggregator, interest articulator, agent of political communication, adjudicator, and agent of political socialization. In brief, the senior bureaucrats are assumed to affect both the input functions and the output gates of the conversion process, especially in developing political systems.

The senior bureaucrats in South Korea do not seem to be an exception to the multifunctional tendencies of development administration. As Henderson suggests, Korea had the long Confucian tradition of "strong, centralized, uncontested bureaucratic rule" even to the extent of retarding pluralist, democratic development.[7] Since the South Korean military leaders seized political power in the 1961 *coup d'état*, they have relied heavily upon the highly centralized bureaucratic structure to achieve their professed goals of planned change.[8]

At the early stage of their military control, these bureaucrats initiated a number of major changes in the civilian bureaucracy to render it conducive to their own reformist and developmental outlook. Specifically, according to Lee, the tradition of bureaucracy based on seniority and accustomed to routine was transformed into one based on merit and motivated to introduce changes. Moreover, they brought in new blood, especially professional military officers, to the high responsible administrative positions.[9] As a result, the senior bureaucrats were known to be more positive, innovative, adaptive, and more inclined to promote change than ever before in the exercise of their developmental leadership. The degree of structural differentiation and functional specialization increased in government agencies.[10]

Despite the emphasis upon this administrative development, one cannot deny the preponderant political control over the bureaucracy. The president, prime minister, cabinet ministers, and ruling party members of the National Assembly may influence the way in which senior bureaucrats are recruited, transferred, and promoted. Most important, the open-ended growth of President Pak's extremely powerful and authoritarian control machinery, centered in his Blue House, tends to hinder the functional autonomy of all subsystems of a political system, including the bureaucracy. It is the Blue House that, in effect, possesses the ultimate authority to determine or at least sanction developmental priorities, resource allocation, and bureaucratic performance. The political constraints superimposed upon bureaucratic behavior are undoubtedly substantial and pervasive.

Nevertheless, the president and his executives have no alternative but to depend upon the vast bureaucracy to produce demonstrable achievements of development that can in turn be used to enhance their legitimacy. They need the cooperation and assistance of able, efficient, and dedicated senior bureaucrats; indeed, the political and bureaucratic elite are mutually interdependent in a functional way, if not in a structural hierarchy.

The senior bureaucrats, by virtue of their technical expertise and managerial skills, are therefore encouraged to take an active part in formulating ambitious economic plans, initiating new governmental programs, and controlling national resources. Whereas the total general expenditure of the national budget was only 57 billion won in 1961, it reached 647 billion won in 1972, which constituted 16.6 percent of the gross national product. Meanwhile, the wholesale price index showed a little less than a threefold increase during the same period. As the scope of their multifunctional responsibilities and the amount of their financial resources expanded, the number of senior bureaucrats also increased. In the process, they assumed a vital role of leading and managing the direction and substance of national development.

Since the bureaucrats are, for all practical purposes, removed from the arena of direct political accountability, they may act as trustees of public interest and/or as agents of popularly elected political elite. If the wishes and perspectives of these political elite are held more or less given or constant, the senior bureaucrats are likely to pursue what they perceive to be the priorities and requirements of development administration. This possibility suggests that much of their administrative leadership is conditioned by their values and attitudes toward national development.

In view of the presumed impact of the values and attitudes of senior bureaucrats upon their developmental leadership, our study is designed to illustrate and examine these values and attitudes in the broad context of the social background and administrative experience of the bureaucrats. It is our primary hypothesis that the three major dimensions of developmental administrative leadership—social background, administrative experience, and developmental orientation—are functionally interrelated in a significant fashion. Special attention is paid to the comparison of social, administrative, and developmental attributes between career civil servants and those who were recruited from the military. It is further hypothesized that the military-turned-civilian bureaucrats share a common social background, administrative functions, and developmental perspectives, which can clearly be distinguished from those held by regular career bureaucratic elite.

In order to examine these hypotheses and other related issues, we interviewed 176 out of 203 senior bureaucrats who, as of January 1972, held Grade II-A positions, which corresponds to the level of central bureau director and provincial lieutenant governor. One interview case was discarded for lack of sufficient information. The interviews, which were conducted from December 1971 to January 1972, elicited from each bureaucrat responses to the following items and questions:

(A) *Social Background.* Age, place of birth, father's education and occupation, class origin, educational attainment, college major, religious affiliation, competence in foreign languages, exposure to foreign countries, military experience, length of military service, timing of retirement.

(B) *Administrative Experience.* Method of recruitment, age of starting bureaucratic career, starting administrative grade, interagency mobility, speed of promotion, age at which grade II was reached, length of administrative service, functional assignment.

(C) *Development Orientations.* Planning for the future, mastery over one's environment, task accomplishment, institutional change, public-minded ethos, political development, locus of developmental leadership, administrative role perception.

SOCIAL BACKGROUND

Our data (see table 1) show that the overwhelming majority of senior bureaucrats, unlike their political superiors, were born and raised in the southern half of the Korean peninsula. The territorial division since 1945 caused North Koreans to be underrepresented in the top bureaucratic echelons; only 14.3 percent (N=25) come from P'yŏngan, Hamgyŏng, and Hwanghae provinces. Moreover, North Koreans in the upper echelons are heavily concentrated in the older age groups, which suggests that the proportion of North Koreans in the bureaucracy is gradually declining.

It has been claimed that in the allocation of leadership positions and national resources the Pak administration has favored Pak's own Kyŏngsang (southeastern) region, and has discriminated against the southwestern region, particularly the Chŏlla provinces. The information we gathered partially confirms this claim, but not to the extent many have expected. The Kyŏngsang provinces have produced 41 senior bureaucrats (23.4 percent), almost twice as many as have the Chŏlla provinces. If these figures are compared with the total population in these provinces, we find that even if the degree of representation of the Kyŏngsang provinces is higher than it is for the Chŏlla provinces, it is lower than the degree of representation of Seoul or Ch'ungch'ŏng provinces.

TABLE 1

BIRTHPLACES OF ADMINISTRATIVE LEADERS

	Number	*Percentage*
Central provinces	45	25.8
Southeastern provinces	41	23.4
Southwestern provinces	43	24.5
Northern provinces	25	14.3
Other places	20	11.4
No information	1	0.6
Total	175	100.0

NOTE: Central = Seoul, and Kyŏnggi and Kangwŏn provinces; southeastern = Pusan and Kyŏngsang provinces; southwestern = Chŏlla, Ch'ungch'ŏng, and Cheju provinces; northern = P'yŏngan, Hamgyŏng, and Hwanghae provinces.

The educational levels of the fathers of most of the senior bureaucrats were higher than are those of the average Korean in the preliberation period; the fathers were almost all literate. Whereas two out of five fathers had the traditional, informal education in Chinese classics, the rest had received some formal education —10.3 percent in primary schools, 26.3 percent in secondary schools, and 22.3 percent in colleges. This record contrasts sharply with the fact that only 20 percent of Koreans had had any formal schooling by 1945 and less than 1 percent of them had been college educated.[11]

There is a low degree of occupational continuity from fathers to sons. As table 2 demonstrates, 16.5 percent of the fathers of senior bureaucrats held positions in the bureaucracy as their principal occupation. A little less than half of them were farmers—the predominant occupation for preliberation Korean households—and one out of five fathers were merchants or businessmen. The others were doctors, teachers, journalists, or held miscellaneous jobs. The diversity of the fathers' primary occupations notwithstanding, senior bureaucrats grew up in relatively comfortable economic conditions. Even though not many fathers reached the upper class in terms of socioeconomic status, the majority (73.1 percent) belonged to the middle class. Only one out of twenty fathers was identified as a member of the lower class.

TABLE 2

PRINCIPAL OCCUPATIONS OF FATHERS OF ADMINISTRATIVE LEADERS

	Number	*Percentage*
Farmer	82	46.9
Merchant	33	18.9
Bureaucrat	29	16.5
Other occupations	27	15.4
No information	4	2.3
Total	175	100.0

If top bureaucratic positions constitute an element of the upper social stratum in South Korea, there is considerable upward social mobility achieved by senior bureaucrats from the level of their fathers, but compared with the rest of the South Korean population, they were endowed with the advantageous circumstances of their fathers' educational and economic achievements. These characteristics may not be a necessary determinant of the career patterns of senior bureaucrats, but some correlations will be indicated later.

In our sample one out of five persons were Christian, but the traditional belief systems, Confucianism and Buddhism, were practiced by 17.7 percent and 11.4 percent respectively. A greater number of senior bureaucrats (36.6 percent) indicated no particular religious preference. The degree of religious secularization is far more extensive among younger bureaucrats than among older ones, who prefer Confucianism or Buddhism. Those whose fathers had been farmers tended towards Confucianism and Buddhism, which is perhaps indicative of the close association between rural origins and traditional values.

The average age of Korean administrative leaders as of January 1972 was forty-six, which is younger than their counterparts in the United States and Japan (see table 3).[12] The majority of them (63.5 percent) were in their forties; ages for the youngest and oldest were thirty-six and fifty-nine, respectively. As Lee argues, the presence of young higher civil servants is a reflection of a policy of rejuvenating the central bureaucracy by the Pak administration. Lee suggests that the younger bureaucrats attain their position more on the basis of merit and are more inclined to institute changes than are their older colleagues.[13] As the Pak government grew older and the bureaucratic system stabilized, the average age of higher civil servants or senior bureaucrats increased; it was forty for Grade II-A in 1962, between forty-one and forty-five in 1967, and forty-six in 1972.[14] The radical surgical operations on the bureaucracy conducted by the coup leaders have been gradually replaced by a normal procedure of bureaucratic turnover.

TABLE 3

AGE LEVELS OF ADMINISTRATIVE LEADERS

	Number	Percentage
35-39	18	10.3
40-44	61	34.9
45-49	50	28.6
50-54	34	19.4
55-59	9	5.1
No information	3	1.7
Total	175	100.0

It is remarkable that the senior bureaucrats in Korea attained a very high level of formal education. All of them except three were college-educated, and 41.1 percent had obtained advanced graduate degrees (see table 4). This record of college training is even better than the comparable record in the United States, where, although not so many were college-educated, 60.1 percent of the American bureaucratic elite had postbaccalaureate degrees in 1963.[15] Our Korean data indicate an appreciable increase in the educational levels of senior bureaucrats for the past decade; for example, in 1962 only 9.3 percent of those in Grade II-A had not advanced beyond the secondary school level.[16] For the financial source of their college education, most of them relied upon their parents completely or in part, and less than 10 percent worked through college.

TABLE 4

EDUCATIONAL LEVELS OF ADMINISTRATIVE LEADERS

	Number	Percentage
Primary school	1	0.6
Secondary school	2	1.2
College	100	57.1
Master's degree	51	29.1
Doctorate	21	12.0
Total	175	100.0

The increasing level of educational attainment of the bureaucrats is probably the result of a combination of three main reasons. First, the pervasive enthusiasm for higher education in Korea has produced a large number of college-educated people available for bureaucratic service. Second, the pattern of recruitment and promotion for upper level managerial posts was favorable to those who had college training. Third, after entering administrative service, a tendency particularly notable among those who came from military service was for bureaucrats to earn college (N=8) and advanced degrees (31 masters, 11 doctorates) at home or abroad, often to obtain the degrees necessary for bureaucratic advancement. Of course, merely obtaining a high degree of formal education does not always guarantee correspondingly superior intellectual professional quality. In a discussion of Korean public administration, Koh questions the relevance of college education to efficient administration on the grounds that many colleges in Korea are no more than "diploma mills."[17] But, on the other hand, most of the senior bureaucrats have been trained in the major Korean universities and reputable foreign schools. In order to enter the bureaucracy, they took stiff examinations in competition with many college-educated applicants and the usual ratio of available administrative positions to serious applications rarely exceeded one to fifty in the 1950s and 1960s.

Closely related to the formal educational level of the bureaucrat is the kind and extent of specialized knowledge obtained in college. The traditional pattern in Korea, especially the examination system in the Confucian classics, long perpetuated the generalist character of the bureaucracy; given the pre-eminence of the "scholar-bureaucrat," the specialist had been relegated to low, technical positions. This pattern was further reinforced by the Japanese colonial administration with its well-known emphasis on the generalist. A number of Western scholars—Joseph LaPalombara, Milton Esman, and Edward W. Weidner, to name a few—have emphasized the primary importance of the functional specialist as developmental administrators. Other scholars like Morstein Marx and Ralph Braibanti have attached a higher priority to administrative generalists as "guardian bureaucrats" than to specialists as "modern medicinemen." One can say that each developing nation is required to have a proper "mix" of generalists and specialists in accordance with its specific developmental stage and needs.

It is still true that the majority of Korean higher civil servants majored in the social sciences (41.7 percent) or humanities (24.0

percent) in college; 32.6 percent were trained in natural sciences and engineering. The number of top bureaucrats with science majors has nearly doubled over the past several years, and that of social science majors has declined by one-third. This change may indicate that as the Korean government becomes more extensively involved in the management of complex scientific and technological issues, it needs and thus promotes more bureaucrats who are equipped with special skills.

Unlike their counterparts in the United States, a very small minority of Korean bureaucrats were born in foreign countries—three in Japan, two in China, and one in the U.S. Almost all of them were born and educated to varying degrees under Japanese colonial rule. They can therefore read and speak Japanese, and nine out of ten had visited Japan. We cannot measure the exact consequences of the nature of their education and exposure to Japan as a developed state, but we can safely surmise that these circumstances must have had substantial effects on the socialization experience of the bureaucrats. The foreign language competence of senior bureaucrats is not limited to Japanese; many of them (75.5 percent) can also read or speak English. Korean bureaucrats frequently note that proficiency in English facilitates their work and helps their advancement, especially in the ministries that deal with foreign companies or countries. Moreover, they have traveled widely in foreign countries; over 90 percent have made trips abroad at least once, and 30 percent more than five times. Hence, they have had extensive opportunities to observe and study a variety of foreign administrative systems. Their experience abroad may have broadened their developmental outlook, which has made it easier for them to transcend narrow national boundaries in conceptualizing developmental goals and choices.

A large number of the higher civil servants (43.4 percent) have served in some form of military service either before or during their bureaucratic careers. This is a result of the Korean War and subsequent national defense policy, which practiced universal conscription. In addition, some professional military officers have sought their postmilitary occupations in civilian public administration, especially since the military *coup d'état* of 1961. Initially, the military oligarchs brought a large number of their trusted and experienced officers into high administrative positions, and some of these men subsequently decided to remain. The massive military involvement in civilian administration was achieved on the basis of two assumptions: first, professional military officers could effectively transfer skills obtained in the military into their civilian administrative roles; second, these officers constituted a pure, reliable, and dedicated core group in the civilian administration so that the military oligarchs' political objectives could be carried out in a systematic way.

Needless to say, military participation in civilian public administration had a far-reaching effect on bureaucratic structures and norms. Cole and Lyman state that "in certain characteristics, particularly time orientation, work habits, and managerial outlook, the military early became one of the most 'modernized' institutions in Korea, out of balance in this respect with most government and educational institutions."[18] Hence, we hypothesize that there is a significant difference of socioeconomic attributes, administrative functions, and developmental outlooks between career civil servants and those who were recruited from the military.

In new nations, Janowitz suggests, "the military establishment is recruited from the middle and lower-middle classes, drawn mainly from rural areas or hinterlands," moreover, "military education contributed to an innovating outlook toward modernization."[19] It is also believed that as the size of military establishment and the level of military technology increase, the transferability of skills from military to civilian functions grows.

Among those bureaucrats who had military experience, 29 served less than six years, and 47 served more than six years. If we assume that military service of six or more years is a crude index of military professionalism, then about 27 percent of our samples can be classified as former professional soliders. Of 59 persons whose timing of retirement from military service is identified, 36 retired before the 1961 coup and 23 after. This means that at least 13.1 percent of senior bureaucrats were recruited from the military in the postcoup period. Most of the military-turned-civilian bureaucrats started their military service as officers in the army. The other service categories—navy, air force, and marine corps—are underrepresented in the top civilian bureaucratic echelons. At the time of their military retirement, these erstwhile military bureaucrats had reached high ranks—two generals, twenty-nine majors and colonels, and twenty-five lieutenants and captains.

Compared with career civilian bureaucrats, ex-military bureaucrats are considerably younger (see table 5). The military officers who joined the civilian bureaucracy before 1961 were much younger than the post-1961 entrants, but the former professional military personnel with more than six years of military experience were older than nonprofessional ones. As we will discuss later, the significant age differences between professional and nonprofessional military people or between those who retired before or after the coup are closely associated with the different methods and ranks of initial administrative appointments.

TABLE 5

CIVILIAN-MILITARY BACKGROUNDS OF ADMINISTRATIVE LEADERS:
A COMPARISON

	Civilian	Military	C (contingency coefficient) G (Goodman's Gamma)
Age group			C = .33 (p < .01)
35-39	7	11	G = −.49
40-44	26	35	
45-49	29	21	
Over 50	36	7	
No information	1	2	
Educational level			C = .22 (p < .01)
College	64	36	G = .38
Graduate	40	32	
College major			C = .19 (p < .05)
Humanities	24	18	G = .17
Social sciences	46	27	
Natural sciences	26	31	
Class origin			C = .16 (p < .20)
Upper	15	19	G = −.28
Middle	76	52	
Lower	8	4	

NOTE: The levels of statistical significance are based on chi-square tests. When the requirements for chi-square tests are not met, they are used for exploratory purposes only.

The total number of persons for each variable used in this and following tables may not add up to 175 due to incomplete information. Those for whom information on a given variable is unavailable are excluded from statistical computations, and these data are not reported in the tables. For educational levels, three persons who did not attend college are not included in computations.

About one-fourth of those who had some military experience come from North Korea. The figure is higher still among the professional military personnel, no doubt because of the presence of many North Koreans in the armed forces, one of a few major occupational opportunities open to them in South Korea. More than three-fourths of all bureaucrats from North Korea have had military service—an appreciably higher proportion than is true for other bureaucrats. However, most of them were recruited into the civilian bureaucracy before 1961. In other words, the military *coup d'état* did not lead to any substantial participation of military personnel from North Korea in the civilian bureaucracy. Of those military officers who entered the bureaucracy after 1961, the largest number (more than one-third) came from the Kyŏngsang region.

Similar to Janowitz's generalization, Scalapino contends that South Korea's military rulers in the early 1960s, who came from rural and poor backgrounds, have a rural orientation that despises the immoral, corrupt, and selfish urban political life.[20] As far as our data are concerned, however, the fathers of ex-military senior bureaucrats were better educated, more affluent, and less likely to engage in rural occupations than were those of career civil servants. This contrast remained even when the extent of military professionalism was controlled. Even though the bulk of military officers have been drawn from poor, rural families, only those ex-military bureaucrats who enjoyed favorable backgrounds have successfully competed with career civil servants to climb the upper ladder of the bureaucratic hierarchy.

The ex-military bureaucrats are better educated than their civilian counterparts; more than half of them have received postgraduate degrees, while less than one-third of civilian careerists have. The high educational achievement of ex-military men may mean either that they needed a good formal educational basis to enter the civilian administration or that, because of their probable inferiority complex vis-à-vis career bureaucrats, they made special efforts to obtain postgraduate credits in an attempt to raise their own status. A small number of them have taken leaves of absence to pursue their educations abroad, but many others have earned advanced degrees in a variety of graduate programs in Korea. For instance, the Graduate School of Public Administration, Seoul National University, alone has provided a special graduate program for about 830 incumbent senior bureaucrats and high military officers since 1961. It is not surprising that unlike their civilian peers, more senior ex-military bureaucrats have majored in natural sciences and engineering than in the social sciences, in part because some of them obtained bachelor's degrees in natural sciences at their service academies. They are as proficient in foreign languages—both Japanese and English—as civilian bureaucrats, and they have traveled abroad as frequently.

Contrary to our initial hypothesis, our data failed to demonstrate any substantial disadvantage that ex-military senior bureaucrats might have suffered due to their special socioeconomic background. Instead, they had equal or even better levels of parental background, formal education achievement, linguistic competence, and foreign experience than their civilian colleagues. Nevertheless, we should note that they include a greater proportion of North Koreans, younger persons, and technically trained functional specialists.

ADMINISTRATIVE EXPERIENCE

The typical senior civil servant took a competitive examination to start his bureaucratic career at the age of thirty, and served sixteen years thereafter. This late bureaucratic beginning reflects both the lateral entry of some senior members and the widespread military experience. It took about twelve years for him to rise from low rank to his present Grade II-A, and he continued to hold that grade for four more years. However, our data show a great variation of administrative recruitment and promotion procedures, which may indicate the relative fluidity of bureaucratic norms and the profound effect of drastic political changes.

Two main methods, regular civil service examination and the special recruitment procedure, were used to procure bureaucrats. Only 48 percent of our sample took the regular, open, and competitive entrance examination; the rest was recruited by the special qualifying examination method, which varied to accommodate the government's particular needs and the applicants' qualifications. The latter method, which was less competitive than the former, was frequently employed to allow the lateral entry of new civil servants, even though the practice adversely affected the morale of incumbent career civil servants. The difference in age levels was not a significant factor in the adoption of regular or special recruitment methods. The more educated the applicants were, the more often special routes of entrance were used; furthermore, administrative generalists (those who studied social sciences) took the regular method far more frequently than functional specialists (those whose majors were in natural sciences).

Higher civil servants started their administrative careers at different ranks. As table 6 indicates, only 27 senior bureaucrats (15.4 percent) held the lowest grade and the largest number (37.7 percent) began at Grade III. Only 22 persons (12.6 percent) entered civilian public administration at their present grade, Grade II. According to our data, the younger they are now, the higher the starting administrative grades these civil servants assumed; the more educated they were, the higher grades they obtained. If all other conditions were more or less equal, functional specialists started at higher grades than administrative generalists.

TABLE 6

METHODS OF RECRUITING ADMINISTRATIVE LEADERS

	Regular	Special	C (contingency coefficient) G (Goodman's Gamma)
Age group			C = .10
35-39	11	7	G = .13
40-44	30	31	
45-49	23	27	
Over 50	19	24	
No information	1	2	
Educational level			C = .14 (p < .10)
College	54	46	G = .27
Graduate	29	43	
College major			C = .28 (p < .01)
Humanities	20	22	G = .27
Social sciences	46	27	
Natural sciences	17	40	
Grade at hiring			C = .43 (p < .01)
G-V	14	13	G = .42
G-IV	29	18	
G-III-B	30	11	
G-III-A	3	22	
G-II	2	20	
Misc.	6	7	

The political elite are increasingly aware of and adaptive to the rapid change that Korea's economic and social conditions have undergone. They are, for instance, emphasizing the greater functional differentiation of administrative task or positions. In order to examine this aspect of Korean bureaucracy, we classified bureaucratic positions into six broad functional categories—symbolic (foreign affairs, public education), distributive (social service, public works), regulative (legal sanctions), extractive (taxes, customs), economic (national planning), and technological (research activities). It must be pointed out at the outset that this classification scheme is not prima facie self-evident; there are some positions that indicate the overlap of two or more functional characteristics.

In table 7, we can see the strong correlations that the different administrative functions bear with age, educational level, and college major. It is immediately apparent that the younger bureaucrats are overrepresented in economic and symbolic functions, and the older ones are overrepresented in distributive and technological categories. The highly educated ones are charged with distributive, regulative, and technological responsibilities. While the humanists (history, literature) are heavily concentrated in symbolic areas, the social scientists (law, political science, economics) are active in economic, regulative, and extractive functions, and technological and distributive fields are largely assigned to the natural scientists. This distribution is perhaps suggestive of a personnel administration policy that allocates senior bureaucrats according to their functional specialties.

TABLE 7

FUNCTIONS OF ADMINISTRATIVE LEADERS

	S	D	R	X	E	T	C (contingency coefficient) G (Goodman's gamma)
Age group							
35-39	1	1	5	3	6	2	
40-44	10	12	6	5	17	11	
45-49	8	19	6	5	6	6	
Over 50	3	11	6	4	4	15	C = .40 (p < .01)
(No information	1	0	0	1	0	1)	G = −.01
Total	23	43	23	18	33	35	
Educational level							
College	18	19	12	10	22	19	C = .26 (p < .05)
Graduate	5	23	10	7	11	16	G = .04
College major							
Humanities	10	10	7	5	6	4	
Social sciences	10	15	13	10	19	6	C = .46 (p < .01)
Natural sciences	3	17	2	2	8	25	G = .32

NOTE: S = symbolic; D = distributive; R = regulative; X = extractive; E = economic; T = technological.

The length of administrative service was uneven; seventy-six persons (43.4 percent) served less than fifteen years, but a little over one-third of our sample spent more than twenty years of their adult life in the civilian public administration. The data suggest that despite the frequent lateral appointment of senior members, the top bureaucratic elite have a fairly high degree of professional commitment to administrative leadership roles. The length of service depended to some extent upon function—those who had symbolic, distributive, and technological responsibilities served longer in the administration than did the rest.

Almost three-fourths of the bureaucrats gained their entire administrative experience in one or two closely related departmental units, but the degree of interagency mobility was a little higher than it is in the United States and Japan (see table 8). This difference is perhaps indicative of the relatively less differentiated and more mobile structure of the Korean public administration. Different ages and educational levels did not appreciably determine horizontal mobility. Nevertheless, natural scientists were slightly more mobile than social scientists and humanists except that only two out of twelve persons who worked for more than four agencies were natural scientists. The frequency of interagency transfer did not correlate significantly with the length of administrative service, but it differed according to different functional categories. Mobility was limited in symbolic and distributive areas; it was quite substantial for those engaged in regulative, extractive, economic, and technological work, as a large number of administrative agencies require the service of experts or specialists in such areas as financial management, legal matters, economic planning, and research operations.

TABLE 8

INTERAGENCY MOBILITY OF ADMINISTRATIVE LEADERS

	Number of Agencies Served				C (contingency coefficient)
	1	2	3	4+	G (Goodman's gamma)
Age group					
35-39	9	4	5	0	
40-44	25	21	10	5	
45-49	24	18	6	2	
Over 50	20	8	11	4	C = .26 (p <.20)
(No information	1	1	0	1)	G = .01
Total	79	52	32	12	
Educational level					
College	41	33	20	6	C = .17 (p <.20)
Graduate	37	17	12	6	G = −.11
College major					
Humanities	24	7	7	4	
Social sciences	32	20	15	6	C = .24 (p <.10)
Natural sciences	32	23	10	2	G = .08
Administrative functions					
S = symbolic	18	5	0	0	
D = distributive	19	14	8	2	
R = regulative	10	6	6	1	C = .35 (p < .01)
X = extractive	7	3	5	3	G = .25
E = economic	12	14	6	1	
T = technological	13	10	7	5	

A majority of senior bureaucrats spent more than ten years in the administration before reaching their present grade. It must be noted that nearly two-thirds assumed Grade II-A before they were forty-five years old. This process of vertical mobility was closely related to their social background and administrative role. As expected, fewer years were needed to promote younger bureau chiefs than were needed to promote older ones. The better educated they were, the shorter the time needed to rise to their present grade. There seems to be a significant difference between promotion patterns for natural and social scientists, but both groups were more rapidly promoted than humanists. Evidently, competence in the English language helped the promotion of senior bureaucrats in Korea. It is an apparent asset for senior administrators who are dealing with international problems and foreign companies.

Those who climbed up from the lowest rank, understandably, took more time to reach Grade II than did the lateral entrants. Our data (see table 9) show that the speed of vertical mobility depended upon different functional responsibilities. The bureaucrats with regulative and extractive functions were quickly promoted; those

TABLE 9

PATTERNS OF PROMOTION OF ADMINISTRATIVE LEADERS

	Years in Service before Reaching Grade II					C (contingency coefficient) G (Goodman's gamma)
	Under 4	5-9	10-14	15-19	Over 20	
Age group						
35-39	2	10	6	0	0	
40-44	15	15	20	6	2	
45-49	10	10	5	15	10	
Over 50	4	5	7	5	22	C = .56 (p < .01)
(No information	1	0	2	0	0)	G = .45
Total	32	40	40	26	34	
Educational levels						
College	14	20	26	17	23	C = .36 (p < .01)
Graduate	18	20	14	9	8	G = −.31
College majors						
Humanities	7	9	8	8	9	
Social sciences	11	20	20	9	12	C = .30 (p <.05)
Natural sciences	14	11	12	9	10	G = −.08
Administrative functions						
S = symbolic	5	4	4	6	3	
D = distributive	7	16	2	6	11	
R = regulative	6	5	3	2	7	
X = extrative	6	2	5	2	3	
E = economic	3	6	15	6	2	C = .43 (p <.01)
T = technological	5	7	11	4	8	G = .04

bureaucrats in technological fields were promoted least rapidly, which may mean that legal and financial specialization is an effective instrument for bureaucratic success as judged by promotion.

It is noteworthy that the regional origin of senior bureaucrats had some relation to their administrative experience. For example, the southeasterners—those from the Kyŏngsang region—were more frequently recruited by the special method and at higher grades than were the southwesterners from the Chŏlla and Ch'ungch'ŏng regions. Although both groups were equal in educational attainment, age distribution, functional specialization, and interagency mobility, the former were more rapidly promoted than the latter. The result may be indicative of personal advantages enjoyed by the southeasterners in the administrative system.

When father-son relations are compared, we find that the sons of bureaucrats have had more successful or dynamic administrative careers than the sons of farmers. They also rose more quickly to their present rank and moved more frequently among different administrative agencies than the sons of farmers. They are slightly overrepresented in regulative and extractive functions, but underrepresented in the technological research field. We do not necessarily attribute the relative rapidity of their mobility, both horizontal and vertical, to their parenthood; it may have been prompted by their higher educational background and/or heavier emphasis upon social sciences. Moreover, their concentration in important regulative and extractive functions may have contributed to their administrative success.

Even if we do not confirm one of our initial hypotheses that there is a consistent correlation between social background and military experience among senior bureaucrats, our data corroborate the hypothesis that serving in the military significantly affects their administrative careers.

A glance at table 10 reveals no distinct difference between recruitment methods for those who do or do not have military experience, but we can see more results in table 11. Whereas only 12 (41 percent) of the nonprofessional military personnel were recruited by the special method, this method was used to recruit 31 (66 percent) of the professional military personnel. Moreover, of 23 military officers who were recruited after the 1961 coup, all but 2 took the special channel of transition into the civilian bureaucracy. No doubt the Pak government has bypassed the regular competitive examination methods to staff itself with professional military officers.

TABLE 10

CIVILIAN-MILITARY BACKGROUND AND ADMINISTRATIVE EXPERIENCE

	Civilian	*Military*	*C (contingency coefficient)* *G (Goodman's gamma)*
Recruitment			
Regular	51	33	C = .08
Special	48	43	G = .16
Grade at hiring			
G-V	24	3	C = .40 (p < .01)
G-IV	34	13	G = .62
G-III-B	20	21	
G-III-A	7	18	
G-II	6	16	
Age at G-II			
Under 39	17	32	C = .34 (p < .01)
40-44	35	29	G = .56
45-49	25	9	
Over 50	18	2	
Mobility (agencies served)			
1	47	32	C = .06
2	28	24	G = .07
3	17	15	
4+	7	5	
Promotion (years before Grade II)			
Under 4	8	24	C = .49 (p <.01)
5-9	13	27	G = .73
10-14	21	19	
15-19	24	2	
Over 20	32	2	
Functions			
S = symbolic	13	10	C = .11
D = distributive	23	20	G = −.03
R = regulative	15	8	
X = extractive	10	8	
E = economic	16	17	
T = technological	22	13	

Related to this recruitment pattern is the higher starting administrative grade assigned to former military officers than to civilian neophytes. Nearly three out of five nonmilitary bureaucrats started either at Grade V or IV, but these two low grades were given to only one out of five of the military personnel, in part a consequence of the frequent lateral entry of professional military people and of those who were recruited after the 1961 coup. Hence, 14 out of 22 persons who joined the civilian bureaucracy at Grade II were professional military, and at least 11 of these did so in the postcoup period. In other words, one-half of those who were hired from the military after 1961 were initially assigned to Grade II.

TABLE 11

MILITARY PROFESSIONALISM AND ADMINISTRATIVE EXPERIENCE

	Nonpro-fessional Military	Profes-sional Military	C (contingency coefficient) G (Goodman's gamma)
Recruitment			
Regular	17	16	C = .17 (p < .10)
Special	12	31	G = .47
Total	29	47	
Grade at hiring			
G-V	0	3	C = .49 (p < .01)
G-IV	8	5	G = .48
G-III-B	14	7	
G-III-A	4	14	
G-II	2	14	
Mobility (agencies served)			
1	16	16	C = .15
2	7	17	G = .32
3	5	10	
4+	1	4	
Promotion (years before Grade II)			
Under 4	2	22	C = .56 (p < .01)
5-9	15	12	G = .47
10-14	10	9	
15-19	1	1	
Over 20	0	2	
Functions			
S = symbolic	6	4	C = .22 (p < .20)
D = distributive	6	14	G = .12
R = regulative	3	5	
X = extractive	2	6	
E = economic	9	8	
T = technological	3	10	

It was noted earlier that the typical senior civil servant begins his bureaucratic career at the age of thirty, but the former military officer assumes his new civilian job at a much older age, after many years spent in military service. Once they are recruited into civilian public administration, senior bureaucrats have had a relatively uniform pattern of interagency mobility irrespective of their military experience and of the extent of their military professionalism. The mobility was higher, however, among those who were transferred from the armed forces after 1961, suggesting that they were freely dispatched to a wider range of administrative agencies as a kind of mobile and loyal guardian of the Pak government.

No clear-cut relationship between military experience and administrative functions appeared in our data. Table 11 indicates that the nonprofessional military bureaucrats were more active in economic and distributive functions, but less active in regulative and technological areas. The professional military were overrepresented in distributive (veterans' affairs), extractive (taxes and customs), and technological fields, which together embraced 64 percent of the professional military bureaucrats. Unlike the general similarities of horizontal mobility and functional responsibilities, the speed of promotion was much faster for ex-military bureaucrats than it was for the rest. Consequently, the former reached Grade II at younger ages than did the latter. Moreover, the professional military made the fastest advancement to their present grades. This finding not only reflects their initial appointments at high administrative grades, but also demonstrates that their long military experience, personal ties, and managerial skills were unmistakably helpful in their rapid bureaucratic ascendancy under the Pak government, which has been dominated by former military political executives. On the basis of backgrounds and interests shared with the political elite, they enjoyed better prospects for promotion and performed more influential roles in political-administrative relations than career civil servants. One can only conjecture that the latter were not always happy or secure about the initial, lateral intrusion of professional military officers, who, in effect, disrupted the integrity of established bureaucratic norms and attitudes. As both groups continued to interact in the same bureaucratic environment and to diffuse their respective erstwhile "subcultures," it can be assumed they gradually became accustomed to the inevitable mixture of military and civilian value systems and behavioral norms. If so, it is highly likely that they came to regard each other more as allies than as competitors for the common goal of developmental administrative leadership.

DEVELOPMENT ORIENTATIONS

One of our original hypotheses is that the social background and administrative experience of the senior bureaucrats are significantly related to their internalized cognitive, affective, and evaluative orientations toward development. It can be suggested that these development orientations to a great extent determine their commitments and capabilities for formulating and executing national developmental goals. The consensus and cleavage patterns of their development orientations may represent the degree to which they are effectively integrated and coordinated in pursuing administrative leadership.

The development orientations may encompass a wide range, but we assume that the most important components include values and attitudes favoring (1) planning for the future, (2) mastering one's environment, (3) task accomplishment, (4) institutional change, (5) a public-minded ethos, and (6) political development. It is further assumed that the awareness by the bureaucratic elite of developmental leadership and perception of their administrative roles are integral parts of their development orientations.[21] It is not the purpose of our present study to assess the interrelationship of these values and attitudes; we are primarily interested in ascertaining the direction (positive or negative) and intenstiy (strong or weak) of the development orientations of senior bureaucrats and examining the associations between these orientations and social and administrative experiences.

Planning for the Future: Our data, first of all, show a substantial consensus among the bureaucratic elite in their ideas about planning for the future. The overwhelming majority rejected—either strongly (58.9 percent) or moderately (29.1 percent)—the claim that since the future is unpredictable, it is more desirable to take routine action than to adopt a long-range plan. Only a negligible minority (5.1 percent) agreed with the statement, and a few more (6.9 percent) remained neutral or ambivalent. These results are not surprising because the Pak government has given top priority to long-range planning, particularly in economic fields. The successful completion of the first two five-year economic development plans, along with the beginning of the third five-year plan (1972–76), may have increased the group's commitment to planning for the future irrespective of their social and administrative experience. They were also innovative and assertive, as shown by their willingness to take risks; all but 5 percent disagreed with the idea that it is better not to start new tasks because they are dangerous.

Mastery over One's Environment: Almost three-quarters of those interviewed expressed self-confidence in their ability to master environmental conditions; namely, they agreed strongly (40.6 percent) or moderately (32.0 percent) with the statement that if a man makes a serious attempt, he can overcome natural and physical obstacles. A little more than 15 percent disagreed, and the rest were noncommittal. The distribution of these responses is obviously skewed toward the affirmative, but one may still ask if the different verbal responses to the statement are in any way related to the differing social backgrounds and administrative experience of the bureaucrats.

As table 12 indicates, the responses are most significantly associated with differences in the levels of formal education. More than one out of five senior bureaucrats with postbaccalaureate degrees disagreed with the statement; so did one out of ten less educated bureaucrats. In other words, the more educated, the less posi-

TABLE 12

RESPONSES TO THE STATEMENT, "IF A MAN MAKES A SERIOUS
ATTEMPT, HE CAN OVERCOME NATURAL AND PHYSICAL OBSTACLES"

	Agree (N=127)	Neutral (N=21)	Disagree (N=27)	C (contingency coefficient) G (Goodman's gamma)	
Class origin					
Upper	27	2	5	C = .27	(p< .01)
Middle	92	15	21	G = .12	
Lower	8	4	0		
Educational level					
College	79	11	10	C = .19	(p < .05)
Graduate	46	10	16	G = .35	
Military service					
No	74	14	11	C = .15	(p < .20)
Yes	53	7	16	G = .16	
Professional military					
No	23	2	4	C = .19	(p < .05)
Yes	30	5	12	G = .28	
Administrative years					
Less than 10 years	16	4	8	C = .28	(p < .20)
10-14	34	4	10	G = .28	
15-19	25	8	4		
20-24	26	2	1		
More than 25 years	26	3	4		
Promotion (years before Grade II)					
Under 4	21	3	8	C = .25	(p < .20)
5-9	25	6	9	G = .28	
10-14	30	5	5		
15-19	22	3	1		
Over 20	28	3	3		

NOTE: Among all social and administrative variables used in this study, only those variables that indicate some statistical significance are reported in this and following tables.

tive was the belief that one could surmount environmental obstacles, a finding that suggests that more educated persons are acutely conscious of the complex relations between man and his environment and are therefore more aware of the limited human or administrative ability to control natural and physical conditions. We also found that the higher their subjectively identified class origins were (on the basis of their fathers' economic status), the more confident were the responses. One phenomenon to be noted is that none of the bureaucrats with lower-class origins disagreed with the statement, but one-third of them took an ambivalent position.

Military experience has some relationship to beliefs about control of one's surroundings, although the level of statistical significance is not very high. Contrary to our initial expectations that experience in military service would contribute to being able to control one's future, we find less optimistic responses in ex-military bureaucrats than in career civil servants. The former groups gave twice as many negative responses as did the latter. Moreover, the professional military person was more negative than the nonprofessional. If this finding is not caused by extraneous factors, one might argue that the ex-military bureaucrats, especially those who had prolonged service records, tended to project their past military experience, which recognized the natural and physical constraints of military activity, into their new bureaucratic functions. Other social attributes—age difference, college major, religious affiliation, and father's occupation—did not show any appreciable relationship with the statement.

In addition, it is interesting that the longer the administrative service the bureaucrats had, the more positive were their responses, a tendency that suggests that as they accumulated administrative experience, they became more confident and optimistic about their capabilities. Those who had limited bureaucratic experience or were rapidly promoted to their present position of leadership were likely to be rather cautious or unsure about their power to overcome natural and physical obstacles. Our data failed to support the thesis that the relatively young, rapidly promoted bureaucrats felt more confident than their older colleagues.

Commitment to Task Accomplishment: Closely related to the beliefs about control over one's environment is the manner in which the bureaucrats are committed to fulfilling their responsibilities. Asked if they agreed or disagreed that all tasks must be accomplished no matter what means are used, about 62 percent answered affirmatively, 24 percent negatively. The emphasis on high achievement indicated by the inclination to get things done regardless of the methods employed has been a major moral imperative of the Pak government, which despises a slow, incremental approach toward national development.

We see in table 13 that the higher the economic condition of the bureaucrat's father, the less positive were his responses. The bureaucrats of lower-class origins were most interested in task accomplishment, a finding consistent with some sociological studies that show a high interest in achievement among lower middle-class adults in a given organizational unit. Former officers were slightly more positive about the need for task accomplishment than were their civilian peers, but the civilian-military cleavage was not very strong. Among senior bureaucrats who had prior military service, the professional officers responded affirmatively more than the

TABLE 13

RESPONSES TO THE STATEMENT, "ALL TASKS MUST BE ACCOMPLISHED
NO MATTER WHAT MEANS ARE USED"

Variables	Agree (N=108)	Neutral (N=25)	Disagree (N=42)	C (contingency coefficient) G (Goodman's gamma)	
Class origin					
Upper	19	7	8	C = .19	(p < .20)
Middle	81	18	29	G = -.08	
Lower	8	0	4		
Professional military					
No	17	6	6	C = .14	(p < .20)
Yes	32	7	8	G = -.17	
Military retirement					
Postcoup	16	5	2	C = .16	(p < .10)
Precoup	22	6	8	G = .23	
Promotion (years before Grade II)					
Under 4	22	6	4	C = .25	(p < .20)
5-9	25	6	9	G = .14	
10-14	22	6	12		
15-19	21	1	4		
Over 20	16	6	12		
Functions					
S = symbolic	15	1	7	C = .31	(p < .10)
D = distributive	30	5	8	G = .02	
R = regulative	8	4	11		
X = extractive	9	5	4		
E = economic	25	3	5		
T = technological	21	7	7		

others. More important, those who retired from military service after the 1961 coup were the most strongly dedicated to accomplishing their tasks by any means. We infer from these data that those who have given extended military service, which emphasizes the priority of task accomplishment, have been sufficiently conditioned to sustain the same attitude in their civilian bureaucratic milieu. In particular, military officers who joined the civilian bureaucracy in the postcoup period shared with their ex-military political leaders a strong commitment to utilize all conceivable methods for the primary purpose of task accomplishment. As far as the end-and-means relationship is concerned, military organizations in general are perhaps less concerned with the choice of means required to accomplish objectives than is the civilian bureaucracy.

The senior bureaucrats who had been rapidly promoted to their present rank agreed more readily than did those who had been promoted more slowly. About 12 persons (35 percent) of those who required more than twenty years to reach Grade II disagreed with the necessity for accomplishing given tasks by whatever means necessary, but only 4 persons (12 percent) of those who spent less than four years to reach Grade II were so inclined. This points to two possible interpretations: either bureaucrats for whom achievement is important enjoy rapid promotion, or rapid promotion encourages a strong commitment to task achievement. Those in regulative, extractive, and symbolic administrative functions gave fewer affirmative answers than did those in economic and distributive functions, who gave more affirmative responses. Successful execution of ambitious economic plans and developmental projects may have fostered a strong preference for getting things done by any means. Methods of administrative recruitment, interdepartmental mobility, and length of bureaucratic service do not indicate any significant correlation with orientation toward task accomplishment.

Need for Institutional Change: The behavioral implications of the bureaucrats' beliefs about environmental control and task accomplishment are probably associated with their willingness to effect an administrative and legal change required for developmental goals. A little over half of those interviewed agreed that administrative institutions and laws must be easily changed to meet new needs. The remainder were almost equally divided between negative and neutral responses. The lower percentage of positive responses to this question, compared with the preceding two statements, may reflect a considerably high degree of what might be termed "institutional conservatism" or "administrative formalism." In other words, some of those who refused to accept the statement may have done so not because they were opposed to a change per se, but because they could fulfill their tasks without administrative or legal change.

Table 14 shows that bureaucrats with graduate degrees looked more favorably on institutional and legal changes than others did. College majors, too, showed some connections with the responses: technical or functional specialists agreed more than social scientists and humanists, but the humanists were more ambiguous than the other two groups. Military service and its length are not significantly relevant to the responses. The ex-military bureaucrats who started their civilian administrative responsibilities after 1961 were more committed to the need for institutional and legal changes than were precoup retirees.

TABLE 14

RESPONSES TO THE STATEMENT, "ADMINISTRATIVE INSTITUTIONS AND LAWS MUST BE EASILY CHANGED TO MEET NEW NEEDS"

	Agree (N=98)	Neutral (N=36)	Disagree (N=41)	C (contingency coefficient) G (Goodman's gamma)	
Educational level					
College	54	20	26	C = .17	(p < .10)
Graduate	43	14	15	G = -.11	
College major					
Humanities	21	11	10	C = .20	(p < .20)
Social sciences	40	16	17	G = -.11	
Natural sciences	36	7	14		
Military retirement					
Postcoup	13	6	4	C = .17	(p < .10)
Precoup	21	3	12	G = .09	
Functions					
S = symbolic	12	7	4	C = .29	(p < .10)
D = distributive	29	9	5	G = .06	
R = regulative	8	7	8		
X = extractive	9	3	6		
E = economic	19	8	6		
T = technological	21	2	12		

It is worth noting that the adherents of Buddhism and Confucianism were far less positive about institutional and legal adaptation than the Christians and those who expressed no religious preferences. The traditional and conservative norms among Buddhists and Confucianists seem to have influenced their reluctance to effect too much change in the established legal and administrative frameworks. Not surprisingly, the senior bureaucrats whose primary responsibilities fall in regulative areas expressed the least interest in institutional and legal change. On the other hand, those with economic and distributive functions were the most strongly interested in change. The divergence of these attitudes indicates a likelihood that the assignment of a given administrative specialty tends to promote the attitudes toward development most appropriate to that specialty. As discussed earlier, the economic specialists show a set of common values and attitudes that are likely to facilitate execution of their responsibilities with regard to major developmental plans.

Public-minded Ethos: The conflict between public and private interests presents a difficult challenge to the bureaucratic leaders who are responsible for the management of developmental policies. They may wish to attach a higher value to public-mindedness so that collective goals of national development can be accomplished effectively; on the other hand, they may hesitate to sacrifice too much of the individual's interest simply for the sake of protecting the public one. In an attempt to examine this dilemma, we asked the bureaucratic leaders whether individuals must always be ready to sacrifice themselves for public interest and obligations.

As table 15 shows, nearly 70 percent of them agreed that this should be the case; and only 17 percent disagreed. A substantial majority of them seem to embrace what Wilson and Banfield call the "unitarist" or "holistic" ethos, a disposition to think in terms of an interest of the whole rather than an individual or parochial interest.[22] Even though age difference is not a significant variable to account for different reactions, we should point out that about 11 percent of those who are over fifty disagreed with the statement, while 28 percent of those in their thirties did so. Hence the younger bureaucrats appear to be less public-minded or more individualistic than their older colleagues.

The differences in educational specialization can explain to a significant extent the variation in opinions about both public interest and institutional changes. Again, a larger percentage of natural scientists than of social scientists or humanists agreed that the public interest should take precedence; the highest proportion of negative responses came from the humanists.

We expected that the ex-military bureaucrats, reflecting their training, would be more readily disposed to accept the priority of

TABLE 15

RESPONSES TO THE STATEMENT, "INDIVIDUALS MUST
ALWAYS BE READY TO SACRIFICE THEMSELVES FOR PUBLIC
INTEREST AND OBLIGATIONS"

	Agree (N=120)	Neutral (N=25)	Disagree (N=30)	C (contingency coefficient) G (Goodman's gamma)	
College major					
Humanities	27	6	9	C = .23	(p < .10)
Social sciences	46	16	11	G = .17	
Natural sciences	44	3	10		
Military service					
No	68	18	13	C = .16	(p < .20)
Yes	52	7	17	G = .07	
Professional military					
No	22	3	4	C = .20	(p < .05)
Yes	30	4	13	G = .29	
Military retirement					
Postcoup	17	1	5	C = .21	(p < .05)
Precoup	23	3	10	G = .20	
Recruitment					
Regular	51	17	16	C = .18	(p < .10)
Special	69	8	14	G = -.28	
Promotion					
Under 4	24	2	6	C = .35	(p < .01)
5-9	24	3	13	G = -.02	
10-14	29	6	5		
15-19	22	3	1		
Over 20	20	9	5		

the public over individual interest than their civilian counterparts, but the reverse is found in our data. The distribution of positive responses was almost identical in both military and civilian groups, but there were twice as many negative responses given by the military as by the civilians. Moreover, the bureaucrats with a professional military background disagreed more than the nonprofessional military. This departure from expectation, in effect, refutes the simplistic notion that experience in military organizations, where individual sacrifices are constantly demanded for public or collective interest, instills a strong dedication to public interest among former military officers. Edward Shils argues that "life in the military has an equivocal relationship to the growth of individuality." Though military organization may impose an oppressive discipline that suppresses individuality, Shils maintains that a young soldier who is away from his kinship group and his local

community removes himself from a force that inhibits individuality, "giving him a wider horizon and training him in skills which
are judged from the standpoint of efficiency, enhance his self-
esteem, and his sense of individual responsibility."[23] It must be
emphasized, however, that compared with those who transferred
from the military to the civilian bureaucracy before 1961, the postcoup military retirees were more positive about public interest.
Military service appears to be less relevant to the variation in the
bureaucrats' opinions toward a public-minded ethos than the timing and circumstances of their transition from military to civilian
service.

The varied processes of initial administrative appointment and
subsequent vertical mobility were closely associated with the way
in which the senior bureaucrats perceived the relative importance
of the public or private interests. Those who took advantage of
special recruitment methods to begin their administrative careers
were more public-minded than those recruited by regular means.
Once admitted to the administrative organization, those who were
rapidly promoted to their present ranks were more public-minded
than those who advanced slowly.

Attitude toward Political Development: In South Korea much of
the conception of development and modernization has centered on
economic development. As Eisenstadt correctly contends, however, the primacy of the economic sphere in development and
modernization is refuted by the impossibility of explaining the
conditions of economic development and the functions of a modern
economic system in economic terms alone.[24] When the economic
system surpasses the take-off stage, a viable political and social
structure, preferably an open, competitive one, may have to be
developed to provide a sound and legitimate basis for sustained
economic growth. As senior bureaucrats are assuming increasing
control over the pace and substance of economic as well as political
development in Korea, we attempted to learn something about
their attitudes toward political development. The bureaucrats were
asked to respond to the familiar claim that for the purpose of anti-
Communist struggles, the freedom of press and civil liberties can
be restricted.

More than 70 percent of those interviewed expressed their
agreement with the statement, while less than 13 percent responded
in the negative. We may infer that, as expected, the Korean bureaucratic leaders are staunchly anti-Communist or predominantly authoritarian with regard to civil liberties and political freedom. It

seems distinctly evident that they were more seriously concerned with the presumed threat from North Korea than with the development of liberal political practices. Conditioned by these attitudes, they were undoubtedly well prepared to welcome and implement the state of national emergency that President Pak declared in December 1971 on the grounds of North Korea's renewed aggressive intentions.

However, table 16 shows that despite the pervasive anti-

TABLE 16

RESPONSES TO THE STATEMENT, "FOR THE PURPOSE OF ANTI-COMMUNIST STRUGGLES, THE FREEDOM OF PRESS AND CIVIL LIBERTIES CAN BE RESTRICTED"

	Agree *(N=123)*	*Neutral* *(N=30)*	*Disagree* *(N=22)*	*C (contingency coefficient)* *G (Goodman's gamma)*	
Age group					
35-39	11	5	2	C = .23	(p < .20)
40-44	41	12	8	G = -.21	
45-49	31	10	9		
Over 50	37	3	3		
Class origin					
Upper	21	8	5	C = .23	(p < .05)
Middle	95	19	14	G = -.09	
Lower	7	3	2		
Educational level					
College	67	16	17	C = .19	(p < .05)
Graduate	54	14	4	G = .23	
Military service					
No	69	14	16	C = .14	(p < .20)
Yes	54	16	6	G = -.37	
Professional military					
No	17	10	2	C = .23	(p < .01)
Yes	37	6	4	G = -.37	
Military retirement					
Postcoup	19	3	1	C = .15	(p < .20)
Precoup	23	9	4	G = -.24	
Recruitment					
Regular	55	14	15	C = .15	(p < .20)
Special	68	16	7	G = -.24	
Promotion (years before Grade II)					
Under 4	27	2	3	C = .28	(p < .10)
5-9	26	9	5	G = .19	
10-14	28	10	2		
15-19	18	5	3		
Over 20	21	4	9		

Communist campaign, which has become a semi-official political religion in South Korea, at least twenty-two senior bureaucrats were ready to cherish democratic freedom and civil liberties more highly than anti-Communist rhetoric. A negative response to the statement does not mean that these "liberals" were necessarily soft on communism. It probably represents their realization that anti-Communist slogans had too frequently been invoked as an effective instrument to rationalize the restrictions of press freedom and civil liberties.

The older bureaucrats, those in their fifties, who had been educated under the Japanese colonial rule in the 1930s, were the most authoritarian; those in their thirties were most ambivalent, indicating perhaps that the younger bureaucrats are caught in the cross-pressures of the two opposing tendencies. The democratically inclined secondary education they had obtained in the postliberation period is likely to have rendered them sufficiently appreciative of the democratic political norms. At the same time, they belong to a generation that received intense indoctrination against communism. If confronted with a choice between democratic values and an anti-Communist crusade, they are bound to be confused and indecisive.

The more formal education the bureaucrats attained, the more authoritarian an orientation they manifested. The social scientists showed the least authoritarian tendency; one-half of the liberals were social scientists. So far as their parents were concerned, middle-class persons were most authoritarian and those of lower-class origins were least authoritarian. This places the higher-class people in a relatively centrist position in the authoritarian-liberal continuum. The extent and kinds of military experience are also intimately associated with the attitudes toward political development. The former military officers were somewhat more authoritarian than career civil servants; sixteen out of twenty-two liberals had no record of military service. Among the ex-military bureaucrats, the longer they had served in the military, the more authoritarian were the political beliefs they expressed. These findings enable us to support the thesis that military service, especially long-term service, contributes to shaping the bureaucrats' strong anti-Communist stand or highly authoritarian attitudes toward liberal democratic values. In particular, those who retired from the military after the coup manifested the strongest propensity to sacrifice democratic norms in the name of anticommunism. Only one of twenty-three bureaucrats who retired after the coup can be classified as a liberal. The relative insensitivity to the value of civil liberties of former military officers may make it easier for them to choose any means for the purpose of task accomplishment. Those who were specially recruited to the civilian bureaucracy or rapidly promoted to their present positions were far more authoritarian than their colleagues.

Locus of Developmental Leadership: No matter how positively and intensely the senior bureaucrats may agree with the need for national development, the way they translate their development orientations into actual administrative behavior seems to be contingent upon how they perceive themselves as development leaders and administrative functionaries. As participants in the management of development strategies, how important and competent do they consider themselves in the broad context of South Korea's political and social system? More importantly, how do they view their roles in the determination and execution of developmental goals, policies, and programs? In order to gain some insight into these issues we asked the senior bureaucrats to rank political, administrative, economic, and cultural fields in importance for leading South Korea's development and to choose the most important role of the civilian bureaucracy from the list of establishment of developmental goals, formulation of public policies, and execution of governmental programs.

As table 17 demonstrates, there is substantial conceptual incongruence in the choice of the most important field for developmental leadership. One out of three considered politics the most important field, but the rest chose economy, culture, and administration, in that order. Even though only 19 percent of the bureaucrats attached the highest priority to their own field of responsibility (administration), almost 37 percent ranked their own area second in the four-way selection. They are therefore conscious of their own importance in leading South Korean development.

Primary importance assigned to political leadership may reflect the daily administrative experience that much of bureaucratic activity is constrained by political circumstances. Another possible reason for incongruent self-identification is the propensity not to recognize functionally specific boundaries between political, administrative, economic, and cultural areas. The fusion, rather than differentiation, of these four areas is likely to be the general conceptual framework of the bureaucrat.

The younger bureaucrats recognized the primacy of political and economic fields more frequently than the older ones did. As to the

TABLE 17

Locus of Developmental Leadership

	Politi-cal (N=64)	Adminis-trative (N=33)	Eco-nomic (N=40)	Cul-tural (N=36)	C (contingency coefficient) G (Goodman's gamma)	
Age group						
35-39	8	0	6	3	C = .30	(p< .05)
40-44	24	10	14	12	G = .01	
45-49	15	13	10	12		
Over 50	17	10	9	7		
Educational level						
College	41	18	24	17	C = .20	(p < .10)
Graduate	23	14	15	18	G = .15	
College major						
Humanities	15	9	3	14	C = .33	(p < .01)
Social sciences	24	10	26	12	G = .15	
Natural sciences	25	13	10	9		
Professional military						
No	15	3	5	5	C = .21	(p < .05)
Yes	17	12	9	9	G = .17	
Recruitment						
Regular	23	16	25	18	C = .23	(p < .05)
Special	41	17	15	18	G = .23	
Promotion (years before Grade II)						
Under 4	13	6	5	8	C = .43	(p < .01)
5-9	18	4	9	9	G = .04	
10-14	11	10	10	8		
15-19	10	7	5	4		
Over 20	11	5	11	7		

importance of administration, the former were far less enthusiastic than the latter. None of those in their thirties gave the highest rank to his own field; instead, they were most seriously preoccupied with the importance of political and economic areas. The level of formal education did not make any difference in attitudes toward the importance of administration. The cultural field was more frequently emphasized by those with graduate degrees and the major in college accounted for great variation in the reactions. The humanists assigned a negligible importance to economics (7.1 percent), but a substantially greater role to culture (33.3 percent). Conversely, the social scientists ranked economics first, while politics was particularly stressed by the natural scientists. The data suggest that the differences in educational specialization between social scientists and humanists are directly related to the differences in their attitudes toward the relative priorities of economic and cultural fields for South Korean development. The social scientists mentioned the central importance of administration far less frequently (13.7 percent) than humanists (21.4 percent) and natural scientists (22.8 percent).

The impact of military service was not clear. The only exception was that those who had a professional military background were more willing to emphasize the role of administration, and to deemphasize the role of politics than were those with a nonprofessional military record. Unlike almost all aspects of development orientations we have discussed so far, the issue of developmental leadership bears a statistically distinct relationship to administrative recruitment patterns. The specially appointed persons, presumably due to the predominantly political nature of their recruitment, emphasized politics at the expense of economy, but the exact reverse is evident among those who went through the regular competitive methods of administrative recruitment. There was no discrepancy in the way both groups of bureaucrats ranked the relative importance of administration. Again, those who had been promoted promptly were more readily inclined to rank politics highly (but to downgrade economy) than were those who had been promoted slowly. Other administrative variables, including functional responsibilities, interagency mobility, and bureaucratic seniority, were not directly related to the bureaucrats' conception of developmental leadership.

Perception of Administrative Role: While the senior bureaucrats gave diverse responses in assessing the central locus of developmental leadership and downgraded their own importance in contrast to political, economic, and cultural areas, a sizable majority of them (72 percent) regarded the establishment of developmental goals as their primary administrative responsibility; 18.3 percent mentioned the formulation of public policies, and 9.1 percent the execution of administrative programs (see table 18). Apparently, they transcended a narrow, implementative perception of their administrative role, and vigorously asserted their legitimate participation in setting the goals and priorities of South Korea's national development. Indeed, positive identification of their multifunctional responsibilities is a result of their deep and active involvement in development administration for the past decade or so.

The data indicate a close linkage between the perceptions of the

TABLE 18

PERCEPTION OF ADMINISTRATIVE ROLE

	Establish-ment of develop-mental goals (N=126)	Formu-lation of public policies (N=32)	Execution of govern-mental programs (N=16)	C (contingency coefficient) G (Goodman's gamma)	
Age group					
35-39	13	2	3	C = .26	(p < .10)
40-44	46	12	2	G = .01	
45-49	30	12	8		
Over 50	34	6	3		
Class origin					
Upper	30	2	2	C = .25	(p < .05)
Middle	86	27	14	G = .26	
Lower	10	2	0		
Educational level					
College	72	15	12	C = .16	(p < .20)
Graduate	52	16	4	G = -.03	
College major					
Humanities	34	5	3	C = .24	(p < .05)
Social sciences	56	9	7	G = .30	
Natural sciences	34	17	6		
Professional military					
No	22	6	1	C = .14	(p < .20)
Yes	32	11	4	G = .20	
Promotion					
Under 4	27	2	3	C = .32	(p < .05)
5-9	27	11	2	G = .16	
10-14	32	3	5		
15-19	18	6	2		
Over 20	21	8	4		
Functions					
S = symbolic	14	6	3	C = .36	(p < .01)
D = distributive	28	12	3	G = -.09	
R = regulative	20	0	3		
X = extractive	16	1	1		
E = economic	26	2	5		
T = technological	22	11	1		

bureaucrats and their class origins as measured by parental economic conditions. The upper-class persons were most strongly committed to determining developmental goals; however, those of middle-class origins were less strongly committed to this than lower-class persons. Consequently, the bureaucrats of middle-class origins perceived a much narrower scope of administrative role than the other two groups. None of the lower-class officials named the execution of administrative programs as his primary responsibility; all of them were mainly interested in establishing developmental goals or formulating public policies. If the middle-class bureaucrats can be called conservative because of their narrow, cautious self-perception, those of upper- and lower-class backgrounds may be termed progressive—one type that deviates from the implementative view of public administrators.

The age variable is somewhat associated with role perceptions as shown in table 18, but the distribution of responses does not yield a clear interpretation. The only notable exception is a rising and then falling correlation between age differences and emphasis on public policy formulation. As ages increase from the thirties to the forties, the number of officials who found their primary administrative role in the decision of public policies increases; once the oldest age group is reached, the number tapers off considerably.

The differences in formal academic achievement did not change the bureaucrats' perception of their roles, but those who obtained graduate degrees were more interested in policy formulation and less concerned with program execution than were their peers. More important to varying role perceptions was the specialization of their college education. The humanists, compared with social and natural scientists, were much more assertive about their role in determining developmental goals, but less preoccupied with policy formulation and program implementation. Since the humanists were educated in the broad subjects of the humanities, they might feel more comfortable and competent in dealing with values and priorities of development than with the technical aspects of public policies and administrative programs. Likewise, the administrative generalists were more interested in goal-setting roles than the functional specialists were.

No statistically significant relationship emerges between military experience and perception of administrative role. Compared with career civil servants, however, ex-military bureaucrats were less interested in program execution, but more interested in policy formulation. It must be added that both groups of bureaucrats were equally concerned with the establishment of developmental goals. The bureaucrats who retired from professional military service were less interested in goal-setting roles, and more interested in program implementation, than were those of nonprofessional military background.

The administrative specialties in which the bureaucrats were engaged affected their views of their roles. Those who were involved in economic, extractive, and regulative functions were strongly committed to a goal-setting role, and less interested in policy formulation, than were those whose administrative responsibilities were in symbolic, distributive, and technological areas. On the other hand, those in economic, regulative, and symbolic functions were more seriously concerned with program execution than with other functional specialists. The distribution of role perceptions is similar for those engaged in economic and regulative functions; a similar pattern was found for the bureaucrats with distributive and technological responsibilities.

CONCLUSION

Admittedly, our study and its implications are limited in a number of important respects. First, the data are drawn from a single administrative rank—Grade II-A, but 86 percent of those who held that rank in January 1972 were successfully interviewed. We are therefore not able to offer a general, comparative statement about civil servants in South Korea as a whole. Second, since we failed to obtain objective biographical materials about those interviewed, we were forced to rely solely on the information provided by the respondent at the time of the interview. This procedure may have created some inconsistencies, for example, class origins and competence in foreign languages. Third, the statistical analysis is derived mainly from simple tabulations. Controls were not widely employed and it is difficult to point out possible spurious associations that may occur between variables. Although we made some inferences that are suggestive of correlations between social background, administrative experience, and attitudes toward development, no causal or unidirectional relations can be safely established. Most important, there is, of course, no sure way of knowing the exact relationship between expressed perceptions and operative beliefs or administrative performance, as the verbal articulation of their values and attitudes toward development may not be an indicator of their real cognitive, evaluative, and effective orientations. It must be reiterated that our study is based upon the assumption that our data bear some relation to their real attitudes toward development.

The preceding discussion suggests that the bureaucratic elite in Korea agree substantially in espousing a positive, confident, and futuristic orientation toward various aspects of national development. An overwhelming majority of them attach a top priority to their own active roles in determining developmental goals. Nevertheless, it must be stressed that the degree of their congruence is higher on "terminal values"—such as attitudes about planning for the future (88 percent) and controlling one's environment (73 percent)—than on "instrumental values"—such as task accomplishment by any means (62 percent) and institutional change (56 percent).[25] The only question that generated diverse responses was concerned with the central locus of developmental leadership. No clear evidence emerges regarding what fields are most necessary to successful development.

Each category of attitudes of the bureaucrats toward development that we have examined is significantly associated with some variables in their social background and administrative experience. Just as Edinger and Searing have found in a comparative analysis of German and French elite, some social and administrative variables are better "predictors" than are others of the South Korean bureaucratic elite's development orientations.[26] Judged by the *scope* and *strength* of explanatory capabilities, the most important variables are educational level and pattern of promotion, each of which is capable of explaining four out of eight categories of development orientations.[27] These two variables are followed by class origins, college majors, military professionalism, military retirement, and administrative functions, which account for three categories. A number of other variables—age groups, military service, recruitment methods, administrative mobility, and length of administrative service—have relatively weak explanatory power. Since both social and administrative variables are more or less equally relevant to the variation in development orientations, it is difficult to ascertain the relative importance of social background and administrative experience in explaining the differences in development orientations.

The generation gap is often cited as a key variable in the study of elite attitude, but our data demonstrate that age group is a poor predictor of the orientations toward such categories as environmental control, task accomplishment, institutional change, and public-mindedness. Since similar attitudes obtain for all ages, no significant relations can be established between age groups and attitudes toward development. In the case of the bureaucratic elite in South Korea, it cannot be stated that youthful bureaucrats are more interested in development than their older colleagues.

Our data failed to corroborate the hypothesis that the military-turned-civilian bureaucrats share common developmental perspectives that can be clearly distinguished from those held by career civil servants. Military service, as a variable, has only very weak explanatory power with regard to the bureaucrats' attitudes toward controlling their environment, public-mindedness, and political development; and it does not account for the variation in other attitudes. In general, therefore, serving in the military has an insignificant effect on bureaucrats' opinions about national development. As Lovell and others suggest in their studies of the military in five developing countries, we must resist a temptation to explain the attitudes and actions of the military personnel solely as a function of their participation in the military establishment.[28]

More significant variables are how long the ex-military bureaucrats served in the armed forces and when they retired. In fact, the differences in development orientations between those who did or did not have military experience is much less noticeable than it is between professional and nonprofessional military personnel or between ex-military bureaucrats who had retired before and after the coup. This finding indicates that even though both groups of military and civilian backgrounds tend to share development orientations, the intramilitary differences in values and attitudes toward national development are by no means negligible. Even among the bureaucrats with military experience, for example, those who entered civilian public administration after the 1961 *coup d'état* agree more with the necessity for public-mindedness, task accomplishment, and institutional change than did those who retired before the coup.

One aspect of the bureaucrats' development orientations that deserves serious attention is their general propensity to place a lower priority on democratic political norms than on national security and economic growth. They are sufficiently predisposed to constrain civil liberties and free press for the sake of anti-Communist struggles, to demand individual sacrifices for public interest, and to use whatever methods are necessary for achievement of specific tasks. Hence, they appear to be more authoritarian and unitarist than democratic and individualistic. Such a tendency promotes a commitment to economic development, but it may hinder Korea's democratic political processes, which implies that while the bureaucrats satisfy all the prerequisites for becoming efficient development administrators, the elite may still be less than responsive to the demands and aspirations of their clients. If this democratic responsiveness is not enhanced, the image that they often project to the general public as being arrogant, selfish, and corrupt may not change. The problem is further compounded by the jealous guarding by the elite of their own roles in establishing developmental goals and policies for the nation. They are reluctant to share their goal-setting and policy-making roles with the National Assembly, political parties, voluntary associations, or other political groups. This assertive preception of their roles is combined with the extension of their responsibilities for extracting, managing, and allocating national resources. Although bureaucratic development in itself may not be politically dysfunctional, Riggs contends that the presence of a strong administrative leadership inhibits the development of political institutions essential to viable democratic government.[29] The crucial problem here is how the bureaucratic elite can strike a judicious balance between the burden of efficient development administration and the requirements of responsive public service that does not exceed a reasonable boundary of their legitimate concern.

NOTES

1. Milton J. Esman, "The Politics of Development Administration," in *Approaches to Development: Politics, Administration, and Change*, ed. John D. Montgomery and William S. Siffin (New York: McGraw-Hill, 1966), p. 80.

2. For a brief review of the literature concerning this question, see Lee Sigelman, *Modernization and the Political System: A Critique and Preliminary Empirical Analyses* (Beverly Hills, Calif.: Sage Publications, 1971), pp. 24–29.

3. Joseph LaPalombara, "Theory and Practice in Development Administration: Observations on the Role of the Civilian Bureaucracy," in *Comparative Administration Group Occasional Papers* (Bloomington: International Development Research Center, Indiana University, 1967), p. 3.

4. See Jerry L. Weaver, "Bureaucracy During a Period of Social Change: The Guatemalan Case," in *LADAC Occasional Papers* (Austin: Institute of Latin American Studies, University of Texas, 1971).

5. Gabriel A. Almond and G. Bingham Powell, Jr., *Comparative Politics: A Developmental Approach* (Boston: Little, Brown & Co., 1966), p. 158.

6. Richard L. Harris, "The Effects of Political Change on the Role Set of the Senior Bureaucrats in Ghana and Nigeria," *Administrative Science Quarterly*, December 1968, pp. 386–401.

7. Gregory Henderson, *Korea: The Politics of the Vortex* (Cambridge: Harvard University Press, 1968), p. 3. For the historical development of Korean bureaucracy, see Dong-Suh Bark, *The Study of Korean Administration* (Seoul: Pŏmmunsa, 1972), pp. 19–27.

8. See Chung Hee Park, *Ideology of Social Reconstruction* (Seoul: Dong-A Publishing Co., 1962), pp. 207–10.

9. Hahn-Been Lee, *Korea: Time, Change, and Administration* (Honolulu: East-West Center Press, 1968), pp. 169–72.

10. See, for example, In-Joung Whang, "Leadership and Organizational Development in the Economic Ministries of the Korean Government," *Asian Survey*, October 1971, pp. 992–1004.

11. Henderson, *Korea*, p. 89.

12. The average age of senior American bureaucrats was fifty in 1963 according to David T. Stanley, *The Higher Civil Service* (Washington: Brookings Institution, 1964), p. 25. For the Japanese bureau chiefs whose average age was forty-eight in 1959, see Akira Kubota, *Higher Civil Servants in Postwar Japan: Their Social Origins, Educational Backgrounds, and Career Patterns* (Princeton, N.J.: Princeton University Press, 1969).

13. Lee, *Time, Change, and Administration*, pp. 169–70.

14. For the earlier figures, see Dong-Suh Bark, "The Problem of Korean Higher Civil Servants: Their Social Background and Morale," in *Some Problems in Public Administration in Developing Countries* (Honolulu: East-West Center Press, 1966); and Dong-Suh Bark, "The Training Needs of Korean Higher Civil Servants," *Korean Journal of Public Administration* (Seoul), 6, no. 1 (1968):95–124.

15. John J. Corson and R. Shale Paul, *Men Near the Top: Filling Key Posts in the Federal Service* (Baltimore, Md.: Johns Hopkins Press, 1966), p. 14.

16. See Bark, "Korean Higher Civil Servants," p. 18.

17. Byung Chul Koh, "Developmental Administration in South Korea," in *Studies in the Developmental Aspects of Korea*, ed. Andrew C. Nahm (Kalamazoo: Institute of International and Area Studies, Western Michigan University, 1969), p. 8.

18. David C. Cole and Princeton N. Lyman, *Korean Development: The Interplay of Politics and Economics* (Cambridge, Mass.: Harvard University Press, 1971), p. 36.

19. Morris Janowitz, *The Military in the Political Development of New Nations: An Essay in Comparative Analysis* (Chicago: University of Chicago Press, 1964), p. 28.

20. Robert A. Scalapino, "Which Route for Korea," *Asian Survey*, September 1962, p. 11.

21. The selection and use of these categories stemmed from a survey of the literature concerning development administration, political culture, and achievement orientation. The most useful references to our study include: Gabriel A. Almond and Sidney Verba, *The Civic Culture: Political Attitudes and Democracy in Five Nations* (Boston: Little, Brown & Co., 1965); Jose Veloso Abueva, "Conditions of Administrative Development: Exploring Administrative Culture and Behavior in the Philippines," in *CAG Working Papers* (Bloomington: International Development Research Center, Indiana University, 1966); Robert T. Daland, "Bureaucracy in Brazil: Attitudes of Civilian Top Executives Toward Change," in *LADAC Occasional Papers* (Austin: Institute of Latin American Studies, University of Texas, 1972); and Joseph A. Kahl, "Some Measurements of Achievement Orientation," in *Studies in Comparative International Development* (St. Louis, Mo.: Social Science Institute, Washington University, 1965).

22. See James Q. Wilson and Edward C. Banfield, "Political Ethos Revisited," *American Political Science Review*, December 1971, pp. 1048–62.

23. Edward Shils, "The Military in the Political Development of the New States," in *The Role of the Military in the Underdeveloped Countries*, ed. John J. Johnson (Princeton, N.J.: Princeton University Press, 1962), p. 36.

24. S. N. Eisenstadt, "Continuity of Modernization and Development of Administration: Preliminary Statement of the Problem," in *CAG Occasional Papers*

(Bloomington: International Development Research Center, Indiana University, 1965), p. 2.

25. As discussed in Glenn D. Paige, "Toward a Developmental Political Leadership Profile for a Total Society" (appendix, this volume).

26. Lewis J. Edinger and Donald D. Searing, "Social Background in Elite Analysis: A Methodological Inquiry," *American Political Science Review*, June 1967, pp. 428–45.

27. The scope refers to the number of development orientations each social or administrative variable explains, and the strength is measured by chi-square whose level of significance is less than .10. For a similar use of both concepts, see Edinger and Searing, "Social Background in Elite Analyses."

28. See John P. Lovell, ed., *The Military and Politics in Five Developing Nations* (Kensington, Md.: Center for Research in Social Systems, 1970).

29. Fred W. Riggs, "Bureaucrats and Political Development: A Paradoxical View," in *Bureaucracy and Political Development*, ed. Joseph LaPalombara (Princeton, N.J.: Princeton University Press, 1963), pp. 120-67; for a counterargument, see Lee Sigelman, "Do Modern Bureaucracies Dominate Underdeveloped Polities? A Test of the Imbalance Thesis," *American Political Science Review*, June 1972, pp. 525-28.

5. Popular Perceptions of Political Leadership

SUNG-CHICK HONG and YOUNG HO LEE

INTRODUCTION

Political stability is clearly one of the foremost concerns of any political system. Stability depends on the extent to which the citizens have supportive orientations toward the political system.[1] The stability of a regime can be maintained by force, but such artificial stability is generally short-lived and not as durable as stability based on voluntary support of the citizens, which is why even a dictatorship tries to create an image of legitimacy in order to be accepted as a proper and appropriate form of government.[2] When such legitimacy is achieved, voluntary support for the system is forthcoming, and there is less need to resort to force.

What, then, makes for citizen support of a political system or a political institution? A necessary prerequisite to political stability is that the citizens must feel allegiance to the government;[3] and it is important that the citizens accept the system or institution as proper and appropriate and that they be satisfied with its performance.[4]

The situation can be examined from the opposite perspective. What if the citizens do not show allegiance? Gurr suggests that rebellion will be the likely result. He uses the concept of "relative deprivation," which is defined as "actors' perception of discrepancy between their value expectations and their value capabilities." Value expectations are, according to Gurr, "the goods and conditions of life to which people believe they are rightfully entitled," and value capabilities, "the goods and conditions they think are capable of getting and keeping."[5] It follows then: *perceived performance/expectation = support quotient where perceived performance refers to the system's performance as perceived by the citizens, and expectation refers to the level of performance as expected by the citizens. Finally, support quotient refers to the likelihood the citizens will be predisposed to support the system.*

According to this formula, the likelihood of citizen support depends more or less equally on two variables: perceived performance and expectation. Even if perceived performance is low, satisfaction is likely if expectation is even lower. Even if performance is high, disappointment, or, to use Gurr's terminology, deprivation, is likely if expectation is even higher.[6] It is assumed here that repeated satisfaction leads to allegiance, repeated disappointment to alienation.[7]

The present study deals with South Korean citizens' perceptions and expectations with regard to the performance of their political leadership on the basis of data obtained in April and May 1972. The study employs a research technique whereby the respondents themselves decide whom they want to regard as political leaders. Also, some questions in the survey deal with citizens' perceptions of government officials as defined by each respondent, respectively. As ordinary citizens come into extensive contact with government or political leadership through government officials, how they perceive the performance of these officials seems to be important in forming their attitudes toward the political system and the regime.

Since the present study focuses on citizen perceptions of political leadership, not on the political system as a whole or its various institutions, it can speak only of the extent of citizen support for the political leadership and not of the extent of support of the system as such. It must be argued, however, that by examining the attitudes toward political leadership, we can make conjectures of the citizens' opinions of the whole system. Accordingly, it will not be too farfetched to discuss support of or alienation from the system in South Korea on the basis of the present analysis.

Political leadership performance can be evaluated from many different perspectives. The perspectives of the present study are three—responsiveness, legitimacy, and effectiveness—chosen as major criteria of democratic leadership, as citizen allegiance or alienation will depend significantly on these variables. If, in the perceptions of the citizens, a political leadership scores low on the scales of responsiveness, legitimacy, and effectiveness, a general pattern of alienation will probably result. On the other hand, if the leadership scores high on these measures, a climate of allegiance is likely to prevail.

It may be generally assumed that there is an important relationship between actual leadership performance and citizen perception of leadership performance. If leadership performance is poor by some objective criteria, it may be expected that the people will hold unfavorable opinions about it, in which case, leadership performance is influencing citizen perceptions. At the same time, the latter may influence the former: the people's attitudes toward leadership, particularly their expectations or demands, even when not always verbalized, are likely to have some effect on leadership behavior. Political leadership, whether democratic or authoritarian, responds to citizen expectations.[8] An authoritarian leadership may be at least partly the result of the leadership's compliance with an authoritarian political culture.

In the present study, the Korean people's perceptions of political leadership are elicited through a survey that includes the following five groups: (1) high school students, (2) university students, (3) farmers, (4) journalists, and (5) legislative aides of the members of the National Assembly. Legislative aides are further divided into two groups: those serving the legislators of the party in power, the Democratic Republican party (DRP), and those serving the legislators of the opposition, New Democratic party (NDP).

It must be emphasized that the present study is not based on a survey of a representative sample of the population of South Korea. For example, among the urban population, only certain segments are included—journalists, students, and legislative aides; the ordinary city dwellers are not represented at all. Also excluded from the sample are some important occupational groups—teachers, public employees, the military, doctors, and lawyers. Their exclusion has been largely dictated by limitations of available research resources. Through analysis of the perceptions held by the five groups represented in the study, however, it is possible to get a reasonably reliable picture of the perceptions of the general population.

It must also be mentioned here that the field work for the present study was done prior to the reforms of October 1972. Since the reforms involved many significant political changes, it is possible that citizen perceptions of the political world have also changed. Particularly, their expectations may have been significantly altered. Whether the data presented in this paper depart significantly from current political realities can be verified only through new research.

POLITICAL AND SOCIAL SATISFACTION

How satisfied or dissatisfied are Koreans with the general performance of their political system? Almond and Verba define "system affect" as "generalized attitudes toward the system as a whole: toward the 'nation,' its virtues, accomplishments, and the like."[9] If one is satisfied with the general performance of the system, he is likely to give allegiance to the system. If the contrary is the case, he is likely to feel alienated.

Except for the farmers, the Koreans interviewed turned out to be generally dissatisfied with the performance of their political system. Those interviewed were asked whether, considering her many difficult problems, it could be said that Korea was doing all right in political matters. The qualifying phrase, "considering her many difficult problems," was likely to encourage affirmative answers, yet the number of respondents agreeing was extremely small, except in the case of the farmers (see table 1).

TABLE 1

GENERAL POLITICAL SATISFACTION

"Considering her many difficult problems, it may be said that Korea is doing all right in political matters"

Respondents	True	False	No Idea	No Response	Total
			(In percentages)		
High school students (N=898)	18.8	36.3	43.9	1.0	100.0
University students (N=413)	10.9	51.6	37.0	0.5	100.0
Farmers (N=235)	66.4	9.4	23.8	0.4	100.0
Journalists (N=165)	3.6	53.9	40.7	1.8	100.0
Legislative aides (N=33)	27.3	48.5	24.2	0.0	100.0
DRP (N=13)	54.0	8.0	38.0	0.0	100.0
NDP (N=13)	8.0	68.0	23.0	0.0	100.0
All respondents (N=1744)	22.0	38.2	38.9	0.9	100.0

Among high school students, negative responses were twice as frequent as affirmative ones. Among university students, the affirmative-negative ratio was about one to five. Journalists were even more negative, ratio of their responses being about one to fifteen. Legislative aides were relatively moderate in their dissatisfaction with the performance of the political system; ratio was less than one to two. When we separated the legislative aides serving the legislators of the opposition party from those serving the legislators of the party in power, we found the former group extremely dissatisfied, in contrast to the latter who were more satisfied with the general performance of the political system. An earlier survey had shown that there are extremely strong interparty differences in political perceptions among Korean legislators.[10] The present study shows that such interparty differences are found also among legislative aides.

There is a consensus among observers of the Korean political scene that the farmers have been given the worst deal by the successive governments. The current administration has admitted to this and has promised to correct the situation through the third five-year economic development plan.[11] Ironically, it is the farmers, of all groups included in the survey, who seemed most satisfied with the political system. Only 9 percent of them felt that Korea was not "doing all right in political matters." Admittedly, some farmers may have given an affirmative response just to be "safe," as they may have had doubts about their anonymity. It may also be that farmers as a group, unlike most other groups in Korean society, are more tolerant of poor performance or political dissatisfaction. Furthermore, farmers may have lower political expectations, and thus would be expected to be less dissatisfied with even relatively poor performance. If dissatisfaction is regarded as a function of what Lerner calls the want-get gap,[12] the farmers' lower expectations may cause a smaller want-get gap in this case.

According to Almond and Verba, dissatisfaction with governmental performance is political alienation; they state that "if they [citizens] are aware of the impact of the government, but dissatisfied, we can call them alienated subjects."[13] A study has shown that the Korean people's awareness of the impact of the government on themselves is relatively high.[14] The data reported in table 1 indicate that the level of general political satisfaction on the part of the Korean people is relatively low, meaning that they are also dissatisfied with this impact. Does this then mean that there is relatively widespread political alienation in Korea? This seems to be the case, and Almond and Verba's two conditions of alienation are satisfied.

Campbell distinguished political detachment from political alienation, and stated that

> the detached person may simply never have learned to communicate at the community level. . . . He lives within a restricted life space without much sense of restriction and without great affect toward the outside world. Our surveys show us, however, that there is a different kind of individual whose orientation toward the world of politics is not simply one of detachment, but of suspicion, distrust, hostility, and cynicism. These people believe that political office holders are corrupt, self-seeking, and incompetent, that the whole political process is a fraud and a betrayal of the public trust.[15]

As will be shown later, the present study as well as others show that there is indeed such distrust and cynicism among the Korean people about the political process.[16] Therefore, regardless of the definition we employ, a strong case may be made for the view that what is observed in Korea is a phenomenon of alienation that is, according to Milbrath, "a more active rejection of politics than the passive withdrawal or detachment or anomie."[17]

It is difficult to separate completely political satisfaction from societal satisfaction, or political alienation from societal alienation. Political satisfaction or dissatisfaction can be considered a subcategory of societal satisfaction or dissatisfaction, one's attitude toward society being more general and inclusive. A high level of political satisfaction does not mean a high level of societal satisfaction. Conversely, a high level of political alienation may not always be followed by a high level of societal alienation, for in no nation does the polity fully absorb society.

To determine the level of societal satisfaction the respondents were asked whether they thought they were getting the rewards they deserved from the society (see table 2). As expected, the responses indicated a relatively high level of societal dissatisfaction. Negative responses far outnumbered positive ones for all groups except the farmers. The journalists and legislative aides showed the highest level of dissatisfaction; there were thirteen dissatisfied journalists for each satisfied one, and seventeen dissatisfied legislative aides for each satisfied one. Whereas some of the legislative aides serving the legislators of the party in power felt satisfied with

TABLE 2

GENERAL SOCIETAL SATISFACTION
"Do you think you are getting the rewards you deserve from
the society?"

Respondents	Yes	No	No Idea	No Response	Total
			(In percentages)		
High school students (N = 898)	19.9	33.0	45.8	1.3	100.0
University students (N = 413)	6.8	42.9	49.1	1.2	100.0
Farmers (N = 235)	31.5	28.5	40.0	0.0	100.0
Journalists (N = 165)	5.5	70.3	22.4	1.8	100.0
Legislative aides (N = 33)	3.0	51.5	45.5	0.0	100.0
DRP (N = 13)	8.0	38.0	54.0	0.0	100.0
NDP (N = 13)	0.0	62.0	38.0	0.0	100.0
All respondents (N = 1744)	16.6	38.7	43.6	1.2	100.0

society's rewards, none of those serving the legislators of the opposition party did. University students were next, with dissatisfied students outnumbering satisfied ones six to one. Among high school students also, negative responses outnumbered affirmative ones by more than three to two. The farmers were the only respondents who were more affirmative than negative; but the margin of difference was small and 40 percent were undecided. Thus, even among the farmers, fewer than one-third of the respondents were satisfied with the performance of the social system.

From the data reported thus far, it is apparent that South Koreans in general feel dissatisfied not only with the performance of the political system, but also with society in general.

RESPONSIVENESS

Responsiveness is one of the most important conditions of democratic leadership. A responsive leader is one who pays close attention to what the people want and tries to adopt policies with the greatest potential benefit.[18] Responsive leadership is not so simple as it may appear for what the people want may not always be what is best for them.[19] Our task here is not to develop a formula that would enable leaders to strike a balance between the two demands of democratic leadership, but to find out how responsive the various segments of Korean society perceive the political leadership to be.

The respondents were asked whether they felt that Korean leaders in general tried hard to understand what the people think (table 3). Both college and high school students reacted strongly in the negative, negative responses outnumbering positive ones by five to two among high school students and three to one among university students. In all, less than 15 percent of the students felt that leaders were aware of the thoughts of their constituents. The journalists also responded negatively, but not so much so as the students, of whom 25 percent considered leaders to be responsive, 32 percent did not, and 42 percent could not decide. Legislative aides as a group were divided almost evenly, but attitudes differed between the legislative aides of the party in power and those of the opposition party. Again the farmers stood out as an exception—positive responses were five times more frequent than negative ones. In general, South Koreans, with the exception of the farmers and the legislative aides of the party in power, did not perceive their leaders to be responsive to or mindful of public opinion.

TABLE 3

ATTENTIVENESS TO PUBLIC OPINION

"Korean leaders in general try hard to understand what people think"

Respondents	True	False	No Idea	No Response	Total
			(In percentages)		
High school students (N = 898)	14.5	36.5	48.7	0.3	100.0
University students (N = 413)	14.8	42.6	42.1	0.5	100.0
Farmers (N = 235)	55.3	10.2	34.1	0.4	100.0
Journalists (N = 165)	25.5	31.5	41.8	1.2	100.0
Legislative aides (N = 33)	27.3	27.3	39.4	6.0	100.0
DRP (N = 13)	46.0	15.0	38.0	0.0	100.0
NDP (N = 13)	15.0	46.0	23.0	15.0	100.0
All respondents (N = 1744)	21.4	33.8	44.2	0.6	100.0

If not susceptible to public opinion, are leaders perceived to be at least interested in public welfare? To ascertain the responsiveness of leaders to the needs of the people, the respondents were asked whether leaders in general cared a lot about the troubles and welfare of the people (table 4). Only the farmers thought so, positive answers outnumbering negative ones, five to three. The journalists were the most extreme in disagreeing with the statement, followed by university students, high school students, and legislative aides.

If the people do not know what is good for them, why pay much attention to what they think or feel? Public opinion *is* held in rela-

TABLE 4

RESPONSIVENESS TO PEOPLE'S NEEDS

"Leaders in general care a lot about the troubles and welfare of the people"

Respondents	True	False	No Idea	No Response	Total
			(In percentages)		
High school students (N = 898)	6.6	61.0	32.1	0.3	100.0
University students (N = 413)	5.3	69.3	24.9	0.5	100.0
Farmers (N = 235)	48.5	28.9	20.9	1.7	100.0
Journalists (N = 165)	3.6	70.9	24.9	0.6	100.0
Legislative aides (N = 33)	12.1	57.6	30.3	0.0	100.0
DRP (N = 13)	8.0	38.0	54.0	0.0	100.0
NDP (N = 13)	15.0	62.0	23.0	0.0	100.0
All respondents (N = 1744)	11.8	59.5	28.2	0.5	100.0

tively high regard in South Korea—at least by the people we interviewed. A majority in all five groups felt that even though public
opinion is determined so much by ignorance and emotion, it is still
a very helpful guide to policy making (table 5). Among the students
and legislative aides, for each person who agreed with the statement there were six who disagreed. None of the legislative aides of
the opposition party accepted the statement. The journalists were
strongly defensive of public opinion: for each one who agreed there
were fourteen who disagreed. Even the farmers were more or less
in the mainstream; those who disagreed outnumbered those who
agreed by eight to five.

TABLE 5

WISDOM OF PUBLIC OPINION

"Public opinion is determined so much by ignorance and emotion
that it is not very helpful as a guide for policy making"

Respondents	True	False	No Idea	No Response	Total
			(In percentages)		
High school students (N = 898)	11	68	21	1	100.0
University students (N = 413)	10.2	68.8	20.3	0.7	100.0
Farmers (N = 235)	25.1	41.7	31.5	1.7	100.0
Journalists (N = 165)	5.5	76.4	17.6	0.6	100.0
Legislative aides (N = 33)	9.1	57.6	33.3	0.0	100.0
DRP (N = 13)	23.0	46.0	31.0	0.0	100.0
NDP (N = 13)	0.0	62.0	38.0	0.0	100.0
All respondents (N = 1744)	11.9	65.1	22.3	0.8	100.0

What if there is a conflict between the leader's personal convictions and public opinion? Which should prevail? The results of
asking whether leaders should act in accordance with their convictions rather than in accordance with public opinion are tabulated in
table 6. The data reported in tables 5 and 6 suggest that public
opinion is highly regarded. One would therefore expect political
leaders to pay close attention to it. The majority of South Koreans
think that in fact they do not; the likelihood of disappointment or
alienation therefore seems great.

Views of Korean citizens notwithstanding, the public is not capable of sound and balanced judgment on complex foreign and
domestic policy issues, not only in politically underdeveloped
societies where the masses are relatively uninformed and unin-
terested in politics, but also in advanced democracies.[20] Many of
today's policy issues are too complicated for an ordinary citizen to

TABLE 6

LEADER'S CONVICTIONS VERSUS PUBLIC OPINION

"Leaders should act in accordance with their convictions rather than in accordance with public opinion"

Respondents	True	False	No Idea	No Response	Total
			(In percentages)		
High school students (N = 898)	19.5	54.8	24.7	1.0	100.0
University students (N = 413)	21.1	48.9	29.5	0.5	100.0
Farmers (N = 235)	39.6	36.2	19.2	4.9	100.0
Journalists (N = 165)	20.0	41.8	36.4	1.8	100.0
Legislative aides (N = 33)	36.4	33.3	24.2	6.1	100.0
DRP (N = 13)	54.0	15.0	31.0	0.0	100.0
NDP (N = 13)	15.0	38.0	31.0	15.0	100.0
All respondents (N = 1744)	22.9	49.3	26.3	1.6	100.0

have sufficient information and analytic ability to make a sound judgment on them. For the sake of efficiency in the decision-making process, leaders and top policy makers would be well advised to exploit the country's experts.

To ascertain whether South Korean leaders are attentive to expert opinion, the respondents were asked whether they thought that leaders took experts' views into consideration when making policy decisions (table 7). In contrast to the farmers, who, in a four to one ratio, felt that leaders did take experts' opinions into account, and the legislative aides, who were divided evenly, an overwhelming majority of the three remaining groups reacted negatively. The university students and journalists disagreed with the statement, five to one; the high school students opposed the statement, seven to two.

Th⌐t experts' opinions are not considered in policy-making is not surprising as the survey shows a relatively widespread view that intellectuals do not often have useful, practical opinions to offer. Respondents were asked whether they felt that although intellectuals sometimes had useful things to say about national affairs, more often their views were far removed from reality (table 8). For all groups except the journalists, twice as many respondents felt that intellectuals' views were often out of touch with reality. The lesser vehemence with which journalists were more negative than positive about the utility of expert views is understandable as journalists themselves are intellectuals and would be defensive about their role in the political process; yet, even they were not certain about the practicality of intellectual opinions. On the basis

TABLE 7

ATTENTIVENESS TO EXPERTS' OPINIONS
"Leaders take experts' views into consideration when making policy decisions"

Respondents	True	False	No Idea	No Response	Total
			(In percentages)		
High school students (N = 898)	12.0	43.9	43.5	0.6	100.0
University students (N = 413)	9.4	49.4	40.4	0.7	100.0
Farmers (N = 235)	46.9	11.5	40.4	2.1	100.0
Journalists (N = 165)	9.7	49.1	40.6	0.6	100.0
Legislative aides (N = 33)	27.3	27.3	45.5	0.0	100.0
DRP (N = 13)	46.0	8.0	46.0	0.0	100.0
NDP (N = 13)	15.0	38.0	46.0	0.0	100.0
All respondents (N = 1744)	16.1	41.0	42.1	0.8	100.0

TABLE 8

USEFULNESS OF INTELLECTUAL OPINION
"Intellectuals have useful things to say about national affairs, but more often their views are far removed from reality"

Respondents	True	False	No Idea	No Response	Total
			(In percentages)		
High school students (N = 898)	50.8	20.9	27.7	0.6	100.0
University students (N = 413)	56.9	19.6	23.2	0.2	100.0
Farmers (N = 235)	37.9	23.4	37.0	1.7	100.0
Journalists (N = 165)	41.8	28.5	26.7	3.0	100.0
Legislative aides (N = 33)	51.5	12.1	36.4	0.0	100.0
DRP (N = 13)	77.0	8.0	15.0	0.0	100.0
NDP (N = 13)	31.0	15.0	54.0	0.0	100.0
All respondents (N = 1744)	49.7	21.5	28.0	0.9	100.0

of this question alone, the farmers were least anti-intellectual, which may be another instance of their being uncritical, as they are in almost all political or social matters. Students had little use for intellectuals' opinions. University students, who are aspiring intellectuals themselves, were even more anti-intellectual than were high school students. The most anti-intellectual of the five groups were, however, the legislative aides. Aides of the legislators of the party in power were overwhelmingly against the usefulness of intellectuals' views; aides of the legislators of the opposition party were only mildly skeptical. If their perceptions reflect their legislators' views, anti-intellectualism is strong among the politicians of the DRP. Since many people in Korea do not value highly the usefulness of intellectual views, the public may not feel seriously disappointed if government and political leaders fail to pay close attention to what the country's intellectuals have to say about policy issues.

The word for compromise in the Korean language carries a slightly immoral connotation, and Koreans in general think little of political compromise, not understanding that democratic politics is the politics of compromise.[21] As a result, most respondents in the survey agreed it was all right for politicians to indulge in a casual give and take but that they should not compromise with their conscience and convictions (table 9). In almost every group, approximately 80 percent agreed. In the case of high school students and legislative aides, nearly nine out of ten did so. Party affiliation made no difference in the opinions of the legislative aides.

TABLE 9

CONSCIENCE VERSUS COMPROMISE

"It is all right for politicians to indulge in a casual give and take but they should not compromise with their conscience and convictions"

Respondents	True	False	No Idea	No Response	Total
			(In percentages)		
High school students (N = 898)	86.8	6.6	5.9	0.8	100.0
University students (N = 413)	80.9	8.7	9.7	0.7	100.0
Farmers (N = 235)	71.5	11.9	15.3	1.3	100.0
Journalists (N = 165)	79.4	9.7	9.7	1.2	100.0
Legislative aides (N = 33)	87.9	3.0	9.1	0.0	100.0
DRP (N = 13)	92.0	0.0	8.0	0.0	100.0
NDP (N = 13)	92.0	8.0	0.0	0.0	100.0
All respondents (N = 1744)	82.6	8.0	8.5	0.9	100.0

In summary, the responsiveness of South Korean leaders to either public opinion or to the people's needs is perceived to be relatively low. As a large majority value highly the wisdom of public opinion, leadership performance in this regard disappoints popular expectations. Leaders are also perceived to be relatively inattentive to experts' views, but disappointment results as a large proportion of the population is skeptical of utility of intellectual opinion. When conflict arises between his own judgment or convictions and public opinion, a leader is expected to subordinate his views to public opinion. Contradictorily, when it is a case of deciding whether a leader should follow his convictions or compromise with others, the former course should be followed. Among the five groups, only the farmers seem relatively satisfied with their leaders' performance. The other groups seem generally alienated. The attitudes of the legislative aides are a function of party affiliation.

LEGITIMACY

To determine to what extent political leaders in Korea are perceived to be legitimate, the respondents were asked whether they felt that leaders in their country were generally qualified for their positions (table 10). University students and journalists were very skeptical about the qualifications of their leaders. For both groups about 45 percent were undecided or refused to commit themselves; 51 percent felt leaders were not qualified; fewer than 4 percent felt that their leaders were. The high school students were also skeptical about the qualifications of the leadership; over 60 percent of them were uncommitted, and another 31 percent felt that leaders were not qualified. Only 8 percent of the high school students felt the qualifications of political leaders were adequate. Legislative aides were about evenly divided on this question. Still, over 60 percent were undecided, thus leaving less than 20 percent who were positive about their leaders' qualification. The farmers were again an exception: a majority of them (52 percent) felt that their leaders were qualified, 9 percent did not, and 39 percent were undecided.

TABLE 10

QUALIFICATION OF KOREAN LEADERS

"Leaders in our country are generally qualified for their positions"

Respondents	True	False	No Idea	No Response	Total
			(In percentages)		
High school students (N = 898)	8.0	31.1	60.4	0.6	100.0
University students (N = 413)	3.4	50.9	45.5	0.2	100.0
Farmers (N = 235)	51.9	8.5	38.7	0.9	100.0
Journalists (N = 165)	3.6	50.9	45.5	0.0	100.0
Legislative aides (N = 33)	18.2	18.2	60.6	3.0	100.0
DRP (N = 13)	15.0	23.0	62.0	0.0	100.0
NDP (N = 13)	15.0	8.0	77.0	0.0	100.0
All respondents (N = 1744)	12.6	34.4	52.5	0.5	100.0

Whether qualified or not, are leaders perceived by the citizens to be at least dedicated to their work? The respondents were asked whether they thought that leaders were in general doing their best to fulfill their responsibilities (table 11). There were more persons who felt that leaders were derelict in their responsibilities than otherwise. Only for the farmers was this not true. For all other groups, a minority ranging from one-tenth to one-third felt that leaders were conscientiously trying to fulfill their responsibilities.

TABLE 11

DEDICATION OF LEADERS

"Leaders in general are doing their best to fulfill their responsibilities"

Respondents	True	False	No Idea	No Response	Total
			(In percentages)		
High school students (N = 898)	21.4	30.0	47.8	0.9	100.0
University students (N = 413)	13.6	44.3	41.9	0.2	100.0
Farmers (N = 235)	51.1	20.9	26.4	1.7	100.0
Journalists (N = 165)	9.7	44.2	44.2	1.8	100.0
Legislative aides (N = 33)	33.3	27.3	36.4	3.0	100.0
DRP (N = 13)	54.0	0.0	46.0	0.0	100.0
NDP (N = 13)	23.0	31.0	38.0	8.0	100.0
All respondents (N = 1744)	22.7	33.4	43.0	1.0	100.0

Our respondents perceive that their political leaders are not only unqualified for their jobs but also are not dedicated to their work. How do such people manage to occupy leadership positions? It is mostly a matter of having the right connections. A strong majority in each of the five groups interviewed agreed that personal connections were more important than ability to be politically successful (see table 12). On this question, even the farmers were no exception. More than three-quarters of the high school and university students, approximately two-thirds of the farmers and journalists, and a little over half of the legislative aides agreed that connections are more important than ability.

The respondents were also asked whether leaders in general valued personal loyalty more than ability in selecting their aides (table 13). Again a strong majority felt that this was true.

As many as four-fifths among the high school and university students and journalists responded affirmatively. Among the farmers and legislative aides, as many as two-thirds responded affirmatively.

If ability is an insignificant factor in political success, or if leaders look first not for ability but for personal loyalty from their prospec-

TABLE 12

RELATION BETWEEN PERSONAL CONNECTIONS AND POLITICAL SUCCESS
"Personal connections are more important than ability to be
politically successful"

Respondents	True	False	No Idea	No Response	Total
			(In percentages)		
High school students (N = 898)	76.7	6.5	16.4	0.5	100.0
University students (N = 413)	78.0	2.7	19.1	0.2	100.0
Farmers (N = 235)	62.6	23.4	14.0	0.0	100.0
Journalists (N = 165)	66.7	4.2	29.1	0.0	100.0
Legislative aides (N = 33)	54.6	6.1	39.4	0.0	100.0
DRP (N = 13)	38.0	15.0	46.0	0.0	100.0
NDP (N = 13)	69.0	0.0	31.0	0.0	100.0
All respondents (N = 1744)	73.7	7.6	18.4	0.3	100.0

TABLE 13

IMPORTANCE OF PERSONAL LOYALTY IN POLITICAL RECRUITMENT
"Leaders in general value personal loyalty more than ability in
selecting their aides"

Respondents	True	False	No Idea	No Response	Total
			(In percentages)		
High school students (N = 898)	80.3	5.0	14.1	0.6	100.0
University students (N = 413)	86.9	3.6	8.7	0.7	100.0
Farmers (N = 235)	61.7	15.7	20.9	1.7	100.0
Journalists (N = 165)	83.6	2.4	12.7	1.2	100.0
Legislative aides (N = 33)	60.6	15.2	24.2	0.0	100.0
DRP (N = 13)	38.0	31.0	31.0	0.0	100.0
NDP (N = 13)	77.0	0.0	23.0	0.0	100.0
All respondents (N = 1744)	79.3	6.1	13.8	0.8	100.0

tive aides, it follows that many unqualified persons manage to occupy leadership positions in the Korean political structure. Personal connections or loyalty are often ascribed resources, not
achieved assets, and therefore the political recruitment process
may still be seen as ascriptive.

The results of the four questions indicate that the current political structure in South Korea enjoys relatively little legitimacy in the
eyes of the South Korean people. A majority think that political
leaders are in general unqualified, not dedicated, and become
politically successful not because of their superior ability but on
account of their good political connections.

VIEWS OF GOVERNMENT OFFICIALS

The survey questions analyzed thus far were concerned with popular perceptions of South Korean "leaders" or "politicians." As it was up to each respondent to define his terms, it is entirely possible that different meanings have been attached to them. Some may have included relatively low echelon leaders; others may have included only high level leaders. Some may have had in mind only incumbents; others may have included opposition leaders as well. The survey could have specified more precisely what categories of persons were to be included, but the social climate persuaded the researchers to be more ambiguous and so avoid any suspicion being cast on the survey.

The five questions to be analyzed in this section deal with a defined group—government officials. This term has some ambiguity, of course. Some may think of only high-ranking officials; others of only low-ranking ones; and still others of both. One may also question the validity of including government officials in a discussion of political leaders. There are two justifications: first, a broad definition of political leadership can include government officials; second, in the experience of ordinary citizens, usual contact with the political leadership of the country is with or through government officials. Accordingly, the attitudes of ordinary citizens toward political leadership or even the political system may be their attitudes toward government officials. Political allegiance or alienation may consequently depend on how citizens feel about government officials.

To determine attitudes toward government officials, the respondents were asked to react to five statements. The first dealt with the public-mindedness of officials, asking whether government officials tended to put their private interests above public interests (table 14). A strong majority of every group, including the farmers, agreed that they did. There were differences, however, between the groups' appraisal of the motivations of government officials. The university students were the most negative, followed closely by the journalists and high school students and the legislative aides. The surprising result was that even the farmers were aware of the lack of public-mindedness; approximately 58 percent of them agreed that private interests take precedence over public interests in determining the actions of public officials.

The fairness of government officials is also suspect (see table 15). Only an extremely small fraction of all groups except the farmers thought government officials are in general fair and just in perform-

TABLE 14

PUBLIC-MINDEDNESS OF GOVERNMENT OFFICIALS
"Government officials in general tend to put their private interests
above public interests"

Respondents	True	False	No Idea	No Response	Total
			(In percentages)		
High school students (N = 898)	78.7	7.2	13.6	0.5	100.0
University students (N = 413)	83.1	6.1	10.9	0.0	100.0
Farmers (N = 235)	57.9	17.9	22.1	2.1	100.0
Journalists (N = 165)	80.0	10.3	9.7	0.0	100.0
Legislative aides (N = 33)	63.6	18.2	18.2	0.0	100.0
DRP (N = 13)	62.0	8.0	31.0	0.0	100.0
NDP (N = 13)	62.0	23.0	15.0	0.0	100.0
All respondents (N = 1744)	76.8	8.9	13.8	0.5	100.0

TABLE 15

FAIRNESS OF GOVERNMENT OFFICIALS
"Government officials are in general fair and just in performing
their duties"

Respondents	True	False	No Idea	No Response	Total
			(In percentages)		
High school students (N = 898)	5.5	62.8	31.5	0.2	100.0
University students (N = 413)	2.7	77.0	20.1	0.2	100.0
Farmers (N = 235)	41.3	30.6	27.2	0.9	100.0
Journalists (N = 165)	6.1	74.6	18.8	0.6	100.0
Legislative aides (N = 33)	9.1	48.5	42.4	0.0	100.0
DRP (N = 13)	23.0	15.0	62.0	0.0	100.0
NDP (N = 13)	0.0	54.0	46.0	0.0	100.0
All respondents (N = 1744)	9.8	62.7	27.2	0.3	100.0

ing their duties. Disagreeing with the statement were about three-quarters of the university students and journalists, nearly two-thirds of the high school students, and half of the legislative aides. There was a pronounced difference between the legislative aides of the party in power and those of the opposition party. The farmers were as usual much more favorable toward the officials than were the other groups. However, even among the farmers only 41 percent felt that government officials were fair and just; the rest felt otherwise or were undecided.

Only a small portion of the respondents felt that government officials tended to observe laws and regulations fairly closely (see table 16). About 6 percent of the university students and journalists and less than 10 percent of the high school students felt that government officials were law-abiding, as did only one out of every six legislative aides, legislative aides of the opposition party being somewhat more skeptical. The farmers again proved to be an exception in that nearly one-half of them responded positively.

TABLE 16

EXTENT TO WHICH GOVERNMENT OFFICIALS ARE LAW-ABIDING

"Government officials tend to observe laws and regulations fairly closely"

Respondents	True	False	No Idea	No Response	Total
			(In percentages)		
High school students (N = 898)	9.5	57.1	33.1	0.3	100.0
University students (N = 413)	5.8	70.0	24.2	0.0	100.0
Farmers (N = 235)	48.5	23.4	26.4	1.7	100.0
Journalists (N = 165)	6.1	58.2	35.8	0.0	100.0
Legislative aides (N = 33)	15.2	36.4	45.5	3.0	100.0
DRP (N = 13)	15.0	8.0	69.0	8.0	100.0
NDP (N = 13)	15.0	38.0	46.0	0.0	100.0
All respondents (N = 1744)	13.7	55.3	30.6	0.5	100.0

Government officials were considered inefficient by most respondents. Asked whether they thought government officials were in general speedy in performing their duties, except for the farmers, only a small percentage of each group responded affirmatively (see table 17). Less than 4 percent of the journalists, 6 percent of the university students and the legislative aides, 20 percent of the high school students, and 45 percent of the farmers felt that government officials were efficient.

TABLE 17

SPEEDINESS OF GOVERNMENT OFFICIALS

"Government officials in general are speedy in performing their duties"

Respondents	True	False	No Idea	No Response	Total
			(In percentages)		
High school students (N = 898)	19.5	54.8	24.7	1.0	100.0
University students (N = 413)	5.6	76.8	17.4	0.2	100.0
Farmers (N = 235)	44.7	33.2	20.4	1.7	100.0
Journalists (N = 165)	3.6	81.2	14.6	0.6	100.0
Legislative aides (N = 33)	6.1	78.8	15.2	0.0	100.0
DRP (N = 13)	15.0	62.0	23.0	0.0	100.0
NDP (N = 13)	0.0	85.0	15.0	0.0	100.0
All respondents (N = 1744)	13.3	63.1	23.0	0.7	100.0

Responses were also negative when respondents were asked whether the government managed to achieve maximum effect given limited budgetary resources (see table 18). The university students and journalists overwhelmingly disagreed with this claim, only 4 percent in either group feeling the government was usually efficient. The next most negative groups were the high school students and the legislative aides; 11 percent of the former and 18 percent of the latter felt that the government made efficient use of its money. Again the farmers were quite uncritical, as 42 percent of them felt that the government was efficient.

TABLE 18

EFFICIENCY OF THE GOVERNMENT
"The government manages to achieve the maximum effect given limited budgetary resources"

Respondents	True	False	No Idea	No Response	Total
			(In percentages)		
High school students (N = 898)	10.9	48.0	40.8	0.3	100.0
University students (N = 413)	4.4	60.5	35.1	0.0	100.0
Farmers (N = 235)	41.7	17.9	37.0	3.4	100.0
Journalists (N = 165)	4.2	64.2	29.7	1.8	100.0
Legislative aides (N = 33)	18.2	57.6	21.2	3.0	100.0
DRP (N = 13)	38.0	38.0	15.0	8.0	100.0
NDP (N = 13)	8.0	54.0	38.0	0.0	100.0
All respondents (N = 1744)	13.0	48.6	37.5	0.9	100.0

From the results presented in this section, it appears that, with the exception of farmers, the people in general credit their government officials with few positive qualities. More often than not, officials are regarded as self-seeking, unfair and unjust, not law-abiding, tardy in their work, and inefficient in performing their duties, qualities similar to those ascribed to political leaders.

SUMMARY AND CONCLUSION

The foregoing analysis suggests a strong undercurrent of political alienation in Korean society. Many feel alienated not only from their political leaders but also from government officials. Leaders are in general perceived to be unresponsive and illegitimate; and government officials are perceived to be self-seeking, unfair, not law-abiding, and inefficient. Such negative feelings are more frequent among urban and educated segments of the population than they are among farmers. In general, university students and journalists turn out to be the most negative. Farmers tend to be generally positive and uncritical about the performance of their leaders and government officials. High school students and legislative aides fall in between. Of the last group, it must be said that there is great variation as a function of party affiliation. As a rule, aides of the party in power are less critical than aides of the opposition party, who are critical of the performance of the political leadership and bureaucracy.

As was suggested at the outset, there may be two explanations for the phenomenon of political alienation. Either the actual performance is so poor as to justify unfavorable evaluation, or unrealistically high expectations are not fulfilled, thus producing a large want-get gap or a sense of political deprivation. The situation can be remedied from either direction; political alienation will probably diminish from actual improvement in performance or from lowered expectations.

The politically alienated are, by definition, dissatisfied with the political situation. The dissatisfaction of our respondents is focused on performance of the political leadership. Political alienation does not mean that those who are alienated will rebel against the leadership or the regime. Only the extremely dissatisfied are likely to engage in activities that would have dangerous consequences, and even they probably would not rebel unless they were certain to succeed. It is assumed here that potential rebels go through a more or less rational process of cost-benefit calculation before assuming such grave personal risk as rebellious activities entail.

This study was not designed to find out the incidence of extreme alienation in the Korean population. Probably under most circumstances such an inquiry would be difficult because expression of such extreme alienation itself, even in a survey setting, involves some risk. The present study can thus speak of only the extensiveness of alienation as measured by the questions of the survey. It cannot speak of the intensity of the feeling of alienation held by the people.

NOTES

1. Harold D. Lasswell and Abraham Kaplan propose that political stability depends upon the intensity of conviction between both elite and mass in the political doctrines that sustain the elite. See their *Power and Society: A Framework for Political Inquiry* (New Haven: Yale University Press, 1950), p. 270. Andrew Janos similarly maintains that "a decline in social consensus" is the first step in the process of revolution. He states: "Doubts arise concerning the policies and aspirations of the

ruling classes, and the doubts are followed by popular withdrawal and alienation." See his *The Seizure of Power: A Study of Force and Popular Consent*, Center of International Studies, Research Monograph, no. 16 (Princeton, N.J., 1964), p. 4.

2. See V. O. Key, Jr., *Public Opinion and American Democracy* (New York: Alfred A. Knopf, 1964), pp. 3-4. See also Alex Inkeles, *Public Opinion in Soviet Russia* (Cambridge, Mass.: Harvard University Press, 1950).

3. Gabriel A. Almond and Sidney Verba stress the importance of what they call the "system affect." The "system affect" is further subdivided between "output affect" and "input affect." See their *The Civic Culture: Political Attitudes and Democracy in Five Nations* (Boston: Little, Brown & Co., 1963), chaps. 3 and 13. They maintain: "Political systems, if they are to survive, must also be relatively effective and relatively legitimate; that is, what the government accomplishes must be at least satisfying enough to the citizens so that they do not turn against the government; and the system, if it is to have a long-run potential of survival, must be generally accepted by citizens as the proper form of government." See Almond and Verba, *Civic Culture*, p. 186.

4. See Seymour Martin Lipset, *Political Man: The Social Bases of Politics* (Garden City: Doubleday & Co., 1960), chap. 3, particularly p. 64.

5. See Ted Robert Gurr, *Why Men Rebel* (Princeton: Princeton University Press, 1970), p. 24.

6. Ibid.; see also W. G. Runciman, *Relative Deprivation and Social Justice* (Berkeley: University of California Press, 1966), p. 9, where he states that "if people have no reason to expect or hope for more than they can achieve, they will be less discontented with what they have, or even grateful simply to be able to hold on to it."

7. Repeated disappointment may be equated with frustration. According to Neal E. Miller and associates, frustration produces instigations to various responses, one of which is aggression. If nonaggressive responses do not relieve the frustration, "the greater is the probability that the instigation to aggression eventually will become dominant so that some response of aggression will occur." See their "The Frustration—Aggression Hypothesis," *Psychological Review* 48 (July 1941):339. Thus alienation here must be regarded as a psychological state that is prone to give rise to aggressive behavior. However, alienation is not aggression, nor will it always lend to aggressive behavior.

8. See Key, *Public Opinion*, p. 3.

9. Almond and Verba, *Civic Culture*, p. 63.

10. See several articles in the *Korea Journal* by Young Ho Lee, "Modernization as a Goal Value in Korean Society" (April 1972); "Economic Development and Environmental Quality" (June 1972); "The Korean People's Distributive Consciousness: An Analysis of Attitudes" (September 1972); "Modernization and Tradition: Korean Attitudes" (October 1972).

11. *Chŏson ilbo*, 24 March 1972.

12. Daniel Lerner, "Toward a Communication Theory of Modernization: A Set of Considerations," in *Communications and Political Development*, ed. Lucian W. Pye (Princeton: Princeton University Press, 1963), pp. 327–50.

13. Almond and Verba, *Civic Culture*, pp. 49–62.

14. Young Ho Lee, "The Political Culture of Modernizing Society: Political Attitudes and Democracy in Korea" (Ph.D., diss., Yale University, 1969), chap. 5.

15. Angus Campbell, "The Passive Citizen," *Acta Sociologica* 6 (fasc. 1–2) (1962):14.

16. Sung-chick Hong, *The Intellectual and Modernization: A Study of Korean Attitudes* (Seoul: Korea University Social Research Institute, 1967), chaps. 5 and 6, particularly pp. 146-53.

17. Lester W. Milbrath, *Political Participation: How and Why Do People Get Involved in Politics?* (Chicago: Rand McNally & Co., 1965), p. 79.

18. See Almond and Verba, *Civic Culture*, pp. 341-44.

19. "In the United States, a highly literate country and one richly endowed with modern mass media of communication, not to speak of its plethora of public relations specialists, we are constantly amazed and shaken by recurrent mobilizations of unimpeachable statistical evidence that the public is inattentive to and impressively ignorant about public affairs, whether domestic or foreign." Inis L. Claude, Jr., *The Impact of Public Opinion upon Foreign Policy and Diplomacy* (The Hague: Mouton & Co., 1965), p. 13.

20. Consider, for example, Doris A. Graber's observation: "The folklore concept of the nature of public opinion in a democracy still is a myth. . . . Beyond a highly generalized sense of trust and approval, or distrust and disapproval of policy making by the executive, there apparently is no single well-structured opinon held by most people, a majority, or even a plurality." See her *Public Opinion, the President, and Foreign Policy* (New York: Holt, Rinehart & Winston, 1968), p. 329. Similarly Gabriel A. Almond observes: "Many of the moralistic exhortations to the public to inform itself and to play an active role in policy-making . . . have the virtues and failings of evangelism." See his *The American People and Foreign Policy* (New York: Praeger, 1960), pp. 5-6.

21. See Young Ho Lee, "Public Opinion, Compromise, Conviction in Democratic Politics," *Chosŏn ilbo*, 4 May 1972.

PART IV

Political Leadership in the Communist System

6. Communist Party Leadership

DAE-SOOK SUH

INTRODUCTION

Any study of the Communist leadership in Korea must begin with some aspects of the leadership style fashioned by Kim Il-sŏng. It is easy to overemphasize his leadership because the people's adulation of their leader seems to have surpassed propriety, while their vociferous, and at times effusive, praise for his wise and benevolent leadership is mingled with hard facts of economic progress and political stability. It is not an easy task to analyze his leadership techniques and list the characteristics of his leadership style. Nor is it possible to give a sophisticated analysis of his personal leadership. The paucity of essential materials prohibits a comprehensive study of either Kim's leadership or the North Korean leadership style.

This study is an effort to analyze the Korean Communist leadership style by examining the members of the Central Committee of the Workers' Party of Korea. Nothing in this study is designed to refute Kim's role as the absolute and unchallengeable Communist leader of Korea today. As head of both the party and the government for more than two decades, Kim Il-sŏng may or may not be what the Communists claim him to be: a "peerless patriot, national hero, ever-victorious and iron-willed brilliant commander, one of the genius leaders of the international Communist movement and workers' movement, and the great leader of forty million Korean people."[1]

The basic assumption of this paper is that the system Kim Il-sŏng has built in the North is important and, notwithstanding his charisma, there is every indication that his system may survive him. Furthermore, the effectiveness of his leadership is partly the result of his control of the elite groups, which play an important if subordinate role in his control mechanism. The analysis of these groups is thus basic to the understanding of his leadership.

Given the dominant role that the party plays in every endeavor in the North, this study will examine the elite group consisting of the

159

members of the Central Committee of the Workers' Party of Korea. There are other elite groups, such as the members of the Council of Ministers, members of the Presidium of the Supreme People's Assembly, generals of the People's Army of Korea, justices in the judiciary branch of the government, members of the diplomatic corps, local and provincial level leaders, and others. A study of the North Korean leadership must incorporate analyses of as many segments of the leadership groups as possible; the relationship of the elite groups to the leader, an analysis of Korean Communist ideology as applied to leadership techniques, the interrelationship of the elite groups to the masses, an analysis of intergroup relationships, the organization and training of the cadres, and the like. But these are beyond the scope of this paper.

This study examines one aspect of the Central Committee, the pattern of change in its membership. Because of the Korean Communist revolutionary tradition, the leaders who emerged in the North shortly after the liberation of Korea was largely revolutionaries returned from various revolutionary bases abroad. These leaders had their own followers and these groups were often antagonistic toward each other. Although factional lines based on their revolutionary past were not as clearly drawn as is commonly alleged, much of the earlier struggle for the control of power in the North emanated from these groups' antagonisms. The struggle culminated in the dominance of one group, the partisan group headed by Kim Il-sŏng.

Except for a few important party officials, most members of the Central Committee hold positions in addition to their membership on the Central Committee, such as a diplomatic position, a cabinet ministerial position, etc. The composition of the Central Committee will be analyzed on the basis of the functional role each member plays in other power organizations in the North. A brief descriptive analysis of the Central Committee will also be made as an introductory preface to the study. An effort will be made to identify and analyze general characteristics of the leaders of the Central Committee of the party for a clearer understanding of the Communist leadership in the Democratic People's Republic of Korea.

THE CENTRAL COMMITTEE

According to the official interpretation of the bylaws of the Workers' Party of Korea (WPK), the Central Committee consists not only of the most able leaders of the political, economic, cultural, military, and other fields, but includes members who are held in the highest esteem by the people. The members are elected by the delegates at the time of each party congress, and the membership is limited to a number authorized by the congress.[2]

The members are to hold plenary meetings at least three times a year and, as members of the highest party organ, they are to perform the supreme tasks of the party, among which are: (1) to set the policy of the party; (2) to organize and administer party organizations, to direct party activities, and to represent the party; (3) to select, educate, and assign members to the party cadres; (4) to organize a party political bureau in various government, industrial, social, and cultural organizations, and to control and direct the activities of these bureaus to conform with general party policy; (5) to publish party organs and manage special enterprises such as publication and printing; and (6) to manage party finances.[3]

The Central Committee consists of the following: a Secretariat; Political, Inspection, Auditing, and Military Affairs Committees; and fifteen functional departments.[4] In addition, there are a South Korea Liaison Bureau and nine Provincial and thirteen Municipal Committees.[5] There have been a few structural changes in the party organs, and the bylaws of the party have been amended three times at the Second, Third, and Fourth Party Congresses. However, except for two reorganizations, the party structure remains intact. The two changes were an exchange between the Political Committee and what was termed a Standing Committee, and the creation of a Secretariat and abolition of the vice-chairmanship of the Central Committee. There are extensive structural differentiations at the Central Committee depeartmental level, but these are to accommodate the growth of the party.

The party held five congresses from 1945 to 1970, and five sets of Central Committee members were announced. The First and Second Party Congresses were held less than two years apart (August 28-30, 1946, and March 27-30, 1948); a 43-man committee for the first congress and a 67-man committee for the second were announced. There was an interval of eight years between the Second and Third Congresses, and then the Third and Fourth Party Congresses were held in close proximity (the third was held April 23-29, 1956, and the fourth September 11-18, 1961). There continued to be a steady increase in the membership of the Central Committee; a 71-man committee was named by the third congress and an 85-man committee by the fourth. The Fifth Party Congress was held November 2-12, 1970, nine years after the fourth congress and a 117-man committee was announced.

In addition, two party conferences[6] were held; one in 1958 between the Third and the Fourth Party Congresses and another in 1966 between the Fourth and Fifth Party Congresses. The second party conference announced the formation of an Executive Section consisting of sixty-one men for the conference, somewhat similar to a new Central Committee of the party; but no such section was announced for the first conference in 1958. The party conference can replace members of the Central Committee with new members, but Article 41 of the bylaws stipulates that members newly elected by the party conference must not exceed one-fifth of the total membership of the Central Committee. There is no such restriction for a regularly scheduled party congress.

Although a regular party congress is to be held once every four years, it has never been held on schedule. Irregularities in scheduling congresses are not uncommon in Communist parties of other countries; at the time of the second party conference in 1966, Ch'oe Yong-gŏn remarked that the Fifth Party Congress had been planned for 1965. Furthermore, even the plenary session of the Central Committee, regularly scheduled to meet at least once every four months, seldom meets more than twice a year.[7]

PATTERNS OF CHANGE

Several characteristic features of the party leadership can be readily observed without a detailed analysis of the Central Committee; for example, the emergence of one group—the partisans—as the elite group of the North, the rapidity with which the members of the Central Committee are recruited and demoted, and the high rate of political purges necessary to maintain Kim Il-sŏng's control of the party. These features have become evident through a gradual, and at times violent, process of elimination of leaders of groups that have competed with the partisans. A closer examination of the competing groups within the Central Committee would reveal many characteristics unique to the Korean Communist leadership. It is important to remember that these leaders were scattered in various centers within and outside of Korea. When they returned to the North after the liberation of Korea, there emerged not one or two but many competing groups.

For the purposes of this study, each member of the Central

Committee is identified as a member of one of four known groups of the Korean Communist revolutionary movement: the domestic group, which operated within both Korea and Japan; the Yenan group, which returned from China; the Soviet-Koreans from the Soviet Union; and the partisan group, which participated in guerrilla activities with Kim Il-sŏng in Manchuria. There are a few members of the Central Committee whose revolutionary past is not known, and these men are grouped as unknown revolutionaries. There is also a large number of newly emerging leaders who do not have a revolutionary past prior to the liberation of Korea, but who were recruited into the Central Committee because of their activities in the North after the revolution. These men are grouped as a newly emerging group. In general, the members of this group do not appear at all until the Fourth Party Congress in 1961.

A. Members of the Central Committee

A pattern of change in the membership of the Central Committee can be observed in table 1. Except for the members of the Central Committee of the First Party Congress, less than one-half of the members of each Central Committee were re-elected to the succeeding Central Committee. In each succeeding congress, proportionately fewer members have been elected to the succeeding Central Committee: in the Third and Fourth Party Congresses, only 28 out of 71 members and 31 out of 85 members were re-elected. The Second Party Congress was held less than two years after the first and although some 30 out of 43 members were re-elected, they failed to constitute a majority as the membership of the Central Committee was increased from 43 in the First to 67 in the Second Party Congress. In the history of the Workers' Party of Korea, newly elected members have always constituted a majority in the Central Committee.

The increase in the size of the Central Committee is modest compared with the increase in party membership. Although the size of the committee has almost tripled from the first Central Committee of 43 members to the fifth Central Committee of 117 members, the membership of the party has increased approximately sixfold from 366,000 to more than two million. One might speculate that the chance of becoming a member of the Central Committee today is decreased by a factor of two from what it was at the time of the First Party Congress and by a factor of three from what it was at the time of the Second Party Congress. If a member

TABLE 1

CHANGES IN THE MEMBERSHIP OF THE CENTRAL COMMITTEE
BY GROUPS

Party Congresses	Total	D	N	P	S	U	Y
1 WPK CCM	43	13	—	4	6	8	12
Re-elected to 2 WPK CCM	30	11	—	3	6	2	8
Dropped	12	2	—	—	—	6	4
Died	1	—	—	1	—	—	—
2 WPK CCM	67	21	—	7	14	12	13
From 1 WPK CCM	30	11	—	3	6	2	8
New Members	37	10	—	4	8	10	5
Re-elected to 3 WPK CCM	29	8	—	5	7	2	7
Dropped	35	13	—	—	6	10	6
Died	3	—	—	2	1	—	—
3 WPK CCM	71	23	—	11	11	12	14
From 2 WPK CCM	29	8	—	5	7	2	7
New Members	42	15	—	6	4	10	7
Re-elected to 4 WPK CCM	28	11	—	10	2	3	2
Dropped	42	12	—	—	9	9	12
Died	1	—	—	1	—	—	—
4 WPK CCM	85	19	21	35	3	5	2
From WPK CCM	28	11	—	10	2	3	2
New Members	57	8	21	25	1	2	—
Re-elected to 5 WPK CCM	31	7	2	19	1	2	—
Dropped	52	11	19	15	2	3	2
Died	2	1	—	1	—	—	—
5 WPK CCM	117	9	68	32	2	6	—
From 4 WPK CCM	31	7	2	19	1	2	—
New Members	86	2	66	13	1	4	—

NOTE: WPK = Workers' Party of Korea; 1 WPK = first congress, August 1946; 2 WPK = second congress, March 1948; 3 WPK = third congress, April 1956; 4 WPK = fourth congress, September 1961; 5 WPK = fifth congress, November 1970; CCM = Central Committee Member; D = Domestic Group; N = New Group; P = Partisan Group; S = Soviet-Korean Group; U = Unknown Group; Y = Yenan Group.

of the Central Committee represents the party membership at all, one member of the Central Committee represents approximately twenty thousand members of the party today.

It is significant that, except for the Fifth Party Congress, no one group had approached a majority of any Central Committee. The fifth Central Committee has 68 newly emerging members who constitute the majority, and if we assume that this group consists primarily of new leaders trained and recruited into the Central

Committee by the partisans, the combination of these two groups gives an absolute majority of 100 out of 117 members. The emergence of a majority can be observed in the Central Committee of the Fourth Party Congress; but the consolidation and control of the committee seems far greater in the Fifth Party Congress than it was in 1961.

Also important is the pattern of change in each group. Unlike the others, the members of the partisan group have consistently been re-elected to the Central Committee. Not counting those among the partisan group who died before the subsequent party congress, no partisan was ever dropped from the Central Committee until the present committee. By comparison, a majority of the members of other groups, including the newly emerging elite, is dropped from the Central Committee at each congress. For example, 12 out of 14 members of the Yenan group were dropped between the third and fourth Central Committees. These figures testify to the severity of the purges of 1956 on the Yenan group.[8] The domestic group was more represented than any other group until the Central Committee of the Fourth Party Congress, but this can be explained by the relative abundance of Communists who fought within Korea and Japan. The rate of their demotion is as acute as it is for the Soviet-Korean group, which had relatively few members.

During the 1960s, between the Fourth and Fifth Party Congresses (more specifically, after the second party conference held in October 1966), when signs of an internal struggle within the partisan group were manifest,[9] the partisan group quickly added 13 new members to the Central Committee of the fifth congress to replace the 15 partisans who had been dropped from the Central Committee of the Fourth Party Congress. Such leading partisans as Pak Kŭm-ch'ŏl, Kim Kwang-hyŏp, Sŏk San, Ch'oe Kwang, Kim Ch'ang-bong, and Hŏ Pong-hak were eliminated.

Because of the rapid turnover in membership, it is useful to analyze the durability of the members of the Central Committee. Out of 259 leaders who have served on the Central Committee, only two, Kim Il-sŏng and Kim Il—both partisans—were elected to all five Central Committees. In contrast, 171 members—two-thirds of all men who ever served on the Central Committee—served only once. Very few served twice; as can be seen in table 2, 61 members served twice but 30 of these were those who served in the first and second Central Committees when there were few changes in the party. Because of the short interval between the two Central Committees, virtually all (30 out of 41) were re-elected.

TABLE 2

NUMBER OF TIMES ELECTED TO THE
CENTRAL COMMITTEE BY GROUPS

| | GROUPS | | | | | | |
	Domes-tic	New	Parti-san	Soviet-Korean	Un-known	Yenan	Total
Once	20	84	26	5	28	8	171
Twice	18	2	19	8	5	9	61
Thrice (Party Congresses)							
1.2.3.	(1)[l]			(2)[m]		(4)[n]	
1.3.4.						(1)[o]	
2.3.4.	(1)[h]		(3)[i]	(1)[j]			
2.3.5.				(1)[k]			
3.4.5.	(2)[d]		(2)[e]	(1)[f]	(2)[g]		
Total	4	—	5	5	2	5	21
Four Times							
1.2.3.4.	(3)[a]	—					
2.3.4.5.	(1)[b]						
Total	4	—	—	—	—	—	4
Five Times	—	—	2[c]	—	—	—	2
TOTAL	46	86	52	35	18	22	259

a	Pak Chŏng-ae	f	Nam Il	l	O Ki-sŏp
	Kang Chin-gŏn	g	Kim Hoe-il	m	Han Il-mu
	Han Sŏl-ya		Kim Man-gŭm		Yim Hae
b	Chŏng Chun-t'aek	h	Chŏng Il-yong	n	Ch'oe Ch'ang-ik
c	Kim Il-sŏng	i	Kim Kwang-hyŏp		Hŏ Chŏng-suk
	Kim Il		Kim Kyŏng-sŏk		Kim Tu-bong
d	Ch'oe Wŏn-t'aek		Pak Kŭm-ch'ŏl		Pak Hun-il
	Pak Mun-gyu	j	Yi Song-un	o	Kim Ch'ang-man
e	Ch'oe Hyŏn	k	Pang Hak-se		
	Ch'oe Yong-gŏn				

Only 4 members served four times and 21 served three. Out of the 4 who were elected four times, only 1, Chŏng Chun-t'aek, is a member of the fifth Central Committee. Pak Chŏng-ae, once the most powerful woman leader of the North, now age sixty-five, seems to have retired. The famous peasant leader Kang Chin-gŏn died in 1963 at the age of seventy-eight, and one of the illustrious literary writers of the North, Han Sŏl-ya, was purged in 1962. Of the 21 members who were elected three times, only 8 are currently on the Central Committee. In general, no one is reinstated in the Central Committee after failure to be re-elected to the succeeding Central Committee. There have been only three exceptions: Kim Ch'ang-man and Yun Kong-hŭm, both Yenan Communists now purged, and Pang Hak-se, a Soviet-Korean who reappeared in the Central Committee of the Fifth Party Congress. Pang was once a powerful man as a minister of public security, and he seems to be the only Soviet-Korean in power, now that Nam Il, former vice-premier and foreign minister, is reported to have been purged.[10]

Some preliminary and general observations of the Central Committee and its members can be made. First, it is unmistakably the partisans, who consolidated their strength by eliminating virtually all other groups by 1961, who have unchallenged control of the party. Second, in order to augment the relatively small numbers of partisan leaders, they have trained and recruited a large number of new leaders into the Central Committee. Third, there is rapid change in the membership of the Central Committee. Only 11 members who were elected to the Central Committee at least three times or more are serving on the fifth Central Committee. Fourth, since the majority of the Central Committee are newly elected members serving only a single term, the control of the Central Committee seems to rest with a select few of the partisan group. Fifth, as the partisan members have consolidated their strength with the assistance of the newly emerging group, the opportunity for a factional struggle based upon the past revolutionary groupings seems to have disappeared. For instance, there is not a single member of the Yenan group in the fifth Central Committee, and there are only 2 Soviet-Koreans and 9 domestic Communists enjoying membership at the pleasure of the partisan group. Sixth, since the second party conference of October 1966, there have been definite signs of an intragroup struggle within the partisan group. Such a struggle may have a debilitating effect, but more importantly, it can also be interpreted as a sign of maturity in the North Korean leadership, which may now be eliminating parts of its membership on the basis of policy differences. Seventh, with the appearance of a large number of newly emerging leaders, there exists today, for the first time, a single group that has the majority in the Central Committee. Because of the relative obscurity of these men, it has become increasingly difficult to determine the direction and orientation of the Central Committee. The primary task of the partisan group seems to have shifted from the struggle to eliminate other competing groups to an effort to train correctly and control the leaders of the newly emerging groups. Eighth, and perhaps most important, is that the appearance of a large number of these new leaders has resulted in a fundamental change in the composition of the Central Committee, from the old revolutionaries who participated in the Communist revolutionary activities abroad to newly trained and, more importantly, Korean-trained leaders under the direction of the Workers' Party of Korea.

B. Candidate Members of the Central Committee

Article 33 of the bylaws states that whenever a vacancy exists in the Central Committee, it should be filled by a candidate member of the Central Committee, and Article 34 provides that candidate members have the privilege of participating in the plenary meetings of the Central Committee without a vote; there is no provision stating the functions of the candidate members of the Central Committee. The Central Committee, however, has seldom made public any replacement of the members of the Central Committee with a candidate member. Some of the important replacements were made not with a candidate member but rather with someone who had held no previous position in the party.[11]

The role of candidate members in the Central Committee is not clear. Contrary to the practices of Communist parties in other countries, only a few candidate members are elected to become regular members of the Central Committee of the WPK and fewer still are re-elected as candidate members of the Central Committee. Out of some 160 candidate members (see table 3), only 32 have been elected to regular membership in the Central Committee; almost all others have been dropped. For example, of 20 candidate members in the second Central Committee only 2 remained as candidate members, and only 1 out of 45 candidate members of the third Central Committee was retained in the fourth Central Committee. In the fourth Central Committee, 7 candidate members retained their status, but this is hardly an improvement as they were joined by 48 new candidate members of the fifth Central Committee. Therefore, almost all candidate members in each Central Committee are newly elected members.

The tenure of candidate members is not long: only one member, Yi Chi-ch'an,[12] has served three terms, and only eight members have served twice; prior to the Fifth Party Congress only one other person, Yi Kyu-hwan, had served twice. The seven men

TABLE 3

Changes in the Candidate Membership of the Central Committee by Groups

Party Congresses	Total	D	N	P	S	U	Y
1 WPK CMCC	NONE						
2 WPK CMCC	20	2	—	1	1	14	2
Elected to 3 WPK CCM	5	1	—	1	1	—	2
Re-elected to 3 WPK CMCC	2	—	—	—	—	2	—
Dropped	13	1	—	—	—	12	—
3 WPK CMCC	45	11	3	6	5	12	8
From 2 WPK CCM	1	1	—	—	—	—	—
From 2 WPK CMCC	2	—	—	—	—	2	—
New Members	42	10	3	6	5	10	8
Elected to 4 WPK CCM	12	3	3	6	—	—	—
Re-elected to 4 WPK CMCC	1	—	—	—	—	1	—
Dropped	32	8	—	—	5	11	8
4 WPK CMCC	50	3	33	8	—	5	1
From 3 WPK CMCC	1	—	—	—	—	1	—
New Members	49	3	33	8	—	4	1
Elected to 5 WPK CCM	15	2	6	3	—	4	—
Re-elected to 5 WPK CMCC	7	—	7	—	—	—	—
Dropped	28	1	20	5	—	1	1
5 WPK CMCC	55	—	49	5	—	1	—
From 4 WPK CCM	2	—	1	—	—	1	—
From 4 WPK CMCC	7	—	7	—	—	—	—
New Members	46	—	41	5	—	—	—

NOTE: WPK = Workers' Party of Korea; 1 WPK = first congress, August 1946; 2 WPK = second congress, March 1948; 3 WKP = third congress, April 1956; 4 WPK = fourth congress, September 1961; 5 WPK = fifth congress, November 1970; CCM = Central Committee Member; D = Domestic Group; N = New Group; P = Partisan Group; S = Soviet-Korean Group; U = Unknown Group; Y = Yenan Group; CMCC = Candidate Members of the Central Committee.

who were successful in remaining as candidate members of the fifth Central Committee are all newly emerging leaders whose identities are relatively obscure.[13] There are other peculiarities of the Central Committee; for example, three regular members of the fifth Central Committee were demoted to candidate members.[14]

Some general characteristics of the changing patterns in the candidate membership are similar to those of the regular members of the Central Committee. There is a definite decrease and phasing out of all groups except the partisan. Important, too, is that during the tenure of the second and third Central Committees all candidate members of the partisan group were promoted to regular membership in the Central Committee. As with regular members of the fourth Central Committee, five partisan candidate members were dropped from the Central Committee, but five new partisans were quickly added by the fifth congress.

There are other similarities between regular and candidate members—the rise of the newly emerging group and a low rate of re-election to the succeeding party congresses. Most important, however, seems to be that in the Workers' Party of Korea election to candidate membership of the Central Committee is not a step toward election to regular membership of the Central Committee. Except for partisans, election to candidate membership appears to be a sure way of not getting re-elected to the membership on the Central Committee either as a regular or as a candidate member.

C. Members of the Political and Standing Committees

The highest ranking leaders of the party were those who held positions as chairman, vice-chairman, secretary-general, secretary, and member and candidate member of the Political, Organizational and Standing Committees. Generally speaking, the chairman, vice-chairmen, and secretaries were also members of the Political and Standing Committees, and the number of these leaders has not exceeded seventeen in any one Central Committee.

A detailed description of structural changes is not necessary for the purpose of this study. Only a few relevant changes will be discussed. The offices of chairman and vice-chairman were abolished in the fourteenth plenum of the fourth congress on October 12, 1966, and were replaced with the offices of secretary-general and secretary. The Political Committee was abolished in the third congress, but was reinstated in the fourth, while the Standing Committee was abolished by the time of the fourth congress. According to the party bylaws (of whichever version), the members of the Political or Standing Committees are the highest functionaries of the party who administer general policies of the Central Committee and implement specific policies in between the Central Committee plenums. The members of these committees are elected by the Central Committee, though the method of election has never been revealed.

Details from two plenums were added in table 4 to examine the changes in the vice-chairmanship of the Central Committee more closely. The sixth plenum of the Second Party Congress was held in August 1953 shortly after the conclusion of the Korean War and it reflects a drastic change within the Central Committee. The fourteenth plenum of the Fourth Party Congress, which was held at the time of the second party conference in October 1966, abolished the vice-chairmanship and created the office of a secretary. New secretaries were elected, with a significant proportion coming from the partisan group.

TABLE 4

CHANGES IN CHAIRMAN, VICE-CHAIRMEN, SECRETARY-GENERAL, SECRETARIES OF THE CENTRAL COMMITTEE BY GROUPS

A. *Chairman and Secretary-General*

1 WPK–June 1949	Chairman	Y - Kim Tu-bong
June 1949–October 1966	Chairman	P - Kim Il-sŏng
October 1966–present	Secretary-General	P - Kim Il-sŏng

B. *Vice-chairmen and Secretaries*

(Vice-chairmen)

Party Congresses	*Total*	D	N	P	S	Y	
1 WPK	2	1	—	1	—	—	P - Kim Il-sŏng
							D - Chu Yŏng-ha
Re-elected to 2 WPK	1	—	—	1	—	—	
Dropped	1	1	—	—	—	—	D - Chu Yŏng-ha
2 WPK	2	—	—	1	1	—	P - Kim Il-sŏng
							S - Hŏ Ka-i
From 1 WPK	1	—	—	1	—	—	P - Kim Il-sŏng
New member	1	—	—	—	1	—	
Re-elected to 2 WPK-6CC	NONE						
Promoted to chairman	1	—	—	1	—	—	
Dropped	1	—	—	—	1	—	S - Hŏ Ka-i
2 WPK-6CC	3	1	—	1	1	—	D - Pak Chŏng-ae
(August 1953)							P - Kim Il
							S - Pak Ch'ang-ok
From 2 WPK	NONE						
New members	3	1	—	1	1	—	
Re-elected to 3 WPK	1	1	—	—	—	—	
Dropped	2	—	—	1	1	—	P - Kim Il
							S - Pak Ch'ang-ok

TABLE 4—*Continued*

Party Congresses	Total	D	N	P	S	Y	
3 WPK	5	2	—	2	—	1	P - Ch'oe Yong-gŏn D - Pak Chŏng-ae P - Pak Kŭm-ch'ŏl D - Chŏng Il-yong Y - Kim Ch'ang-man
From 2 WPK-6CC	1	1	—	—	—	—	D - Pak Chŏng-ae
New members	4	1	—	2	—	1	
Re-elected to 4 WPK	3	—	—	2	—	1	
Dropped	2	2	—	—	—	—	D - Pak Chŏng-ae D - Chŏng Il-yong
4 WPK	5	—	—	4	—	1	P - Ch'oe Yong-gŏn P - Kim Il P - Pak Kŭm-ch'ŏl Y - Kim Ch'ang-man P - Yi Hyo-sun
From 3 WPK	3	—	—	2	—	1	P - Ch'oe Yong-gŏn P - Pak Kŭm-ch'ŏl Y - Kim Ch'ang-man
From 2 WPK-6CC	1	—	—	1	—	—	P - Kim Il
New member	1	—	—	1	—	—	
Re-elected to 4 WPK- 14 CC	4	—	—	4	—	—	
Dropped	1	—	—	—	—	1	Y - Kim Ch'ang-man

Party Congresses	Total	D	N	P	S	Y	
				(Secretaries)			
4 WPK-14CC	10	—	2	8	—	—	P - Ch'oe Yong-gŏn P - Kim Il P - Pak Kŭm-ch'ŏl P - Yi Hyo-sun P - Kim Kwang-hyŏp P - Sŏk San P - Hŏ Pong-hak P - Kim Yŏng-ju N - Pak Yong-guk N - Kim To-man
From 4 WPK	4	—	—	4	—	—	P - Ch'oe Yong-gŏn P - Kim Il P - Pak Kŭm-ch'ŏl P - Yi Hyo-sun
New members	6	—	2	4	—	—	
Re-elected to 5 WPK	3	—	—	3	—	—	
Dropped	7	—	2	5	—	—	P - Pak Kŭm-ch'ŏl P - Yi Hyo-sun P - Kim Kwang-hyŏp P - Sŏk San P - Hŏ Pong-hak N - Pak Yong-guk N - Kim To-man

TABLE 4—Continued

Party Congresses	Total	D	N	P	S	Y	
5 WPK	9	1	2	6	—	—	P - Ch'oe Yong-gŏn
							P - Kim Il
							P - Kim Yŏng-ju
							P - O Chin-u
							P - Kim Tong-gyu
							D - Kim Chung-nin
							P - Han Ik-su
							N - Hyŏn Mu-gwang
							N - Yang Hyŏng-sŏp
From 4 WPK-14CC	3	—	—	3	—	—	P - Ch'oe Yong-gŏn
							P - Kim Il
							P - Kim Yŏng-ju
New members	6	1	2	3	—	—	

NOTE: WPK = Workers' Party of Korea; 1 WPK = first congress, August 1946; 2 WPK = second congress, March 1948; 3 WPK = third congress, April 1956; 4 WPK = fourth congress, September 1961; 5 WPK = fifth congress, November 1970; CCM = Central Committee Member; D = Domestic Group; N = New Group; P = Partisan Group; S = Soviet-Korean Group; U = Unknown Group; Y = Yenan Group; 2 WPK-6CC = sixth plenum of the Central Committee of the second congress; 4 WPK-14CC = fourteenth plenum of the Central Committee of the fourth congress.

Kim Il-sŏng replace Kim Tu-bong as chairman of the Central Committee on June 11, 1949, when the North and South Korean Workers' parties were officially merged as the Workers' Party of Korea. The chairman has not changed since then, except that the title of the post has changed from chairman to secretary-general of the Central Committee.

Many of the changes in the vice-chairmanship and secretary are more clearly reflected in the changes in the Political and Standing Committees. A special note should be made to point out the gravity of the intragroup struggle of the partisan group that can be seen in the change from the Fourteenth Plenum of the fourth Central Committee in October 1968 to the Fifth Party Congress in November 1970. All partisans from the third to seventh ranking secretaries of the Central Committee were dropped. For some twenty-two years, from the first congress of August 1946 to the fourteenth plenum of the fourth Central Committee in October 1968, no partisan was ever dropped from the vice-chairmanship. Kim Il was dropped from the Third Party Congress but was quickly reinstated in the Fourth. Leaders of other groups who were dropped from the vice-chairmanship, such as Chu Yŏng-ha of the domestic group, Hŏ Ka-i of the Soviet group, Kim Ch'ang-man of the Yenan group, and Pak Yŏng-guk of the newly emerging group, were never reinstated. The pattern of change in the top leadership of the Workers' Party of Korea can be studied more closely by examining the changes in membership of the Political and Standing Committees. As is obvious from table 5, there was no change in the Political Committee from the First to the Second Party Congress; there is a sharp change, however, in the sixth plenum of the Central Committee, which was held in August 1953, shortly after the Korean War.

TABLE 5

CHANGES IN THE MEMBERSHIP OF THE POLITICAL COMMITTEES

Party Congresses	Total	D	P	S	Y	
1 WPK PCM	5	1	1	1	2	Y - Kim Tu-bong P - Kim Il-sŏng D - Chu Yŏng-ha S - Hŏ Ka-i Y - Ch'oe Ch'ang-ik
Re-elected to 2 WPK PCM Dropped	5 NONE	1	1	1	2	
2 WPK PCM	7	1	2	1	3	Y - Kim Tu-bong P - Kim Il-sŏng S - Hŏ Ka-i P - Kim Ch'aek Y - Ch'oe Ch'ang-ik Y - Pak Il-u D - Chu Yŏng-ha
From 1 WPK PCM New members	5 2	1 —	1 1	1 —	2 1	P - Kim Ch-aek Y - Pak Il-u
Re-elected to 2 WPK-6CC Dropped	2 4	— 1	1 —	— 1	1 2	D - Chu Yŏng-ha S - Hŏ Ka-i Y - Ch'oe Ch'ang-ik Y - Pak Il-u
Died	1	—	1	—	—	P - Kim Ch'aek
2 WPK-6CC PCM (August 1953)	7	1	3	2	1	P - Kim Il-sŏng Y - Kim Tu-bong D - Pak Chŏng-ae S - Pak Ch'ang-ok P - Kim Il P - Pak Kŭm-ch'ŏl S - Pak Yŏng-bin
From 2 WPK PCM	2	—	1	—	1	P - Kim Il-sŏng Y - Kim Tu-bong
New members	5	1	2	2	—	

TABLE 5 — Continued

Party Congresses	Total	D	P	S	Y	
2 WPK-6CC PCM (Cont'd.)						
Re-elected to 3 WPK OCM	3	1	2	—	—	
Dropped	4	—	1	2	1	Y - Kim Tu-bong
						S - Pak Ch'ang-ok
						P - Kim Il
						S - Pak Yŏng-bin

NOTE: Third Party Congress had no Political Committee. This is for an Organizational Committee that performed functions of the Political Committee.

	Total	D	P	S	Y	
3 WPK OCM	7	3	3	—	1	P - Kim Il-sŏng
						P - Ch'oe Yong-gŏn
						D - Pak Chŏng-ae
						P - Pak Kŭm-ch'ŏl
						D - Chŏng Il-yong
						Y - Kim Ch'ang-man
						D - Han Sang-du
From 2 WPK-6CC	3	1	2	—	—	P - Kim Il-sŏng
						D - Pak Chŏng-ae
						P - Pak Kŭm-ch'ŏl
New members	4	2	1	—	1	
Re-elected to 4 WPK PCM	6	2	3	—	1	
Re-elected to 4 WPK CMPC	1	1	—	—	—	D - Han Sang-du

NOTE: The Political Committee was abolished in the Third Party Congress but was reactivated by the Fourth Party Congress. However, the reactivated Political Committee was more of a continuation of a Standing Committee than the Political Committees of previous party congress. The Fourth Party Congress had no Standing Committee and the changes in the Political Committee of the Fourth and Fifth party Congresses will be repeated in Table 6. The newly created candidate membership to the Political Committee is omitted in this table but they are fully recorded in Table 6.

	Total	D	P	S	Y	
4 WPK PCM	11	3	6	1	1	P - Kim Il-sŏng
						P - Ch'oe Yong-gŏn
						P - Kim Il
						P - Pak Kŭm-ch'ŏl
						Y - Kim Ch'ang-man
						P - Yi Hyo-sun
						D - Pak Chŏng-ae
						P - Kim Kwang-hyŏp
						D - Chŏng Il-yong
						S - Nam Il
						D - Yi Chong-ok
From 3 WPK OCM	6	2	3	—	1	
New members	5	1	3	1	—	P - Kim Il
						P - Yi Hyo-sun
						P - Kim Kwang-hyŏp
						S - Nam Il
						D - Yi Chong-ok

TABLE 5 — Continued

Party Congresses	Total	D	P	S	Y	
4 WPK PCM (Cont'd.)						
Re-elected to 4 WPK-14CC PCM	6	—	6	—	—	
Dropped	5	3	—	1	1	Y - Kim Ch'ang-man
						D - Pak Chŏng-ae
						D - Chŏng Il-yong
						S - Nam Il
						D - Yi Chong-ok
4 WPK-14CC PCM	11	1	10	—	—	P - Kim Il-sŏng
						P - Ch'oe Yong-gŏn
						P - Kim Il
						P - Pak Kŭm-ch'ŏl
						P - Yi Hyo-sun
						P - Kim Kwang-hyŏp
						D - Kim Ik-sŏn
						P - Kim Ch'ang-bong
						P - Pak Song-ch'ŏl
						P - Ch'oe Hyŏn
						P - Yi Yŏng-ho
From 4 WPK PCM	6	—	6	—	—	
New members	5	1	4	—	—	D - Kim Ik-sŏn
						P - Kim Ch'ang-bong
						P - Pak Sŏng-ch'ŏl
						P - Ch'oe Hyŏn
						P - Yi Yŏng-ho
Re-elected to 5 WPK PCM	5	—	5	—	—	
Dropped	6	1	5	—	—	P - Pak Kŭm-ch'ŏl
						P - Yi Hyo-sun
						P - Kim Kwang-hyŏp
						D - Kim Ik-sŏn
						P - Kim Ch'ang-bong
						P - Yi Yŏng-ho
5 WPK PCM	11	1	10	—	—	P - Kim Il-sŏng
						P - Ch'oe Yong-gŏn
						P - Kim Il
						P - Pak Sŏng-ch'ŏl
						P - Ch'oe Hyŏn
						P - Kim Yŏng-ju
						P - O Chin-u
						P - Kim Tong-gyu
						P - Sŏ Ch'ŏl
						D - Kim Chung-nin
						P - Han Ik-su
From 4 WPK-14CC PCM	5	—	5	—	—	
New members	6	1	5	—	—	P - Kim Yŏng-ju
						P - O Chin-u
						P - Kim Tong-gyu
						P - Sŏ Ch'ŏl
						D - Kim Chung-nin
						P - Han Ik-su

TABLE 5 — *Continued*

NOTE: WPK = Workers' Party of Korea; 1 WPK = first congress, August 1946; 2 WPK = second congress, March 1948; 3 WPK = third congress, April 1956; 4 WPK = fourth congress, September 1961; 5 WPK = fifth congress, November 1970; CCM = Central Committee Member; D = Domestic Group; N = New Group; P = Partisan Group; S = Soviet-Korean Group; U = Unknown Group; Y = Yenan Group; PCM = Political Committee Members; CMPC = Candidate Members of the Political Committee; OCM = Organizational Committee Members.

Two important events during this period need to be mentioned: one is the merger of the South Korean Workers' Party and the North Korean Workers' Party on June 11, 1949, and the second is the outbreak of the Korean War. The South Korean Workers' Party with its own 31-man Central Committee was merged wtih the 67-man Central Committee of the North Korean Workers' Party, but there was no official announcement of a new Central Committee of the merged Workers' Party of Korea prior to the Third Party Congress in 1956. An 8-man Political Committee and a 14-man Standing Committee of the South Korean Workers' Party were reported.[15] A new 9-man Political Committee of the Workers' Party of Korea was also announced, consisting of five members from the North and four members from the South, who were all members of their respective Political Committees.[16]

A significant change occurred in the leadership of the North during and after the Korean War, and a new line-up shortly after the Korean War reflected almost total elimination of the leaders of the domestic group from the South. No one from the Political Committee of the South Korean Workers' Party was elected to a new Political Committee of the sixth plenum of August 1953. Only one of fourteen members of the Standing Committee of the South Korean Workers' Party was elected to the Standing Committee of the sixth plenum (see table 6). He was soon purged.[17]

The rise of the partisan group can be seen as early as August 1953 by the election of such partisans as Kim Il[18] and Pak Kŭm-ch'ŏl, and in the failure on the part of such important leaders as Ch'oe Ch'ang-ik and Pak Il-u of the Yenan group to be re-elected. Contrary to popular belief, leaders, such as Ch'oe Ch'ang-ik who was not purged until after the Third Party Congress in 1956, were never re-elected to the Political Committee after August 1953. The fall of the Yenan group became obvious when Kim Tu-bong was dropped from the Political Committee. Another member of the Yenan group, Kim Ch'ang-man, was recruited, but his open denunciation of his fellow revolutionaries from Yenan seems to have been the main reason for his prominence. Similarly, the lack of close ties with the mainstay of the domestic group seems to have contributed in no small way to the election of such leaders as Pak Chŏng-ae, Chŏng Il-yong, and Han Sang-du to the Organization Committee of the third Central Committee.

TABLE 6

CHANGES IN THE MEMBERSHIP OF THE STANDING COMMITTEE

Party Congresses	Members Total	D	N	P	S	U	Y	Candidate Members Total	D	N	P	S	U	Y
1 WPK SCM				Data not available										
2 WPK SCM	17	5	—	3	5	1	3							
Re-elected to 2 WPK-6CC	7	2	—	2	1	—	2							
Dropped	9	3	—	—	4	1	1							
Died	1	—	—	1	—	—	—							
2 WPK-6CC SCM	15	5	—	4	4	—	2							
From 2 WPK	7	2	—	2	1	—	2							
New members	8	3	—	2	3	—	—							
Re-elected to 3 WPK	9	2	—	4	1	—	2							
Dropped	6	3	—	—	3	—	—							
3 WPK SCM	11	2	—	5	2	—	2	4	1	—	1	1	—	1
Re-elected from 2 WPK-6CC	9	2	—	4	1	—	2							
New members	2	—	—	1	1	—	—	4	1	—	1	1	—	1
Re-elected to 4 WPK PCM	8	2	—	5	1	—	—							
Promoted to 4 WPK PCM								3	1	—	1	—	—	1
Dropped	3	—	—	—	1	—	2	1	—	—	—	1	—	—

NOTE: A standing committee was abolished in the Fourth Party Congress and a political committee was reinstated in place of the standing committee.

4 WPK PCM	11	3	—	6	1	—	1	4	3	—	—	—	—	1
From 3 WPK SCM	8	2	—	5	1	—	—							
From 3 WPK CMSC	3	1	—	1	—	—	1							
New members								4	3	—	—	—	—	1
Re-elected to 4 WPK-14CC PCM	6	—	—	6	—	—	—							
Promoted to 4 WPK-14CC PCM								1	1	—	—	—	—	—
Dropped	5	3	—	—	1	—	1	3	2	—	—	—	—	1

TABLE 6 — Continued

Party Congresses	Members Total	D	N	P	S	U	Y	Candidate Members Total	D	N	P	S	U	Y
4 WPK-14CC PCM	11	1	—	10	—	—	—	9	—	2	7	—	—	—
From 4 WPK PCM	6	—	—	6	—	—	—							
From 4 WPK CMPC	1	1	—	—	—	—	—							
New members	4	—	—	4	—	—	—	9	—	2	7	—	—	—
Re-elected to 5 WPK PCM	5	—	—	5	—	—	—							
Promoted to 5 WPK PCM								3	—	—	3	—	—	—
Dropped	6	1	—	5	—	—	—	6	—	2	4	—	—	—
5 WPK PCM	11	1	—	10	—	—	—	4	1	2	—	—	1	—
From 4 WPK-14CC PCM	5	—	—	5	—	—	—							
From 4 WPK-14CC CMPC	3	—	—	3	—	—	—							
New members	3	1	—	2	—	—	—	4	1	2	—	—	1	—

NOTE: WPK = Workers' Party of Korea; 1 WPK = first congress, August 1946; 2 WPK = second congress, March 1948; 3 WPK = third congress, April 1956; 4 WPK = fourth congress, September 1961; 5 WPK = fifth congress, November 1970; CCM = Central Committee Member; D = Domestic Group; N = New Group; P = Partisan Group; S = Soviet-Korean Group; U = Unknown Group; Y = Yenan Group; SCM = Standing Committee Members; CMSC = Candidate Members of the Standing Committee.

The partisans outnumbered all other groups by the Third Party Congress, and it seems that the now famous coup of the Yenan and Soviet-Koreans in 1956 in the name of a collective leadership was a futile effort in view of the composition of the Political Committee of the third Central Committee. The partisans attained a majority in the Political Committee of the fourth Central Committee, which became absolute by the second party conference in October 1966, ten out of eleven members being partisans. No partisan was ever denied re-election to the membership or candidate membership of the Political or Standing Committees until the Fifth Party Congress. These five who failed were quickly replaced by five new partisans, so that the Political Committee of the Fifth Party Congress also consists of ten partisans and one member of the domestic group.

The dominance of the partisan group is most obvious in table 7. Out of fifty-four men who served on the Political and Standing Committees, by far the largest number (twenty) were members of the partisan group and five out of nine members who were elected more than four times to the committees were partisans. From this table it can also be seen that the Yenan group was never a serious contender for power in the party; nor were the Soviet-Koreans a threat to the partisans. The members of the domestic group were the second most numerous, but they were ineffective after the Korean War, when most of their leaders were purged.

TABLE 7

FREQUENCY OF RE-ELECTION TO THE POLITICAL AND STANDING
COMMITTEES BY GROUPS: FIVE CONGRESSES AND TWO PLENUMS OF
AUGUST 1953 AND OCTOBER 1966

	D	N	P	S	U	Y	Total
Once	6	4	9	7	2	2	30
Twice	5^a	—	5^b	2^c	—	1^d	13
Thrice	—	—	1^e	1^f	—	—	2
Four times	2^g	—	3^h	—	—	2ⁱ	7
Five times	—	—	—	—	—	—	0
Six times	—	—	1^j	—	—	—	1
Seven times	—	—	1^k	—	—	—	1
Total	13	4	20	10	2	5	54

a Chu Yŏng-ha
   Chŏng Chun-t'aek
   Han Sang-du
   Yi Chong-ok
   Kim Ik-sŏn
b Pak Sŏng-ch'ŏl
   Ch'oe Hyŏn
   O Chin-u
   Kim Tong-gyu
   Kim Yŏng-ju

c Hŏ Ka-i
   Pak Ch'ang-ok
d Kim Ch'ang-man
e Yi Hyo-sun
f Nam Il
g Pak Chŏng-ae
   Chŏng Il-yong

h Kim Kwaung-hyŏp
   Pak Kŭm-ch'ŏl
   Ch'oe Yong-gŏn
i Kim Tu-bong
   Ch'oe Ch'ang-ik
j Kim Il
k Kim Il-sŏng

D = Domestic Group; N = New Group; P = Partisan Group; S = Soviet-Korean Group; U = Unknown Group; Y = Yenan Group.

Three generalizations can be drawn from the study of the Political and Standing Committees. First, except for two occasions, the top leadership in the party has been relatively stable. For example, contrary to the common understanding that there was a spectacular coup and attending purges of a joint force of the Soviet-Koreans and the members of the Yenan group shortly after the Third Party Congress in 1956, almost all members of the Standing Committee of the third Central Committee were re-elected to the Political Committee of the fourth Central Committee. It seems that there were only two occasions when the top leadership of the party was in disarray; once after the Korean War and then shortly before and after the second party conference in October 1966. In general, most of the highly publicized purges were relatively minor changes in the top leadership of the party.

Second, Kim Il-sŏng and his partisans were seriously challenged twice; once by the domestic group during the Korean War and another time by the members of his own partisan group. The more important of these two challenges seems to have been the crisis that occurred quite recently, two or three years prior to the Fifth Party Congress—the intraparty struggle of the partisans. Partisans eliminated in this struggle included such important party and military leaders as Pak Kŭm-ch'ŏl, Yi Hyo-sun, Kim Kwang-hyŏp, Sŏk San, Kim Ch'ang-bong, Hŏ Pong-hak, Ch'oe Kwang, Yi Yŏng-ho, and Yim Ch'un-ch'u. This crisis was important as it signaled a change in the style of competition for leadership from one of factional intergroup struggle to one of intragroup struggle within the dominant group, based, perhaps, on policy differences. One may easily speculate that this struggle was related to the shift, in recent years, of North Korean policy toward the South and to the change from the militant policy pursued by the North during the *Pueblo* incident to a new, more friendly phase by the North toward the South, and the West, today. The demoted partisans were almost all military leaders of some repute.

Third, it seems obvious that neither the Chinese nor the Russians had any significant influence on the top leadership of the party. For example, there was no sharp decrease in the number of Soviet-Koreans when the Russians left the North, nor was there a sharp increase in the membership of the Yenan group when the Chinese were stationed in the North. On the contrary, the Yenan group was almost completely uprooted during the Chinese military presence in the North.

The claim that neither the Russians nor the Chinese exerted any influence on party leadership is strengthened by considering earlier revolutionary activities of the two Korean groups in China and the Soviet Union. Neither the Yenan group nor the Soviet-Koreans had close enough ties with the ruling Chinese and Russian elites to merit their support in the intergroup struggle within the Workers' Party of Korea. There is no convincing evidence that either the Chinese or the Russian Communists made efforts to exert influence in the North through the members of the Yenan or the Soviet group. Had the Russians or the Chinese wanted to exert pressure to control and manipulate North Korea, they had far more effective means, such as economic and military aid, than the Yenan or the Soviet-Koreans did on the WPK Central Committee. The Yenan and Soviet-Koreans, as groups, were never a threat to the partisan group, nor did the fate of these men fluctuate in accordance with the friendly or hostile relations of the Workers' Party of Korea with China or the Soviet Union.

D. *Members of the Inspection, Auditing, and Other Committees*

The members of the Inspection and Auditing Committees are elected by the Central Committee. While a chairman and vice-chairmen of the Inspection Committee are elected by the Central Committee at large, a chairman and vice-chairmen of the Auditing Committee are elected by the members of the Auditing Committee. The bylaws stipulate that the Inspection Committee has a duty to investigate the observance of the bylaws by the members and candidate members of the party; it must also conduct investigations of members who violate the bylaws, neglect party platforms, or weaken the unity of the party. The Inspection Committee also investigates and renders decisions on punishment of members, which are appealed from the provincial committees. The Auditing Committee's function is to inspect the works of various departments and the finances of the Central Committee.[19]

It is obvious from table 8 that almost all members of Inspection Committees are dropped from succeeding Inspection Committees. Out of thirty-six men who served on the committee, only Kim Ik-sŏn, O Yŏng-bong, and Kim Yŏ-jung were re-elected. The chairmen of the committees were not prominent members of the party; although they were all members of the Central Committee except the first chairman, none was a regular member of the Political Committee. It is also significant that except in the case of the present Inspection Committee, all chairmen were from the domestic group. Unlike other Communist parties where the Inspection Committee plays a significant role (for example, the Control Commission of the Chinese Communist Party), the Inspection Committee of the Workers' Party of Korea plays a relatively insignificant role. The large turnover in the membership of the Central Committee and the significant number of high-ranking party officials either demoted or purged suggest that the Inspection Committee might be important, but it seems to be engaged in the investigation of leaders of the provincial and local party organizations, not of high-ranking party officials. All past chairmen themselves were either demoted or purged. None, including the present chairman, has been of the caliber necessary to investigate any member of the Political or Standing Committees.

The rate of re-election to the Auditing Committee is just as low as is the rate of election to the Inspection Committee. Out of forty-nine persons who have served on the committee, only six have been re-elected. The members of the Auditing Committee seem to have been recruited more on a functional than political basis, for the current chairman of the Auditing Committee, Kim Se-hwal, is not even a member of the Central Committee. There are no partisans on the current Auditing Committee, and perhaps the most insignificant group politically, the unknown group, has persistently maintained the highest level of representation.

There are two unofficial but important organizations in the Central Committee; one is the Military Affairs Committee and the other, known as a Liaison Bureau, is said to direct the party's operations in South Korea. The Military Affairs Committee was reported to have been established in December 1962 at the time of the fifth plenum of the fourth Central Committee, when various measures were passed to fortify and strengthen the military forces of the North.

Not enough information exists on these two organizations to document their function and details of their operations, but no one other than the partisans ever headed the two organizations until the current chairman of the Liaison Bureau, Kim Chung-nin,[20] who shares no guerrilla revolutionary past with the partisans. It is also important to note that all those partisans who have headed the Liaison Bureau in the past, Yi Hyo-sun and Hŏ Pong-hak, for example, were purged when they were relieved of their responsibilities. One can speculate that North Korean efforts to direct a revolutionary struggle in the South may not have produced the expected results.

Not enough information is available to analyze the leaders of the Central Committee departments and secretaries of the provincial and municipal committees of the party.

E. Changes in the Membership by Occupation

Except for those who work for the party, every member of the Central Committee, in addition to his membership, holds an outside position. It is useful to analyze the members of the Central

TABLE 8

CHANGES IN THE MEMBERSHIP OF THE INSPECTION AND AUDITING COMMITTEES

A. Inspection Committee

Party Congresses	Total	D	N	P	S	U	Y
1 WPK ICM	11	5	—	—	1	5	—
Re-elected to 2 WPK ICM	NONE						
Dropped all but one who died							
Elected to 2 WPK CCM	3	2	—	—	1	—	—
2 WPK ICM	6	3	—	—	1	2	—
New members	ALL						
Re-elected to 3 WPK ICM	NONE						
Dropped all but one who died							
3 WPK ICM	7	2	—	2	—	2	1
New members	ALL						
Re-elected to 4 WPK ICM	1	1	—	—	—	—	—
Dropped	6	1	—	2	—	2	1
4 WPK ICM	7	1	1	1	—	4	—
From 3 WPK ICM	1	1	—	—	—	—	—
New members	6	—	1	1	—	4	—
Re-elected to 5 WPK ICM	1	—	—	—	—	1	—
Dropped	6	1	1	1	—	3	—
5 WPK ICM	7	—	5	1	—	1	—
From 4 WPK ICM	1	—	—	—	—	1	—
New members	6	—	5	1	—	—	—

NOTE: WPK = Workers' Party of Korea; 1 WPK = first congress, August 1946; 2 WPK = second congress, March 1948; 3 WPK = third congress, April 1956; 4 WPK = fourth congress, September 1961; 5 WPK = fifth congress, November 1970; ICM = Inspection Committee Member; D = Domestic Group; N = New Group; P = Partisan Group; S = Soviet-Korean Group; U = Unknown Group; Y = Yenan Group; Inspection Committee Chairmen: 1 WPK ICM D = Kim Yong-bŏm; 2 WPK ICM D = Chang Sun-myŏng; 3 WPK ICM D = Kim Ik-sŏn; 4 WPK ICM D = Kim Ik-sŏn; 5 WPK ICM P = Kim Yŏ-jung.

B. Auditing Committee

Party Congresses	Total	D	N	P	S	U	Y
1 WPK ACM	NONE	—	—	—	—	—	—
2 WPK ACM	7	2	—	—	1	3	1
Re-elected to 3 WPK ACM	3	2	—	—	—	—	1
Dropped	4	—	—	—	1	3	—

TABLE 8 — Continued

Party Congresses	Total	D	N	P	S	U	Y
3 WPK ACM	17	6	—	—	2	4	5
From 2 WPK ACM	3	2	—	—	—	—	1
New members	14	4	—	—	2	4	4
Re-elected to 4 WPK ACM	1	1	—	—	—	—	—
Dropped	16	5	—	—	2	4	5
4 WPK ACM	17	4	4	5	—	4	—
From 3 WPK ACM	1	1	—	—	—	—	—
New members	16	3	4	5	—	4	—
Re-elected to 5 WPK ACM	3	—	—	—	—	3	—
Dropped	14	4	4	5	—	1	—
5 WPK ACM	15	—	11	—	—	4	—
From 4 WPK ACM	3	—	—	—	—	3	—
New members	12	—	11	—	—	1	—

NOTE: WPK = Workers' Party of Korea; 1 WPK = first congress, August 1946; 2 WPK = second congress, March 1948; 3 WPK = third congress, April 1956; 4 WPK = fourth congress, September 1961; 5 WPK = fifth congress, November 1970; ACM = Auditing Committee Member; D = Domestic Group; N = New Group; P = Partisan Group; S = Soviet-Korean Group; U = Unknown Group; Y = Yenan Group; Auditing Committee Chairmen: 1 WPK ACM none; 2 WPK ACM D = Yi Chu-yŏn; 3 WPK ACM D = Yi Chu-yŏn; 4 WPK ACM P = Kim Yŏ-jung; 5 WPK ACM N = Kim Se-hwal.

Committee on the basis of their occupation; but relatively little information permits but a cursory survey.

Each member of the Central Committee is identified by his occupation at the time of his election to the committee according to the following nine categories: (1) cabinet ministers and workers in the ministries; (2) diplomats and trade representatives; (3) justices, procurator-generals, and members of the judiciary; (4) military officers; (5) party functionaries whose primary occupation is work within the party; (6) members of the presidium of the Supreme People's Assembly; (7) provincial and local organization leaders; (8) leaders of other organizations, such as cultural and educational institutions; and (9) members whose occupation is not known, grouped as unknown group. As is clear from table 9, there are too many unknowns in both the first and fifth congresses to make any meaningful analysis. Furthermore, the First and Second Party Congresses were held prior to the official establishment of the government in the North. It is only the Central Committees of the Third and Fourth Party Congresses that can be meaningfully evaluated.

TABLE 9

CHANGE IN THE MEMBERSHIP OF THE CENTRAL COMMITTEE
BY OCCUPATION

	1 WPK	2 WPK	3 WPK	4 WPK	*	5 WPK	Total
Cabinet Ministers	10	6	24	20	44	25	85
Diplomats	0	1	3	6	9	2	12
Justices	0	1	1	1	2	0	3
Military Officers	3	10	10	18	28	13	54
Party Functionaries	7	19	9	9	18	15	59
Presidium Members	0	4	6	9	15	5	24
Provincial Leaders	6	5	11	17	28	5	44
Others	5	14	6	4	10	8	37
Unknowns	12	7	1	1	2	44	65
Total	43	67	71	85		117	383

NOTE: WPK = Workers' Party of Korea; 1 WPK = first congress, August 1946;
2 WPK = second congress, March 1948; 3 WPK = third congress, April 1956;
4 WPK = fourth congress, September 1961; 5 WPK = fifth congress, November
1970.
*Total of 3 WPK and 4 WPK

Several observations can be made. If any profession dominates, it is administrative workers in the ministries; the bureaucracy contributes the most to the membership of the Central Committee. Military officers and leaders of local organizations are the second largest groups. Since only generals and very high-ranking field officers are included in the military officers' category, the military is quite an important contributor to the membership of the Central Committee, particularly when one considers the large number of provincial and municipal organizations throughout the North. The low rate of representation of the judiciary and diplomatic corps is understandable, but it is important to note the small number of party workers and legislative leaders represented in the Central Committee. The members of the diplomatic corps are a part of the Ministry of Foreign Affairs, and the combined number of cabinet ministers and diplomats gives by far the largest representation of the bureaucracy in the party.

SOME CHARACTERISTICS OF THE COMMUNIST LEADERSHIP IN KOREA

Out of many characteristics that have emerged from this study, several are important and need to be analyzed in more detail. One is the appearance of a large number of newly recruited young leaders who were trained by the Korean Communist system. There is a definite pattern of induced change in the membership of the highest party leadership organ, which replaces the old revolutionaries who were trained abroad with a new group of "revolutionaries" who were trained by Kim Il-sŏng and his partisans. In an effort to encourage the new leaders, Kim has taken pains to explain that a "Korean revolutionary" is not only a Korean who fought against the Japanese in the struggle for Korean independence but, more importantly, he is a worker who contributed to the building of communism in Korea. A revolutionary is also a young soldier who fought the Americans in the Korean War, and a hero of the socialist construction of the North.[21]

In his speech to the party organizers and leaders of provincial and municipal party committees, Kim Il-sŏng stressed the importance of party leaders in Korea. In a metaphor, he explained that a leader of the party, compared to an administrator or a leader of government organizations, is similar to a helmsman compared to an oarsman of a boat. The administrative worker rows in front, while the party chairman directs the boat by taking the rudder in the stern.[22]

A new leader must undergo a thorough training process of criticism and self-criticism. He must also study the past revolutionary records of Kim and his partisans. And he must be determined to fight against revisionism, dogmatism, formalism, factionalism, nepotism, and other forms of decadence.[23] However, the most important element required of a new leader is *tangsŏng*, party spirit. Kim has defined party spirit as nothing but an absolute and unflinching loyalty to the party.[24] An efficient leader is not one who carries a "bag full of criticism" and is effective in pointing out the mistakes of others, but is a person who is thoroughly armed with the party spirit and who is able to give directions to solve the problems of the workers.

Another characteristic that has become obvious from this study is the disappearance of factional groupings in the North. Although Kim has accomplished this by a process of elimination rather than persuasion, the emergence of the partisans and the new leaders in the North has strengthened the party leadership. The process took some two decades, but it is not merely a case of ruthless purges of the old and a reckless recruitment of the new only to consolidate Kim's power; the changes within the partisan group and the failure of many members of the newly emerging group to be re-elected to the Central Committee seem to suggest the disappearance of factional groups in the leadership of the North.

As early as October 13, 1945, Kim Il-sŏng stated his uncompromising principle of noncooperation with those revolutionaries who had once submitted to the Japanese.[25] Many elements of the domestic group were thereby eliminated, but it was not until after the Korean War that Kim was able to push forward his role as helmsman. A direct but unsuccessful challenge by the domestic group, together with the lack of cooperation among the leaders of the Yenan group and the Soviet-Koreans, was fatal to the old revolutionaries. In the name of party unity, Kim has repeatedly stressed the unconditional struggle against antiparty reactionary elements.[26]

A few old revolutionaries of the Yenan group and the Soviet-Koreans (e.g., Kim Ch'ang-man and Nam Il) remained even after the mainstays of their groups were eliminated, but these men stayed on a little longer only at the pleasure of the partisans and by professing a carping criticism of their former comrades.[27] Contrary to common understanding, the rise and fall of these men had little to do with the Chinese or Russian influence in the North; neither the Yenan group nor the Soviet-Koreans were ever serious contenders for power in the North. They were often criticized by other groups for allowing their revolutionary past to influence them, but neither the Chinese nor the Russians seem to have shown any sign of support of them.

Still another characteristic of the Communist leadership is the rapidity with which leaders are replaced. As a general rule, most of those who were not re-elected to the Central Committee were seldom reinstated later, and those eliminated from Political Committees were purged. On the other hand, many newly elected leaders, particularly candidate members of the Central Committee, seem to have returned to work with the people. Rapid change in the leadership minimizes the danger that reactionary elements will inflict serious harm on the party, and the recruitment of large numbers of new leaders affords a greater number of cadre members an opportunity to participate in party leadership.

The general dearth of leaders in the North has necessitated an intensive recruitment of new leaders and retraining of the old, though Kim has recruited neither those who have ever professed loyalty to the Japanese nor those leaders who fled the South. Kim once said, lamenting the reactionary leaders in the party, that had there been enough partisans to man each cell, we would not have had to resort to such a bureaucrat as Hŏ Ka-i to work for the party.[28] There were 12,000 cells in 1946 alone, and to date there are less than 150 partisans in the North. The party has made efforts to train cadres and new intellectuals from the workers and peasants, and has demanded their unflinching loyalty to the party. The party has also made efforts to instill in new leaders a rigid party life and to arm them with socialistic patriotism.[29] To augment the general dearth of leaders in local organizations, Kim has employed what is known as a direct leadership method. He has himself been a much publicized leader on the local level, and has also dispatched to the local level many able leaders from the top leadership of the party to direct the party work for several months at a time.[30]

It is not difficult to be critical of the current leadership in the North. Kim has repeatedly condemned the bureaucratic practices in the party, but it is the bureaucracy that has contributed most to the membership of the Central Committee. He has also condemned the nepotism practiced by other groups in the past, but both his wife and his brother are on the Central Committee. Perhaps more important is the gradual but complete change in the character of the leadership with the vigorous recruitment of new leaders, who replace the leaders of various factional groups of the old Communist movement. The allegation that the North is a garrison state because its leaders are not intellectuals and technocrats but rather militarily oriented guerrillas is made with no knowledge of the changes in the leadership of the North. There may be a shortage of leaders in the North, but those that they have are highly trained and, perhaps, most significant, they have been trained by the Korean Communists themselves and are therefore fully integrated into the Korean Communist system.

NOTES

1. *Minjok ŭi t'aeyang Kim Il-sŏng changgun* [The Sun of the Nation, General Kim Il-sŏng] (P'yŏngyang: Inmun kwahak-sa, 1968), p. 1.

2. Article 32 of the bylaws of the Workers' Party of Korea.

3. For other administrative tasks of the Central Committee, see Articles 31–42 of the bylaws. See the interpretation of the bylaws in *Chosŏn nodong-dang kyuyak haesŏl* [Commentary of the Bylaws of the Workers' Party of Korea] (P'yŏngyang: Chosŏn nodong-dang ch'ulp'an-sa, 1969), pp. 204–15.

4. The fifteen Central Committee departments are: Administrative, Agriculture, Communications, Construction and Transportation, Culture and Arts, Fiscal Planning, Fisheries, Foreign Liaison, Heavy Industry, International, Light Industry and Commerce, Military, Organization and Guidance, Propaganda and Agitation, and Science Education.

5. The nine provincial committees are: Chagang, Hambuk, Hamnam, Hwangbuk, Hwangnam, Kangwŏn, P'yŏngbuk, P'yŏngnam, and Yanggang. The thirteen municipal committees are located in the cities of Ch'ŏngjin, Haeju, Hamhŭng,

Hesan, Kaesŏng, Kimch'aek, Namp'o, P'yŏngyang, Sariwŏn, Sinp'o, Sinŭiju, Song-
nim, and Wŏnsan.

6. Article 41 of the bylaws of the party stipulates that the Central Committee can
call a party conference when necessary to discuss urgent policy and tactical problems of the party.

7. For more information on the Workers' Party of Korea in general, see a few
standard works on the party: Chosŏn nodong-dang yŏksa kyojae [Text of the History
of the Workers' Party of Korea] (P'yŏngyang: Chosŏn nodong-dang, ch'ulp'an-sa,
1964); Chosŏn nodong-dang i kŏrŏ-on yŏngkwang sŭroŭn kil [Glorious Path trodden
by the Workers' Party of Korea] (P'yŏngyang: Chosŏn ch'ŏngnyŏn-sa, 1965); Chosŏn
nodong-dang ŭn chosŏn inmin ŭi chido-jŏk mit hyangdo-jŏk yŏngyang ida [The
Workers' Party of Korea is a Leading and Guiding Force of the Korean People]
(P'yŏngyang: Chosŏn nodong-dang ch'ulp'an-sa, 1960). See a South Korean account
of the party by Pang In-hu, Puk-han Chosŏn nodong-dang ŭi hyŏngsong kwa paljŏn
[The Formation and Development of the Workers' Party of Korea in North Korea]
(Seoul: Asea munje yŏn'gu-so, 1967).

8. This phenomenon is most acute in the unknown revolutionary group throughout the five Central Committees, giving some idea as to the relative insignificance of
the group and thus perhaps giving more credence to the analyses of other groups.

9. Most of the fifteen who failed to get re-elected to the fifth party Central
Committee were active as members of the 61-man Executive Section of the second
party conference prior to October 1966.

10. Pang reappeared first at the time of the second party conference as a member
of the Executive Section of the conference. It was reported in Japan that Nam Il was
demoted and was sent to an obscure place in Southeast Asia.

11. For example, Pak Yŏng-bin, a Soviet-Korean who held no official party position, was recruited as a member of the Standing Committee of the Second Party
Congress at its sixth plenum in August 1953 shortly after the Korean War.

12. Yi Chi-ch'an was also a candidate member of the Executive Section of the
second party conference in October 1966, but he was finally elected to the membership of the Central Committee in the fifth congress. Yi was a manager of the Sup'ung
power plant and has long been a vice-minister of the Ministry of Power and Coal
Industries.

13. These men are Ch'oe Chong-gŏn, Kim Hong-gwan, Kim Kwan-sŏp, Kim
Pyŏng-sam, Paek Sŏn-il, Yang Ch'ung-gyŏm, and Yi Hong-gyun.

14. They are Yi Puk-myŏng, Chang Ch'ŏl, and Yi Chang-su. As a member of the
domestic group, Yi was purged soon after his demotion. Chang Ch'ŏl was a member
of the Central Committee and the Inspection Committee of the Second Party Congress. Yi Chang-su was a member of the Central Committee of the Fourth Party
Congress. It is not clear as to why Yi was demoted and Chang reactivated.

15. The members of the Political Committee of the South Korean Workers' Party
were Hŏ Hŏn, Pak Hŏn-yŏng, Yi Ki-sŏk, Kim Sam-yong, Yi Chu-ha, Yi Sŭng-yŏp, Ku
Chae-su, and Kim Yong-am. The Standing Committee consisted of all members of
the Political Committee and the following: Yi Hyŏn-sang, Kang Mun-sŏk, Ko
Ch'an-bo, Yu Yŏng-jun, Kim O-sŏng, and Song Ŭl-su.

16. They were Kim Il-sŏng, Pak Hŏn-yŏng, Kim Ch'aek, Pak Il-u, Hŏ Ka-i, Yi
Sŭng-yŏp, Kim Sam-yong, Kim Tu-bong, and Hŏ Hŏn. The Committee consisted of
two members each from the partisan and Yenan groups, four members from the
domestic group, and a member from the Soviet group.

17. This is Kang Mun-sŏk. For a denunciation of Kang by Kim Il-sŏng, see Kim

Il-sŏng sŏnjip [Selected Works of Kim Il-sŏng], 1960 ed. (P'yŏngyang: Chosŏn nodong-dang ch'ulp'an-sa, 1960), 4:268.

18. Kim Il was considered to have been purged or reprimanded during the Korean War by Kim Il-sŏng. This view seems erroneous. The person Kim Il-sŏng referred to in his speech at the third plenum of the Second Party Congress on December 21, 1950, is a certain major-general of the same name from the Soviet Union. Other prominent partisans were reprimanded such as Yim Ch'un-ch'u and Ch'oe Kwang, but not Kim Il, and perhaps his election to the Political Committee at this time will attest to this. See *Kim Il-sŏng sŏnjip* [Selected Works of Kim Il-sŏng] (1960 ed.), 3:138-42.

19. See Article 36 for the Inspection Committee and Article 40 for the Auditing Committee.

20. The appointment of Kim Chung-nin represents a significant change from the militant posture of the North under General Hŏ Pong-hak. Kim had participated in Communist activities prior to the liberation of Korea in Hamgyŏng Pukto, and was a member of the *Minjok haebang tongmaeng*. He was also a chairman of the Hambuk Provincial Committee of the party, and has long been a member of the Executive Committee of the North Korean Red Cross. He was also a member of the Central Committee of the *Choguk p'yŏnghwa t'ongil wiwŏnhoe*, an organization consisting primarily of the leaders of South Korean origin, which promotes a peaceful unification of Korea. He was a North Korean representative to the Geneva Conference for the discussion of the repatriation of Koreans in Japan to North Korea.

21. *Kim Il-sŏng chŏjak sŏnjip* [Selected Works of Kim Il-sŏng] (P'yŏngyang: Chosŏn nodong-dang ch'ulp'an-sa, 1968), 2:378–79.

22. Ibid., pp. 338–39; speech on February 26, 1959.

23. Chang Chong-yŏp, *Uri tang ŭi kanghwa paljŏn e issŏsŏ reninjŏk tang-kŏnsŏl wŏnch;ŭk ch'angjokŏk kuhyŏn* [The Creative Realization of the Leninist Party Construction Principles in Strengthening and Development of Our Party] (P'yŏngyang: Chosŏn nodong-dang ch'ulp'an-sa, 1963).

24. *Kim Il-sŏng chŏjak sŏnjip*, 3:158-60.

25. Ibid., 1:1–9.

26. *Tang ŭi konggohwa rŭl wihan t'ujaeng* [The Struggle to Strengthen the Party] (P'yŏngyang: Chosŏn nodong-dang ch'ulp'an-sa, 1956).

27. Kim Ch'ang-man, "Chosŏn nodong-dang yŏksa yŏn-gu esŏ chegi doenŭn myŏtkkaji munje," *Kŭlloja*, no. 1 (January 1960), pp. 10–21.

28. *Kim Il-sŏng chŏjak sŏnjip*, 2:340.

29. Hŏ In-hyŏk, *Urinara esŏŭi sahoechuŭi int'eri ŭi hyŏngsŏng kwa changsŏng* [Formation and Growth of Socialist Intelligentsia in Our County] (P'yŏngyang: Chosŏn nodong-dang ch'ulp'an-sa, 1960). Ch'oe Song-uk, *Uri tang ŭi chuch'e sasang kwa sahoechuŭijŏk aeguk chuŭi* [The Thought of Chuch'e and Socialistic Patriotism in Our Party] (P'yŏngyang: Chosŏn nodong-dang ch'ulp'an-sa, 1966).

30. *Kim Il-sŏng chŏjak sŏnjip*, 3:160-61.

7. The 1972 Constitution and Top Communist Leaders

CHONG-SIK LEE

The first session of the fifth Supreme People's Assembly (SPA) of the Democratic People's Republic of Korea (DPRK) adopted the draft of a new constitution on December 27, 1972. It is an interesting document reaffirming the changes that had taken place in North Korea during the previous two decades. It codified some of the ideological principles and policy lines enunciated by the leadership and introduced some changes in the political structure. New institutions were created and the new offices were filled. This paper will attempt to describe some of the salient features of these changes and examine the new structure of authority in North Korea by analyzing both the functions vested in various offices by the constitution and the nature of the leadership.

THE 1972 CONSTITUTION

That the DPRK needed a new constitution cannot be disputed. The old constitution, adopted in 1948, was a document designed for the "bourgeois democratic" stage in North Korea, while the North Korean leadership claimed to have entered the "socialist era" in 1958. In this sense, the drafting of a new constitution was long overdue. The ideological assumptions embodied in the old constitution as well as the political structure it had instituted had long been obsolete, and there had been a critical need to bring the constitution up to date. North Korean jurists were reported to have been engaged in the task of drafting a new constitution as early as 1960.[1]

Evidently, the North Korean leaders decided that they could no longer postpone the constitutional revision. Kim Il-sŏng declared at the first session of the fifth SPA on December 25, 1972, that

> our realities today urgently demand the establishment of a new socialist constitution legally to consolidate the great achievements of our people in the socialist revolution and building of socialism and lay down principles for the political, economic, and cultural spheres in socialist society.[2]

As to the content of the new constitution, the premier declared:

> The new socialist constitution correctly reflects the achievements made in the socialist revolution and building of socialism in our country, defines the principles to govern the activities in the political, economic, and cultural fields in society and the basic rights and duties of the citizens, and stipulates the composition and functions of the state organs and the principles of their activities. It is to protect by law the socialist system and the dictatorship of the proletariat established in the northern half of the republic and to serve the revolutionary cause of the working class.[3]

The principal aim of the new constitution then is to "protect by law" the socialist system and the dictatorship of the proletariat. Thus, while Article 2 of the old constitution stated simply that "the sovereignty of the DPRK resides in the people" without defining who constituted the people, Article 7 of the new constitution states that the "sovereignty of the DPRK rests with the workers, peasants, soldiers and working intellectuals." The DPRK, according to the new constitution, is a "revolutionary state power which has inherited the brilliant traditions . . . ," (Article 3) and that it "exercises the dictatorship of the proletariat and carries through the class and mass lines" (Article 10).[4]

In practical terms, the basic aim of the leaders in drafting the new constitution was to bring the goals and structures of the state into consonance with those of the Workers' Party of Korea (WPK). Although the old constitution contained a few provisions that can be identified with socialism, for example, nationalization of major industries, mineral resources, forests, and waters, it was virtually indistinguishable from the constitution of a non-Communist, democratic state. Meanwhile, vigorous efforts have been made in North Korea to build a "socialist" system of economy, including collectivization of the farms and abolition of all private commerce, and an intensive program to insure thorough ideological change has been enforced. The leadership evidently felt that this change should be reflected in the new constitution.

It is not surprising, therefore, that the wording of the constitutional provisions dealing with "politics" is similar to the preamble of the rules of the WPK. Article 5 of the new constitution states, for example, that

> the DPRK strives to achieve the complete victory of socialism in the northern half, drive out foreign forces on a nationwide scale, reunify the country peacefully on a democratic basis and attain complete national independence.

This provision can be compared with the following paragraphs from the preamble of the rules of the WPK:[5]

The immediate aim of the WPK lies in guaranteeing the complete victory of socialism in the northern half of the republic. . . .

The WPK struggles for the liberation of the southern half of our country from American imperialist aggressive forces and internal reactionary rule. . . .

The WPK successfully carries out the building of socialism in the northern half of our country by consolidating the socialist system, and by mobilizing the creativity of the people. . . .

With respect to power structure, the anomaly was even greater. Since the conclusion of the war in 1953, the state had effectively been turned into an instrument of the party, or of its supreme, unchallenged leader Kim Il-sŏng, and the entire state mechanism, including the SPA and its Presidium, had been subordinated to the party, which had become a super-state. And yet the old constitution had defined the SPA as the supreme, sovereign organ with the highest authority in the state, empowered to establish basic principles concerning domestic and foreign policies. The premier, being the "principal officer of the DPRK," was required to "obey the SPA in the conduct of its activities" (Article 60). The Presidium of the SPA was charged with supervising the "implementation of the constitution and the laws" under the direction of the premier.

One of the first items the new constitution deals with is the relationship between the party and the state. Article 4 states that "the DPRK is guided in its activity by the *chuch'e* (self-identity) idea of the Workers' Party of Korea, which is a creative application of Marxism-Leninism to our country's reality." The implication here is that the DPRK and the WPK are not only inseparable, but that a hierarchical relationship exists, the party being superior to the state. Premier Kim Il-sŏng confirmed this relationship, as he has done on numerous occasions before, on December 25 by saying, "Under our party's wise guidance, the government of the republic has achieved really great successes . . . in the past years."[6]

With the relationship between party and state redefined, the North Korean leaders overhauled the political structure of the DPRK in order that the structure of authority would conform to the reality of power distribution. In doing so, the myth of legislative supremacy embodied in the old constitution was discarded, the supreme authority of the leader legitimized, and the enormous power of the inner circle of the ruling elite institutionalized. These purposes were attained by (1) the creation of a presidency, (2) the establishment of the Central People's Committee, and (3) the emasculation of the Supreme People's Assembly and its Presidium.

NEW INSTITUTIONS

The Presidency

According to Article 89 of the new constitution, the president is the head of state and represents the DPRK. Under the old constitution, there was no one designated as the head of state, and following the Soviet practice, the chairman of the Presidium of the Supreme People's Assembly (SPA, Ch'oe Yong-gŏn) had represented the state. The new presidency will conform to the reality of the supreme power exercised by Kim Il-sŏng. Few states in the world today, if any, can rival North Korea in the extent of adulation, indeed deification, of its leader. Anyone in doubt should read the following announcement of the Korean Central News Agency (KCNA) released December 28, 1972, reporting the election of Kim Il-sŏng as the new president:[7]

> The first session of the fifth Supreme People's Assembly of the Democratic People's Republic of Korea elected as President of the DPRK Comrade Kim Il-sŏng, the great leader of our party and our people, peerless patriot, national hero, ever-victorious iron-willed brilliant commander and one of the outstanding leaders of the international communist movement and working-class movement, who founded the Workers' Party of Korea, an ever-victorious Marxist-Leninist party, and the Democratic People's Republic of Korea, a genuine worker-peasant state, and leads our revolution along the one road of victory.

The president, elected for a four-year term by the SPA, is given all the powers normally held by a strong president. He convenes and presides over meetings of the cabinet (the Administration Council—*Chŏngmu wŏn*), and serves as the supreme commander of the armed forces and as chairman of the National Defense Commission. He promulgates laws and ordinances of the SPA (a function held by the Presidium of the SPA under the old constitution), the decrees of the Central People's Committee, and the decisions of the SPA Presidium. He is also empowered to issue "orders," grant special pardons, ratify or abrogate treaties, and receive the credentials of foreign envoys. Some of these functions had been performed by the SPA Presidium. It should be noted in passing that while the North Korean president is called *chusŏk* and the South Korean counterpart is called *taet'ongyŏng*, both presidents share similar powers.[8]

Some interesting observations can be made about the vice-president, called for by the new constitution of the DPRK as is also true for the secretary and other members of the Central People's Committee, vice-presidents can be recalled by the SPA on the recommendation of the president. The responsibilities of North Korean vice-presidents are also quite different from those of other countries; Article 99 of the constitution states that the vice-president "assist" the president in his work. Unlike in the United States and elsewhere, vice-presidents do not succeed the president in the event of his incapacitation or death.

The intent behind the provisions of the constitution can be clearly seen by the election of Ch'oe Yong-gŏn and Kang Yang-uk as vice-presidents. Although Ch'oe enjoys the number two position in the Central Committee of the WPK and was granted the illustrious title of vice-marshal of the People's Army of Korea in 1953, his role since 1962 has been totally ceremonial as the chairman of the Presidium of the SPA. He was born in 1900, and his age alone makes it rather difficult for him to play an active role. Kang Yang-uk, on the other hand, is not even a member of the WPK, but rather is chairman of the Korean Democratic Party, a paper organization with small membership. He is a Presbyterian minister and has performed useful functions for the DPRK as a front man, particularly in dealing with foreign countries. He has, for example, toured various foreign countries as the head of friendship delegations. It is alleged that he enjoys a high status in North Korea because of his family ties with Kim Il-sŏng, Kang being a maternal granduncle of the supreme leader. The role of the vice-presidents, therefore, is ceremonial, particularly in dealing with foreign countries.

The Central People's Committee

The Central People's Committee (CPC) is designated the "highest leadership organ of sovereignty of the DPRK."[9] Since the SPA is designated simply as the "highest sovereign organ," presumably the CPC is to exercise leadership over the SPA. The CPC is headed by the president and consists of the two vice-presidents of the DPRK, a secretary, and members of the CPC. At present there is a total of twenty-five persons in the CPC. All these officials are elected by the SPA for a term of four years—all of them except the president are to be elected "on the recommendation of the president" (Article 76). In the CPC are concentrated all the important functions that had been assigned to the SPA and its Presidium under the old constitution. Articles 103 and 104 succinctly summarize these functions.[10]

Article 103—The Central People's Committee exercises the following functions and powers: (1) to shape the internal and external policies of the state; (2) to direct the work of the Administration Council of the local People's Assemblies and People's Committees; (3) to direct the work of judicial and procuratorial organs; (4) to guide the work of national defense and State security; (5) to supervise the execution of the Constitution, the laws and ordinances of the Supreme People's Assembly, the orders of the President of the Democratic People's Republic of Korea and the decrees, decisions and directives of state organs which contravene them; (6) to establish or abolish ministries, executive bodies of the Administration Council; (7) to appoint or remove vice-premiers, ministers and other members of the Administration Council; (8) to appoint or recall ambassadors and ministers; (9) to appoint or remove high-ranking officers and confer military titles of general; (10) to institute decorations, titles of honor, military titles and diplomatic grades and confer decorations and titles of honor; (11) to grant general amnesties; (12) to institute or change the administrative division; (13) to declare a state of war and issue mobilization orders in case of emergency.

Article 104—The Central People's Committee adopts decrees and decisions and issues directives.

According to Article 105, the CPC can establish and appoint members of a number of commissions that deal with internal policy, foreign policy, national defense, justice, and security; it can also create other commissions as needed. Presumably, these commissions will be headed by members of the CPC, but the members are not known. It is probably not too farfetched to compare these commissions to the specialized assistants and their staffs in the offices of presidents of the Republic of Korea and the United States.

The Supreme People's Assembly

The SPA retains only certain nominal powers, almost all important state functions having been taken away from it. It still adopts or amends the constitution, laws, and ordinances; but the likelihood that it would take independent initiative was never present, even under the old constitution. It is also empowered to establish the "basic principles of domestic and foreign policies of the state," but it is for the CPC to "shape" these policies. Otherwise, the SPA is left as a legitimizing organ, "electing" such officers as the president and vice-presidents of the DPRK, the Presidium (or standing committee) of the SPA, and the president of the Central Court and of the Central Procurator's Office. As noted, the SPA elects the members and other officers of the CPC "on the recommendation of the president."

Members of the Political Elite

As was amply shown under the old constitution of the DPRK, constitutional provisions alone do not reveal the actual power relationship between one governmental institution and another. Political institutions are, after all, operated by men, and the ultimate power position of a given agency is determined by the power and influence of the occupants of the respective offices. In order to understand properly the significance of the change in the political structure of the DPRK, therefore, one must analyze the relative strength of the occupants of the new and old institutions.

In most non-Communist societies, assessment of the relative power of a given individual would be extremely difficult, particularly if one intended to do so with any precision. Fortunately for students of Communist societies, the task is made considerably easier by the system of rank ordering of the members of the Central Committee of the ruling parties. Each party congress—"the highest organ of the party"—elects members of the Central Committee to direct all party work in the intervals between party congresses, establish party policies, and otherwise keep the party in operation. In the case of the WPK, the Central Committee in turn elects the Political Committee to direct all the activities of the party. A newly elected member of the Central Committee is assigned a rank order that indicates his status within the party hierarchy. This order, of course, is subject to abrupt change. In the WPK, many party leaders with high rank orders have been purged between congresses, and the rank order attained at a given congress does not automatically indicate status during the years before the next congress.

The fifth Congress of the WPK was held in November 1970, only two years before the structural changes in the government were instituted. There had been no indication during the intervening two years that any substantial change had occurred in the power hierarchy of the Central Committee. One can, therefore, use the rank orders given at the fifth Congress to assess the power status of the top elites of North Korea. The fifth Congress elected 117 full members of the Central Committee and 55 candidate members. As can be seen from table 1, the top elite of North Korea are concentrated in the Political Committee (11 full members and 9 alternate members) and the 13-member Secretariat. Some of the top elite figures serve on both committees.

TABLE 1

SELECT LEADERS OF NORTH KOREA — 1973

Name	WPK CC Rank	WPK Political Comm.	WPK Secretariat	DPRK CPC	SPA Standing Comm.	DPRK Admin. Council	Partisan
Kim Il-sŏng	1	x	Gen. Sec.	x		President	P
Ch'oe Yong-gŏn	2	x	x	x		V. President	P
Kim Il	3	x	x	x		Premier	P
Pak Sŏng-ch'ŏl	4	x		x		V. Premier Ch. Comm. of People's Serv.	P
Ch'oe Hyŏn	5	x		x		Defense	P
Kim Yŏng-ju	6	x	x	x			
O Chin-u	7	x	x	x			P
Kim Tong-gyu	8	x	x	x		V. President	P
Sŏ Ch'ŏl	9	x			x		P
Kim Chung-nin	10	x	x	x			
Han Ik-su	11	x	x		x		P
Hyŏn Mu-gwang	12	c	x	x		Ch. Trans. Comu. Comm.	
Chŏng Chun-t'aek	13	c		x		V. Premier	Died, 1973
Yang Hyŏng-sŏp [See note]	14	c	x	x			
Kim Man-gŭm [See note]	15	c	x	x		V. Premier Ch. Ag. Comm.	
Nam Il	16			x		V. Premier Ch. Light Ind. Comm.	
Ch'oe Yong-jin	17	c					P
Hong Wŏn-gil	18			x		V. Premier Ch. Machine Bldg. Ind. Comm.	
Chŏng Kyŏng-hŭi	19						
Kim Yŏ-jung	20						P
O Paek-yong	21						P
Chŏn Ch'ang-ch'ŏl	22				Sec		
Yu Chang-sik [See note]	28			x			
Hŏ Tam	29			x		Foreign Aff.	
Kim Pyŏng-ha	30			x		Pub. Security	
Yim Ch'un'ch'u	34			x (Sec.)			P
Kim Chwa-hyŏk	35	x					P
Yi Kŭn-mo [See note]	54	c			x		P
Yun Ki-bok	57				x		

TABLE 1 — Continued

Name	WPK CC Rank	WPK Political Comm.	WPK Secretariat	DPRK CPC	SPA Standing Comm.	DPRK Admin. Council	Partisan
Ch'oe Chae-u	58	c			x	V. Premier, Ch. State Plan. Comm.	
O Tăe-bong	60		x	x			
Chŏng Chun-gi	62				x		
Yŏn Hyŏng-muk	63	c	x	x			
Kang Sŏng-san	65	[See note]			x		
Kim Sŏng-ae	67	c			x		
Kye Ŭng-t'ae	73					Foreign Trade	
Kim Yŏng-nam	80				x		
Kim I-hun	98				x		
Kim Kyŏng-yŏn	100					Finance	
Hwang Chang-yŏp	102				Ch'rman		
Yi Myŏn-sang	103				x		
Yŏm T'ae-jun	105				x		
Ch'ŏn Se-bong	148				x		
Yi Chong-ok	[See note]				x	Ch. Heavy Ind. Comm.	
Chŏng Tu-hwan	[See note]					Labor Adm.	
O Hyŏn-ju	[See note]				x		
Hŏ Chŏng-suk	[See note]				V.Ch'rman	V. President	
Kang Yang-uk					x	V. President	
Hong Ki-mun					V.Ch'rman		
Pak Sin-dŏk					x		
Yi Yŏng-bok					x		
Yi Tu-ch'an					x		
Han Sŏng-yong						Ship Machine Bldg. Industry	
Kim Hwan						Chem. Ind.	
Kim Yun-sang						Fishery	
Mun Pyŏng-il						Bldg. Materials Ind.	
Kim Sŏk-ki						Education	
Yi Chang-sŏn						Culture and Art	
Kong Chin-t'ae						External Econ. Aff.	
Pak Im-t'ae						Construction	
Yi Nak-pin						Pub. Health	

NOTE: Between 1973 and 1974, the status of some leaders underwent changes. Yi Kŭn-mo (54) and Yang Hyŏng-sŏp (14) were promoted to full members of the Political Committee; Kang Sŏng-san (65) and Yu Chang-sik (28) were appointed candidate members of the Political Committee. Yu was concurrently appointed a member of the Secretariat of the WPK. A person not on the list, Yi Yong-mu (53) was appointed a member of the Political Committee. Yi reportedly replaced Han Ik-su (11) as the director of the General Political Bureau of the Korean People's Army. Kim Man-gŭm (15) was replaced by Sŏ Kwan-hŭi as the chairman of the

Agricultural Commission. So was not a member of the Central Committee of the WPK in 1970; he was last known as the chairman of the Agricultural Management Committee of the City of P'yŏngyang.

In 1961 Yi Chong-ok was number 11, Chŏng Tu-hwan was number 47, and O Hyŏn-ju was number 63. Hŏ Chŏng-suk was number 34 in 1956 but not in 1961.

WPK = Workers' Party of Korea; SPA = Supreme People's Assembly; CPC = Central People's Committee.

Table 2 presents the functional or specialty areas of the top leaders. When an individual holds an office in a certain functional area for a long period of time, it can be regarded as his specialty area because he would have acquired knowledge and experience in that area even if his earlier education and training were not in that field. Some individuals have occupied offices in different functional areas and have held these different offices for extended periods. In those cases, they have been assigned more than one area of functional specialty. A few individuals dealing with foreign trade were assigned two functional areas, that is, economy and foreign affairs.

The Political Committee of the Workers' Party of Korea

Table 1 reveals some interesting phenomena, some obvious and others not so obvious. For example, those who hold rank orders 1 through 17 (with the exception of number 16, Nam Il) are all on the political committee, which confirms the most important decision-making organ of the North Korean power structure. Nam Il is the only survivor of those who returned from the Soviet Union remaining in the top echelon of North Korean leadership, and he had been tainted by his indirect involvement in the 1956 conspiracy against Kim Il-sŏng. His loyalty and ability, however, had restored the leader's trust in him and he was made a member of the Political Committee after the Fourth Party Congress of October 1961 when he was promoted to rank order number 10 from his previous number 23 position. At the Second Party Conference of October 1966, however, he was not a member of the Political Committee.

Except for Kim Yŏng-ju (number 6) and Kim Chung-nin (number 10), all the members of the Political Committee had been partisans in Manchuria under Kim Il-sŏng, although Ch'oe Yong-gŏn, number 2, had led his own unit in Manchuria and joined Kim Il-sŏng much later. These individuals have thus been closely associated with Kim Il-sŏng for nearly four decades, serving as his subordinates in the most trying circumstances. Kim Yŏng-ju is, of course, Kim Il-sŏng's younger brother, and this blood relationship assures his loyalty to the leader.

TABLE 2

FUNCTIONAL SPECIALITY OF NORTH KOREAN LEADERS

Name	WPK CC Rank	Ad-min/ Gen.	Eco-no-my	Mili-tary & Secur-ity	Party	For-eign Aff.	Mass Aux. Orgs.	Mass media/ Cul-ture	SPA Standg. Comm.	Edu-ca-tion
Kim Il-sŏng	1	x								
Ch'oe Yong-gŏn	2								x	
Kim Il	3	x	x							
Pak Sŏng-ch'ŏl	4		x							
Ch'oe Hyŏn	5			x		x				
Kim Yŏng-ju	6				x					
O Chin-u	7			x		x				
Kim Tong-gyu	8					x				
Sŏ Ch'ŏl	9					x			x	
Kim Chung-nin	10									
Han Ik-su	11			x		x				
Hyŏn Mu-gwang	12		x		x					
Chŏng Chun-t'aek	13		x							
Yang Hyŏng-sŏp	14				x					x
Kim Man-gŭm	15		x							
Nam Il	16		x		x	x				
Ch'oe Yong-jin	17			x	x					
Hong Wŏn-gil	18		x							
Chŏng-Kyŏng-hŭi	19									
Kim Yŏ-jung	20			x		x				
O Paek-yong	21									
Chŏn Ch'ang-ch'ŏl	22				x			x		
Yu Chang-sik	28					x				
Hŏ Tam	29					x				
Kim Pyŏng-ha	30			x (security)						
Yim Ch'un-ch'u	34					x			x	
Kim Chwa-hyŏk	35			x	x					

TABLE 2—Continued

Name	No.						
Yi Kŭn-mo	54	x					
Yun Ki-bok	57	x					x
Ch'oe Chae-u	58	x					
O T'ae-bong	60	x					
Chŏng-Chun-gi	62					x	
Yŏn Hyŏng-muk	63				x		
Kang Sŏng-san	65				x		
Kim Sŏng-ae	67			x			
Kye Ung-t'ae	73	x		x			
Kim Yŏng-nam	80	x				x	
Kim I-hun	98	x					
Kim Yŏng-yŏn	100	x				x	
Hwang Chang-yŏp	102					x	
Yi Myŏn-sang	103					x	
Yŏm T'ae-jun	105	x			x	x	
Ch'ŏn Se-bong	148					x	
Yi Chong-ok		x					
Chŏng Tu-hwan		x		x			
O Hyŏn-ju				x			
Hŏ Chŏng-suk		x			x		
Kang Yang-uk				x		x	
Hong Ki-mun				x		x	
Pak Sin-dŏk				x			
Yi Yong-bok							
Yi Tu-ch'an		x					
Han Sŏng-yong		x					
Kim Hwan		x					
Kim Yun-sang		x					
Mun Pyŏng-il		x					
Kim Sŏk-ki							x
Yi Chang-sŏn						x	
Kong Chin-t'ae		x		x		x	
Pak Im-t'ae		x					
Yi Nak-pin		x					

Note: WPK CC = Worker's Party of Korea Central Committee; SPA = Supreme People's Assembly.

Table 2 also raises some doubt about the status of Ch'oe Yong-jin. Since being elected to the Central Committee in 1956 as a candidate member (rank order 25), he has ascended the ladder rapidly, rising to full membership (number 23) in 1961 and to number 17 in 1970. He has also occupied the all-important position of vice-chairman of the Military Affairs Committee, been vice-premier, and served as a general of the People's Army of Korea. But he was not given any of his previous positions in 1972 nor was he assigned to the CPC. The only two other high-ranking members of the Central Committee who were not elected to the CPC are Sŏ Ch'ŏl (number 9) and Han Ik-su (number 11), which can be easily explained by their memberships in the Standing Committee of the SPA. Sŏ Ch'ŏl, one of the oldest leaders in North Korea, had been serving as the chairman of the Diplomatic Committee of the SPA since 1967 and as vice-president of the Presidium since 1970. Han had been a member of the SPA since 1962, but why the director of the General Political Bureau of the Defense Ministry was assigned to the new SPA instead of the Central People's Committee is not known.

It is also uncertain why low-ranking members of the Central Committee of the WPK, such as numbers 54, 58, 63, and 67 were chosen as candidate members of the Political Committee, although the case of number 67 is obvious in that she happens to be the wife of the supreme leader. The only plausible explanation that can be afforded for the others is that both Yi Kŭn-mo (number 54) and Ch'oe Chae-u are technocrats with expertise in industrial fields. The case of number 63, Yŏn Hyŏng-muk, is less certain.

On the basis of table 2, we can compile table 3, which gives the distribution of expertise or functional specialty in the Political Committee. Kim Il-sŏng and Kim Il, the president and the premier, were excluded from table 3 on the grounds that they are general overseers with considerable knowledge about most of the functional areas, but without specialization in any specific functional area. President Kim Il-sŏng, the former partisan leader, has headed the North Korean political structure since 1946. Kim Il, the former company commander under Kim Il-sŏng in Manchuria, has served as a party functionary in charge of local organizations and as a political officer in the army with lieutenant general's rank, has headed a provincial party branch, and has served as minister of agriculture; but since 1957, he has been in charge of over-all administration as vice-premier, and since 1959, as the first vice-premier. He was made premier in 1972.

The Political Committee of the WPK has six experts on the

economy, four on the military, four on foreign affairs, and four with experience in the party's leadership organizations, a fairly even distribution of functional expertise in areas of concern to the leadership. Possession of the personal confidence of Kim Il-sŏng is the foremost criterion for membership in this all-important body, but functional expertise is also significant in the choosing of certain individuals, particularly the younger candidate members. It is significant that none of the nine full members of the Political Committee, excluding Kim Il-sŏng and Kim Il, can be called experts on the economy, and that all five experts on the economy hold candidate rank. The full members of the Political Committee, on the other hand, represent the military, the party, and foreign affairs, and the recruitment of the candidate members was proportioned accordingly.

TABLE 3

DISTRIBUTION OF EXPERTISE IN THE WPK
POLITICAL COMMITTEE, 1972*

Functional or Institutional Areas	*Full Members*	*Candidate Members*	*Total*
Party	2	2	4
Economy	1	5	6
Military	3	1	4
Foreign Affairs	4	0	4
SPA Standing Committee	2	0	2
Mass Organizations	0	1	1
Education	0	1	1

*Some individuals were counted more than once.

Data on the age of the Political Committee members are not complete, but the following should be of interest (table 4):

The top leaders of North Korea are aging and a majority of the members of the Political Committee are over sixty. Although the exact ages of two full members of the Political Committee (Kim Tong-gyu and Kim Chung-nin) are not known, both are in their late fifties or early sixties. Kim Yŏng-ju is probably the youngest of the full members of the committee, and as noted, is the younger brother of President Kim Il-sŏng.

The three oldest members of the Political Committee will probably retire very soon. The oldest, Ch'oe Yong-gŏn, has played no more than a ceremonial role during the last decade or so, and his retirement or death will have little effect on the operation of the top leadership. The second-oldest member of the Political Committee, Sŏ Ch'ŏl, was assigned to the Presidium of the SPA, a position of relative insignificance, in 1972. The other members of the Political Committee still show signs of vitality, and old age is not likely to be a problem for the North Korean leadership for the next several years, although it is questionable whether it could function effectively for another decade. The problem of succession, therefore, is not an immediate problem for the North Korean leadership although it is a potential problem if one looks ten years ahead.

TABLE 4

AGE OF THE WPK POLITICAL COMMITTEE MEMBERS

Name	CC Rank	Year of Birth
Ch'oe Yong-gŏn	2	1900
Ch'oe Hyŏn	5	1907
Sŏ Ch'ŏl	9	1907
Kim Il	3	1912
O Chin-u	7	1910
Kim Il-sŏng	1	1912
Pak Sŏng-ch'ŏl	4	1912
Kim Tong-gyu	8	1915
Han Ik-su	11	1918
Kim Yŏng-ju	6	1922
Kim Chung-nin	10	

The Secretariat of the WPK Central Committee

The Secretariat of the WPK is a very important political organization as it is the body charged with implementing the lines, policies, and resolutions of the party, as well as supervising routine party work. It is also the highest coordinating body in the administrative sphere, handling all personnel and organizational matters. It should be recalled that Joseph Stalin acquired his initial powers within the Communist Party of the Soviet Union under Lenin because he was appointed general secretary. It is only natural in North Korea today that President Kim would concurrently serve as general secretary.

Until 1966, the WPK had operated under the system of chairman and vice-chairmen, but at the fourteenth plenum of the fourth Central Committee held in October 1966, the WPK adopted the system of Secretariat, electing Kim Il-sŏng as general secretary. After the fifth Congress in November 1970, the Central Committee elected nine secretaries to serve under the general secretary.

As can be seen from table 1, there is substantial overlap between the Political Committee and the Secretariat in that only two lower ranking secretaries are not concurrently members of the Political Committee. A certain division of labor exists among the top leaders of the party: those with major administrative or legislative responsibilities in the government are excluded from the Secretariat, including three full members and six candidate members of the Political Committee. Those excluded from the Secretariat include four vice-premiers and vice-chairman of the National Defense Commission. The secretaries implement the policies of the Political Committee within the party organizations; vice-premiers and vice-chairmen implement policies in the respective government branches. This division of labor again accentuates the primacy of the Political Committee in the entire political system of North Korea.

The Central People's Committee

The powers of the newly created Central People's Committee (CPC) have been noted. The provisions of Articles 103 and 104 support the role defined for the CPC in Article 100, that it is the "highest leadership organ of state power."[11] The powers vested in the CPC are similiar to those powers vested by the party rules in the Political Committee and the Secretariat of the WPK.

Having given total powers to the CPC, the North Korean leadership has established a close link between the leading organs of the WPK and the CPC of the DPRK by monopolizing the membership of the latter. Only two full members of the Political Committee are excluded from the CPC and both of them serve on the Standing Committee of the SPA. Only two candidate members of the Political Committee are not on the CPC: Ch'oe Yong-jin, whose case we discussed, and Mrs. Kim Il-sŏng, whose absence probably does not require elaboration.

Out of twenty-five members of the CPC, on the other hand, there are eight who are not members of either the Political Committee or the Secretariat. The names and other positions of these individuals are as follows (rank order is given in parentheses):

Nam Il (16) Vice-premier and chairman of Light Industry Committee

Hong Wŏn-gil (18) Vice-premier and chairman of Machine Building Industry Committee

Yu Chang-sik (28) Former vice-director of International Department of the CC, director of unidentified department as of May 1972

Hŏ Tam (29)	Minister of Foreign Affairs
Kim Pyŏng-ha (30)	Minister of Public Security
Yim Ch'un-ch'u (34)	Secretary of the CPC: former Secretary-General of the SPA Presidium
Ch'oe Chae-u (58)	Vice-premier and chairman of the State Planning Commission
Yi Chong-ok	Chairman, Heavy Industry Committee
Kang Yang-uk	Vice-president, DPRK

It is obvious that these individuals were appointed to the CPC as they are in charge of the specific functional areas: economy (4); foreign affairs (2); public security (1); and one ex-officio.[12] Evidently, Yim Ch'un-ch'u was made the secretary of the CPC because of his previous experience as secretary-general of the Standing Committee of the SPA. Yim's experience as President Kim Il-sŏng's close follower during the partisan days in Manchuria accounts for his selection. It is also extremely interesting that Yi Chong-ok was restored to power not only as the chairman of the Heavy Industry Committee but also as a member of the CPC. An engineer with some underground experience as a Communist before 1945, he had occupied a number of key government and party positions since 1951, including that of minister, chairman of the State Planning Commission, vice-premier, candidate of the Standing Committee of the Central Committee since 1956, and full membership in the Political Committee in 1961. Since 1959, he also served as one of the powerful vice-chairmen of the WPK. His rank order in the Central Committee had climbed rapidly from number 22 in 1956 to number 11 in 1961. For some reason, however, Yi Chong-ok was dropped from the Political Committee at the second party conference of October 1966 but was eighth in the Executive Section along with Nam Il, among others. While Nam Il preserved his Central Committee rank, Yi had been dropped even from the Central Committee at the fifth congress in November 1970.

The party and government positions represented in the membership of the CPC are evidence of the magnitude of power concentrated in the Central People's Committee. The CPC membership includes:

1. The president and all three vice-presidents of the DPRK.
2. Nine of the eleven full members and eight of the nine candidate members of the Political Committee of the WPK.
3. The general secretary and eleven secretaries of the CC.
4. The premier and all six vice-premiers.
5. All six chairmen of state commissions.

6. The chairman and two of the three vice-chairmen of the National Defense Commission.
7. Ministers of defense, foreign affairs, and public security.

The constitutional provisions concerning the Central People's Committee are effectively buttressed by the appointment of key party and government personnel who are actually in a position to know the true state of affairs and who have the means to implement the decisions reached. There is no doubt that the CPC is a super-power agency in which all executive, legislative, and judicial powers are rolled into one.

While the constitution itself says little about the reasons for creating the Central People's Committee, Kim Il-sŏng offered an explanation in his December 25 speech:

> . . . The new state structure is built in such a way that the activities of administrative bodies are always supervised and controlled by the masses of the people. Under the new state structure, unlike the old one, the People's Committees are separated from Administrative bodies, and the former, which are composed of representatives of the workers, peasants, soldiers and working intellectuals, are to perform the function of exercising day-to-day supervision and control over the latter's activities so that the functionaries of the administrative bodies are able to do away with bureaucracy in their work and serve the people better as their servants.[13]

The above paragraph, which was the only reference to the people's committees, may have been sufficient to justify the separation of the people's committees from the administrative committees at the local level (Articles 124 to 132), but it obviously does not explain the case of the Central People's Committee, which was granted enormous powers aside from simple supervision of the cabinet. I would claim that the CPC was created and power was concentrated in it to dispense with the myth of legislative supremacy as well as the fiction of the separation of power and authority between party and state.

Discarding the fiction of separation of power and authority between party and state is likely to contribute to improved efficiency simply by eliminating duplication of efforts. In the past, party offices at various levels maintained rather elaborate staff personnel in various functional areas who were charged with responsibility for drawing up plans and supervising actual operations. The government agencies also maintained a corresponding staff, duplicating some of the efforts. The Agricultural Department in the party headquarters, for example, would draw up a guideline for the Agricultural Commission in the cabinet, which in turn would draw up a detailed plan and return it to the party department for approval. The implementation of the plan would then be subjected to the supervision of the party staff.

While this system guaranteed the implementation of party policies, there is no doubt that it also entailed a considerable waste of manpower. Friction could also develop between staff members of the party and the government. Although no proof has yet been provided by the North Korean authorities, it is quite possible that the special commissions to be established within the CPC will amalgamate some of the functions performed by the party and government staffs in the past. Since most of the important government functionaries are also party members whose loyalty to the leader and the system should be no different from the loyalty of those who staff party departments, the need to maintain duplicate departments at each level may no longer be present. It should be emphasized, however, that this is simply conjecture.

How do the functional specialties represented by members of the Central People's Committee compare with those represented on the Political Committee? Does the composition of the CPC reveal anything noticeable? Table 5 answers these questions.

TABLE 5

FUNCTIONAL SPECIALITY OF THE MEMBERS OF THE CENTRAL
PEOPLE'S COMMITTEE AND THE PC OF THE WPK*

Functional or Institutional Areas	Central People's Committee	Political Committee WPK
Party	4	4
Economy	9	6
Military	3	5
Foreign Affairs	6	4
Education	1	1
SPA Standing Committee	3	2
Mass Organizations	1	1

*Excludes Kim Il-song and Kim Il. While Nam Il had briefly served as the chief of the General Staff during the Korean War, he was not counted as a military expert because of prolonged absence from military affairs. Chŏng Chun-t'aek, who died in early 1973, was counted both in the PC and the CPC.

The presence in the CPC of three additional economy experts and two additional foreign affairs experts is natural as the CPC has five more members than the Political Committee. What is interesting, however, is the remarkable absence of military security personnel in the CPC; only two vice-chairmen of the National Defense Commission and the minister of Public Security are present in the CPC in spite of the constitutional provision that the CPC "guide the work of national defense and state security." As previously mentioned, Generals Sŏ Ch'ŏl and Han Ik-su were assigned to the Presidium of the SPA rather than to the CPC. General Ch'oe Yong-jin, the other military leader in the Political Committee, was not assigned to the CPC, as noted earlier. Neither were any of the numerous generals serving in the Central Committee of the WPK appointed to the CPC. It should be pointed out that military leaders are heavily clustered in ranks 30 through 53 in the Central Committee (those holding ranks 31, 35, 36, 37, 38, 39, 40, 44, 45, 46, 47, 48, 50, 52, and 53 are high-ranking generals), which indicates that the CPC will have rather limited power over military affairs, and that the conduct of defense will be entrusted to the National Defense Commission.

The National Defense Commission (NDC) is a creature of the CPC in that Article 105 of the constitution grants it the authority to establish the NDC as well as the power to appoint and remove members of various commissions including the NDC, but its independence is assured by other constitutional provisions. Article 93 states that the president of the DPRK shall concurrently serve as the supreme commander of the armed forces and as chairman of the NDC. Article 76 states, on the other hand, that the Supreme People's Assembly shall elect and/or recall the vice-chairmen of the NDC at the proposal of the president of the DPRK.

Finally, the CPC membership list released by the North Korean authorities varies somewhat from the rank orders assigned at the Fifth Party Congress. It is customary in all Communist societies for the order in which individuals are listed to signify the rank of the individuals involved. A change in the order in which the individuals are listed, therefore, signifies certain changes in their status. In December 1972, just two years after the fifth congress of the WPK, the North Korean leadership appears to have decided on certain changes.

The following is the order in which the members of the CPC were listed in all official publications. The number designates the rank order assigned to these individuals at the fifth congress.

2	Ch'oe Yong-gŏn	5	Ch'oe Hyŏn
	Kang Yang-uk	7	O Chin-u
3	Kim Il	8	Kim Tong-gyu
4	Pak Sŏng-ch'ŏl	6	Kim Yŏng-ju

10 Kim Chung-nin	34 Yim Ch'un-ch'u
12 Hyŏn Mu-gwang	63 Yŏn Hyŏng-muk
14 Yang Hyŏng-sŏp	60 O T'ae-bong
13 Chŏng Chun-t'aek	16 Nam Il
15 Kim Man-gŭm	18 Hong Wŏn-gil
54 Yi Kŭn-mo	28 Yu Chang-sik
58 Ch'oe Chae-u	29 Hŏ Tam
Yi Chong-ok	30 Kim Pyŏng-ha

The placement of Kang Yang-uk immediately behind Ch'oe Yong-gŏn is understandable in that Kang was made the second vice-president of the republic. By placing Kim Yŏng-ju, rank 6 in the Central Committee, behind Kim Tong-gyu, the party may be indicating that the current director of Organization and Guidance of the Central Committee of the WPK has encountered some difficulties. Reportedly, Kim has been suffering from "toxic neurasthenia" (mental depression), and has not appeared in public since July 1972, when he was made cochairman of the North-South (Korean) Coordinating Committee. Pak Sŏng-ch'ŏl has been acting for Kim Yŏng-ju since that time. It is also highly significant that six individuals, Yi Kŭn-mo (54), Ch'oe Chae-u (58), Yi Chong-ok (nonmember of the CC), Yim Ch'un-ch'u (34), Yŏn Hyŏn-muk (63), and O T'ae-bong (60) have been placed ahead of those with rank orders between 16 and 30. We alluded to Ch'oe Chae-u earlier. On December 28, 1972, he was concurrently appointed one of the six vice-premiers as well as the chairman of the National Planning Commission. Obviously, Ch'oe is a man on the rise. His status and power is likely to rise faster now that the other technical expert and vice-premier, Chŏng Chun-t'aek, has passed away. It should also be noted that Ch'oe was placed ahead of Nam Il and Hong Wŏn-gil in the list of vice-premiers. Yi Kŭn-mo (54) is also a man on the rise. In October 1973, he was appointed a candidate member of the Political Committee of the WPK.

The State Administrative Council

The cabinet under the old constitution was redesignated *Chŏngmu wŏn*, officially translated as the Administration Council. The old cabinet was responsible only to the SPA and its Standing Committee, but the new cabinet is responsible to the SPA, the president of the DPRK, and the Central People's Committee.[14] The Administration Council is headed by a premier, and consists of six vice-premiers, commission chairmen, and ministers. The new constitution also provides for a Permanent Commission of the cabinet appointed by the premier. The new cabinet no longer engages in the "guidance of local sovereign organs" as provided by the old constitution; no change was introduced in cabinet functions.

Along with the change in the name of the cabinet, the cabinet of the DPRK underwent some structural changes. The thirty-seven old ministries and committees or commissions were reduced to twenty-two units. The State Planning Commission and Agricultural Commission as well as thirteen old ministries were retained with the same titles, five new commissions were created, and some of the old ministries were abolished.

The intent of the reorganization was to provide tighter control by the elite over important economic affairs and to facilitate better coordination between related sectors of the economy. The first point is evinced by five of the seven commissions being headed by the vice-premiers and the other two being headed by Hyŏn Mu-gwang, rank order number 12 of the Central Committee, concurrently a secretary and candidate member of the Political Committee, and Yi Chong-ok, rank order number 11 in the fourth Central Committee. Instead of the vice-premiers supervising indirectly given sectors of the government as in the past, the vice-premiers are now responsible directly for certain areas of the economy. Whether the new commissions, which are in fact superministries, will function more efficiently than the old structure remains to be seen, but the assignment of top leaders as heads of these commissions, and the regrouping of ministries indicate a wish for better coordination among related ministries. The creation of the Commission of Service for the People may indicate the government's desire to meet consumer demands. The head of that commission, Pak Sŏng-ch'ŏl, has also been serving as the acting cochairman of the North-South Coordinating Committee, which was created to conduct the negotiations between North and South Korea.

Who will be appointed to the Permanent Commission of the new cabinet can be seen from the party ranking of the elite assigned to the cabinet. As shown in table 1, ten of the fifteen ministers are not even members of the fifth Central Committee of the WPK and seven of these attained ministerial posts for the first time in 1972. The ministers of the Ship Machine Building Industry and of Public Health were also in the previous cabinet, but they were not in the Central Committee. The minister of Labor Administration had held rank number 47 in the fourth Central Committee, but was dropped from the fifth Central Committee. The ministers of Culture and Chemical Industry were newly promoted from vice-ministerial positions. Four ministers are completely new faces, presumably younger, new elite emerging from the rank and file with technical expertise in their respective fields. The contrast between these new individuals and the old elite who hold such important positions as ministers of People's Armed Forces (Ch'oe Hyŏn, number 5) and Foreign Affairs (Hŏ Tam, number 29) is sharp. The wide gap in status and power between the old and the new elites probably necessitated the establishment of the Standing Committee within the cabinet. The system of a two-layer cabinet would permit the advancement of the younger elite to cabinet rank while avoiding the embarrassment of having old and new cabinet members on equal terms.

The Standing Committee of the Supreme People's Assembly

Earlier it was noted that the 1972 constitution virtually stripped the Standing Committee of the SPA of any real power. All of its previously important functions were transferred to either the president of the DPRK or the Central People's Committee.

The change in the status of the Standing Committee of the SPA was directly reflected in the personnel assigned to it. The Standing Committee of the fourth SPA, elected in December 1967, contained some of the more important leaders of North Korea; the new Presidium consists of individuals best characterized as peripheral figures. Tables 6 and 7 reveal the marked contrast.

The Standing Committee of the fourth SPA contained a number of important party officials. Not only did they hold high party rank, four of the Presidium members were WPK Political Committee members (three, if Pak Chŏng-ae is excluded) and five others were candidate members of the Political Committee. Three of the nine party officials were concurrently secretaries of the WPK. There were indeed the top level leaders of the party. The Standing Committee of the fifth SPA, by contrast, contains only two Political Committee members and a candidate member of the Political Committee, who happened to be Mrs. Kim Il-sŏng. Only three members of the Central Committee of the party holding ranks above 50 are serving in the Standing Committee of the fifth SPA, while nine out of eleven members of the Central Committee serving in the Standing Committee of the fourth SPA held ranks above 41. The chairman of the Standing Committee of the fourth SPA was Ch'oe Yong-gŏn, the holder of number 2 rank in the WPK; the new chairman in the fifth SPA is Hwang Chang-yŏp, rank 102, the president of Kim Il-sŏng University.

TABLE 6

MEMBERS OF THE STANDING COMMITTEE OF THE FOURTH SUPREME PEOPLE'S ASSEMBLY

Name	WPK/CC rank	WPK positions*	Position within the Standing Committee
Ch'oe Yong-gŏn	2	Sec/Pol Com	Chairman
Hong Myŏng-hŭi			Vice-Chairman
Pak Chŏng-ae	7	Pol Com**	Vice-Chairman
Kang Yang-uk			Vice-Chairman
Yi Yŏng-ho	28	Pol Com	Vice-Chairman
Pak Mun-gyu	60		Chief Secretary
Ch'oe Hyŏn	18	Pol Com	
Hŏ Pong-hak	22	Sec/Pol Com (C)	
Kim Yŏng-ju	41	Sec/Pol Com (C)	
Yi Kuk-chin	29		
Ch'oe Kwang	31	Pol Com (C)	
O Chin-u	25	Pol Com (C)	
Kim Tong-gyu	40	Pol Com (C)	
Pak Sin-dŏk			
Kim Yŏ-jung			

*Party position refers to those elected at the Second Party Conference in October 1966. Sec = Secretary; Pol Com = Political Committee; (C) = nonvoting candidate member.

**Pak Chŏng-ae was elected a member of the Political Committee in September 1961 after the Fourth Party Congress, but she was dropped from the committee at the Second Party Conference in October 1966.

TABLE 7

MEMBERS OF THE STANDING COMMITTEE OF THE FIFTH SUPREME PEOPLE'S ASSEMBLY

Name	5th WPK/CC rank	WPK position*	Positions in the Standing Committee of the SP
Hwang Chang-yŏp	102		Chairman
Hong Ki-mun			Vice-Chairman
Hŏ Chŏng-suk			Vice-Chairman
Sŏ Ch'ŏl	9	Pol Com	
Han Ik-su	11	Pol Com/Sec	
Chŏn Ch'ang-ch'ŏl	22		Secretary
Pak Sin-dŏk			
Kim Yŏng-nam	80		
Chŏng Chun-gi	62		
Yŏm T'ae-jun	105		
Kim Sŏng-ae	67	Pol Com (C)	
Kim I-hun	98		

TABLE 7 — *Continued*

Name	5th WPK/CC rank	WPK position*	Positions in the Standing Committee of the SP
Yi Yŏng-bok			
Yun Ki-bok	57		
Yi Tu-ch'an			
Kang Sŏng-san	65		
O Hyon-ju			
Ch'ŏn Se-bong	31		
Yi Myŏn-sang	103		

*Party positions as of November 1970. Pol Com = Political Committee.

The Standing Committee of the fifth SPA is noteworthy for the prominence of intellectuals and others who are well known in South Korea. Only one member of the fourth Presidium could be so classified: Hong Myŏng-hŭi, a famous novelist and scholar. In the fifth Presidium, however, are the following:

Hwang Chang-yŏp, the chairman: president of Kim Il-sŏng University.

Hŏ Chŏng-suk, vice-chairwoman: daughter of Hŏ Hŏn, a famous lawyer of South Korean origin. Hŏ Chŏng-suk earned fame in her own right before 1945 for her socio-political activities and her escape to Yenan, China.

Chŏng Chun-gi: editor-in-chief of *Nodong Sinmun*, the organ of the WPK; chairman of the Korean Reporters' Union.

Ch'ŏn Se-bong: writer; chairman of the Korean Writers' Union.

Yi Myŏn-sang: composer; chairman of the Korean Musicians' Union.

Of particular interest is the election of Hong Ki-mun and Hŏ Chŏng-suk as vice-chairpersons. Hong, son of Hong Myŏng-hŭi referred to above, went to North Korea from Seoul in late 1947; he continued his academic work, became a professor at Kim Il-sŏng University, and was elected to the Academy of Science in 1964. He was elected to the first SPA in 1948 as a representative from South Korea, but since then his only political activity has been confined to membership in the Central Committee of the Committee for the Peaceful Unification of the Fatherland. His only political writings and speeches known to the outside world have been the call for the peaceful unification of Korea supporting, of course, the line of the WPK. Hŏ Chŏng-suk, on the other hand, has served in various ministerial positions since her return from Yenan in 1945, and even after her husband, former vice-premier Ch'oe Ch'ang-ik, was purged in

1956, she continued her political career, being appointed head of the Supreme Court in 1959. But, she was retired from the party's Central Committee in 1961 and no word has been heard about her since. From 1957 until her retirement, she had been prominent in the Democratic Front for the Unification of the Fatherland.

The restoration of Hŏ Chŏng-suk at the age of 70 and her appointment as vice-chairwoman of the Standing Committee of the fifth SPA along with Hong Ki-mun can be interpreted in only one way: the North Korean leadership desired individuals well known in South Korea in officially prominent positions in order that the contacts with South Korean personalities should function more smoothly and the North Korean line of argument should be communicated more effectively. Certainly, South Korean legislators and intellectuals would find it easier to build rapport with old acquaintances than with generals of guerrilla background. While other intellectuals on the Standing Committee are not as well known in the South, they would share more common ground than the other elite of the North, a line of analysis all the more plausible as the election of the members of the Standing Committee occurred only five months after the epochal joint communique of July 4, 1972, that launched the North and South negotiations.

The SPA continues to serve as the legitimizing organ for the DPRK, but the Standing Committee has in effect become an institution concerned with the party's efforts in South Korea.

CONCLUDING OBSERVATIONS

Our analysis of the constitutional revision as well as the personnel assigned to various old and new institutions shows that the constitutional structure of the DPRK was altered to conform to the reality that has existed in North Korea during the last two decades; in the process, the monolithic structure around President Kim Il-sŏng has been further consolidated. Kim Il-sŏng is not only the head of the party, he is also the chief of state, and concurrently head of the military establishment. Although he has wielded power in all three spheres for some time, only in 1972 were these facts legally documented.

The assignment of personnel to various institutions also shows that about fifteen of the president's close followers constitute the inner circle of power or the top echelon elite in North Korea. These men hold membership in the party's Political Committee, form the upper crust of the Central People's Committee, and serve as the premier and vice-premiers of the Administration Council. They also control the army by being vice-chairmen of the National Defense Commission. These men have been with President Kim Il-sŏng for more than four decades, having begun their political careers as guerrillas, and they seem to be implicitly trusted by him, although, if experience of the past several years can serve as a guide, this trust can be abruptly withdrawn. For the moment, however, no doubt can be raised about the power of these men.

The pattern of personnel assignment in the North Korean power structure reveals a trend toward functional specialization among the top elite in North Korea. Until about ten years ago, many of the top elite circulated with relative ease among the military, government, and party posts. But, there now seems to be a trend in North Korea to reduce this movement and to let each individual develop his specialty in a given area. As indicated above, very few professional military men were assigned to party or governmental posts in 1972. Only those with considerable technical expertise become vice-premiers and ministers. Such individuals as Yi Chong-ok were reinstated to important economic posts even after they had been dropped from the Central Committee. We are perhaps witnessing the compartmentalization of the North Korean elite into military, party, and state functionaries. Of course, all components of power revolve around the president and the Political Committee of the WPK, and, as was discussed earlier, the Central People's Committee will serve as another institution where party-state coordination will be realized. But, possibilities always exist for the military to develop into a separate institution with its own special interests. The role of such men as Ch'oe Hyŏn, the minister of defense, O Chin-u, the chief of the General Staff, and Han Ik-su, the director of the General Political Bureau of the Korean People's Army, as a link between the army and the Political Committee is, therefore, important.

Although President Kim Il-sŏng asserted that the new constitution would better reflect the opinion of the masses in the conduct of government business, the power of the Supreme People's Assembly was emasculated. The president's assertion can be accepted only if one pays homage to the idea of democratic centralism, which serves as the guiding organizational principal of all Communist societies. Even so, Kim's interpretation of that concept is far more restrictive than any organizational version hitherto tried in the Soviet Union and other socialist states.

NOTES

1. See L. M. Gudoshnikov, "Among the Lawyers of the Korean People's Democratic Republic," in *Sovetskoe Gosudarstvo i pravo* [Soviet State and Law], no. 10 (1960), p. 116, cited by George Ginsburgs, "Soviet Sources on the Law of North Korea," *Journal of Korean Affairs*, January 1972, p. 61.

2. *Nodong sinmun*, December 26, 1972. For English version, see *Korea Today*, no. 196 (1973), p. 3.

3. Ibid., p. 12.

4. For an English text of the new constitution, see ibid., pp. 24–30.

5. For the English text of the rules of the WPK as amended on September 16, 1961, see Robert A. Scalapino and Chong-Sik Lee, *Communism in Korea*, 2:1331–49 (Berkeley: University of California Press, 1972).

6. *Korea Today*, no. 196 (1973), p. 11.

7. Ibid., p. 2.

8. Article 43 of the new ROK constitution says: The president shall be the head of the State and represents the State vis-à-vis foreign states.

9. Article 100 of the constitution of the DPRK. See FBIS *Daily Report*, January 17, 1973, no. 12, supplement 3, p. 24.

10. See the new constitution in English in *Korea Today*, no. 196 (1973), pp. 24–30.

11. Article 100. The Central People's Committee is the highest leadership organ of state power in the Democratic People's Republic of Korea.

12. *Economy:* Nam Il; Hong Wŏn-gil; Ch'oe Chae-u; Yi Chong-ok. *Foreign Affairs:* Yu Chang-sik; Hŏ Tam. *Public Security:* Kim Pyŏng-ha; *ex-officio:* Kang Yang-uk.

13. *Korea Today*, p. 14.

14. Article 113. The Administration Council bears responsibility for its work before the Supreme People's Assembly, the president of the Democratic People's Republic of Korea and the Central People's Committee.

PART V

Concluding Observations

8. Toward a Theory of Korean Political Leadership Behavior

GLENN D. PAIGE

In this final chapter we will attempt to summarize our impressions about goals, felt needs, methods, and findings in the study of Korean political leadership behavior. We are hopeful that this effort will suggest useful points of departure for subsequent work.

THE QUESTION OF SCHOLARLY GOALS

The clearer we are about the goals in political leadership research, the more aware we are of alternatives, the more rigorous we are about translating goals into research operations, and the more tolerant we are of diverse but high quality efforts to achieve objectives, the more satisfying will be the results of our collective scholarly efforts. At least five main goals are clear.

A primary goal is *to describe, explain, and predict Korean political leadership behavior.* We need a basic description of political leadership behavior. We require theoretical explanations and interpretations of what we are able to describe. And we seek ultimately to predict, within known limits of error, future behavior, either in the laboratory or in the field. We want to understand Korean political leadership behavior in its own context and with an increasing sense of satisfaction in the richness of our description, in the cogency of our interpretations, and in the accuracy of our predictions. Furthermore, we seek a growing sense of total comprehension, which may have to be created out of fragmented, apparently unrelated inquiries.

A second goal, essential to the accomplishment of the first, is *to achieve greater insight into the nature of Korean political leadership behavior by comparing it with political leadership behavior in other societies.* Our discussions include efforts to clarify what is distinctly Korean by comparisons with Chinese, Japanese, Russian, American, or other relevant political leadership behavior. We can appreciate the distinctive qualities of Korean political behavior through combined use of two approaches: a direct attempt to understand Korea on its own terms; and an effort to make comparisons that highlight distinctions. We are interested also in discovering similiarities of outcomes and processes through comparison.

The interest in comparison suggests a third goal, which is to gain a *general understanding of political leadership behavior* by creating concepts and testing hypotheses derived from or applied to Korea. From the experiences gained from these studies on Korea —traditional, colonial, in divided development, and in potential reintegration—we wish to gain knowledge of political leadership behavior that can be generalized.

A fourth goal, which has been ignored in this symposium, but which deserves explicit discussion is *to assist actual or potential leaders in performing their functions.* As the direct application of scholarship to political leadership performance is implied by this goal, its pursuit will affect the kinds of problems that are researched, the research designs employed, and the disposition of the findings. This kind of research, which can be designed to assist incumbents, conventional competitors, and counterconventional leaders in their efforts, is the only kind of research allowed in some societies. Other societies fear such research as potential instigation of a pernicious symbiosis between a manipulative elite and a sycophantic intelligentsia. But where independent, scholarly research has a strong foundation, perhaps socially useful research designed to improve political leadership performance can be accomplished to the mutual benefit of leaders and researchers—as well as the people as a whole.

A fifth goal, which raises the question of the societal usefulness of social science knowledge, is *to improve citizen competence.* Goals would be to make all citizens aware of the nature, qualities, composition, and processes of their political leadership, which should allow citizens to make more informed social choices. It can be argued that the citizenry of future societies should at least have as much information available to them about their leaders as the latter have about them in the form of opinion polls, survey research, and governmental statistics.

As research on Korean political leadership progresses, one or more of these goals in various emphases is likely to be pursued. They should be subjected to continuous critical evaluation by scholars, political leaders, and other citizens.

FELT NEEDS ARISING OUT OF PRESENT RESEARCH EFFORTS

In the course of our discussions, several ways to improve future research on Korean political leadership became clear.

The first is the need for *the creation of a functionally equivalent systematic overview that would facilitate comparative interpretation of Korean political leadership behavior over time.* To illustrate this, consider the problem of comparing the political leadership behavior of (a) the Yi dynasty kings, (b) the Japanese governors-general, (c) the presidents of the Republic of Korea, and (d) the premiers of the Democratic People's Republic of Korea. To make such a combined historical and contemporary comparison we need an explicit theory that would describe and explain the political system of the Yi dynasty, colonial Korea, and the present divided configurations. Several alternative conceptions of a political system are available as point of departure. These include such frameworks as structural-functional analysis, power analysis, Marxist-Leninist class analysis, value allocation analysis, and decision-making analysis. To describe and interpret the roles of king, governor-general, president, or premier requires some kind of understanding of how a given incumbent functions in relation to other elements of society. Simply put, to accomplish this we need to create inductively or to apply deductively some conceptual frameworks that will permit comparison across historical periods. For example, how are we to compare political leadership at the village level during the Yi dynasty, the Japanese occupation, and now in North and South Korea? Or how are we to compare the roles of provincial governors? Each historical period may have its own institutions, role relations, and procedures. Yet each, viewed from a higher level of abstraction, can also be expected to share common elements. In each period, for example, somebody made and somebody attempted to carry out authoritative decisions. And various elements of the population provided support, voiced opposition, or showed indifference.

Another way of expressing the need for functionally equivalent systemic overviews is to state that we do not have a fully satisfactory model of Yi dynasty political processes, we have an even hazier comprehension of Korea under Japanese control, and we still do not have adequate summaries of the political processes in either North or South Korea. The problem may be handled by creating four different models to fit each period, and then seeking to perceive common elements. Or we can approach all four in terms of an a priori conceptual framework, and then adjust the model to take empirical variations into account. Such a model does not now exist in Korean political science, and we suffered from this lack.

A second felt need was for *comparative data on political leader-*

*ship composition and behavior at all levels in North and South
Korea since 1945.* These data can help answer questions such as the
following: (a) Are there distinctive continuities reaching back to the
Yi dynasty? (b) Are different bases of social recruitment associated
with different public policy preferences? (c) What accounts for the
different attitudes of leaders with similar socioeconomic backgrounds? (d) What is the potential range of decision latitude of
political leaders in relation to other societal leaders? (e) Have different value systems espoused by political leaders actually been
translated into concrete social conditions, and so forth? The questions to be asked are many. All we wish to express here is that
comparison of North and South Korean leadership was felt by us to
be essential for the advancement of Korean political leadership
studies. Furthermore, because of Korea's remarkable potential as a
"natural social science laboratory," we believe that research on
Korea can offer some extraordinary insights, which can be
generalized. It is not too much to suggest that the whole subdiscipline of comparative political science might benefit from a penetrating analysis of parallel changes in North and South Korea since
1945.

A third requirement for research on Korea that emerged from our
symposium was a need for *three-dimensional conceptualization*,
by which is meant incorporation of the following three different
viewpoints: (a) the "inside view" of how behavior is interpreted by
Korean political leaders themselves, (b) the conceptualizations and
interpretations known by the emerging multicultural social science
community, and (c) the creative concepts of the individual researcher.

Our discussions led us to appreciate the fruitfulness of viewing
each of these three conceptual strategies as complementary tools in
arriving at sound, scientific understanding. We could envision the
usefulness of moving back and forth among the three points of view
in order to create theory that is (a) faithful to Korean reality and to
Korea's potential distinctiveness, (b) enriched by the accomplishments of the social science community, and (c) sharply challenged
and advanced by the inventiveness of the individual or group in-
vestigator. We suspect that creative interaction among these three
will lead us to the kind of political leadership theory that allows
universal insights to be drawn. Furthermore, the skillful application of these three viewpoints to a given problem offers a means for
liberating the human intellect from the imprisoning dogmas of any
one of the constitutent points of view.

A fourth felt need is obtaining *more precise descriptions and interpretations of political leadership at the highest level of formal authority.* There is some evidence that suggests the critical importance of the king, governor-general, president, or premier for the functioning of the Korean political leadership system, but we need to know more about the daily decision-making contributions of the incumbents of this highest position. We need also to understand more about the processes by which the influence of the central leader diffuses throughout the Korean political system or by which such diffusion is attenuated. Among diffusion processes that we think require investigation are modeling behavior; the tacit encouragement of supportive behavior; persuasion; personnel recruitment, promotion, and assignment behavior; resource allocation reinforcements; direct coercive intervention; and the provision of organizing symbols, concepts, and ideologies. We recognize that careful comparative analysis of the highest formal position is a crucial requirement for the advancement of political leadership studies in any society.

A fifth clear need was for *the engagement of colleagues from the various social and behavioral sciences in the development of Korean political leadership studies.* For example, where questions of personality arose, we felt the need for the insights of personality psychologists. On questions of organizational behavior, we recognized the potentially important contributions of sociologists and anthropologists. In seeking more explicit theoretical models we recognized the potential contributions of economic theorists who might be interested in political leadership behavior. Thus, we reaffirm here the need for the creation of a multidisciplinary community to advance the study of Korean political leadership. It cannot be satisfactorily accomplished by scholars alone. We look forward someday to engaging political leaders themselves and other concerned laymen in the identification of research problems, the perfection of research designs, and the interpretation of research findings.

METHODOLOGICAL REFINEMENT

Our joint research experience taught us that methodological refinement is necessary if the study of Korean political leadership is to advance. Four areas where greater methodological precision would be helpful are clear:

1. *The need for greater precision in the definition of socioeconomic status variables.* As an example, consider the cate-

gory "farmer," which we find listed as the occupation of fathers of bureaucrats. We need to know what kind of farmer (large, small, tenant, owner, etc.), if the data are to be useful. A similar effort is needed to achieve precision in other conventional socioeconomic status variables. For example, not just "educational level," but an indication of the kind of education; not just "religion," but an effort to measure intensity; not just "years of military service," but specification of its content, not just "profession," but specification of the vocation.

2. *The need for perfection of methods that will assist in interpreting the large numbers of "don't know," "no response," or "undecided" responses.* This has been a continuing problem for Korean social science and it arose again in these studies. We discussed several alternative explanations for the "don't know" response and those of a similar nature. These included: (a) biasing effects, including incomprehensibility of the wording of either the question or the "don't know" item itself; (b) effects of interviewer's age, sex, and social status upon the respondent; (c) need for social approval, desire to please the interviewer or sponsors of the survey; (d) fear of political retaliation or punishment for unfavorable responses; (e) conflict among alternative choices leading to inability to decide; (f) disinterest and boredom with the subject and the interview; (g) lack of knowledge or opinion; and (h) modesty and uncertainty about one's opinion.

Among the devices considered to increase the interpretability of these responses was to conduct in-depth interviews with a subsample of respondents to explore explicitly the reasons for such responses. In these interviews each respondent would be given a copy of the frequency distribution of the results and then asked to discuss (a) why "other people" might have given the results and (b) why they themselves had given the response if they had done so. Or, in-depth exploration of alternative reasons for "don't know" responses might be conducted at the end of a regular interview, when the nature of the inquiry had become clearer to the respondent and when, it is hoped, a degree of rapport had been established between the interviewer and respondent. On the basis of these unstructured explorations, we thought that possible reasons such as the eight suggested in the foregoing paragraph might be included as probes to the meaning of "don't know" responses in future survey research.

3. *The need for research designs that permit comparative analysis between leader-based and follower-based viewpoints.*

Such designs have become customary in studies of industrial sociology where, for example, the responses of foremen about supervisory practices are compared with reports on the foreman's behavior obtained from the workers themselves. Clearly, we need to apply this kind of methodology to political leadership studies. If both leaders and followers agree on the description and interpretation of behavior, we may have greater confidence in our results. Where leaders and followers disagree, we have additional data for interpreting the meaning of either response. Leader-follower comparative studies can range from studies of close, staff interactions to mutual perspectives of leaders and followers separated by social distance.

4. *The need for more precise operationalization of concepts coupled with the need for making these concepts more system-relevant.* One of the most stimulating discussions focused upon the concept of "alienation" and its significance for political leadership in the Korean political system. We wanted to know the concrete indicators of this concept and whether these indicators were to be interpreted as disposing the polity toward apathetic resignation or revolutionary agitation. Several other concepts posed the same problem: what are their empirical referents and how do they function in a larger context of empirical or theoretical relationships?

SOME CHARACTERISTICS OF KOREAN POLITICAL LEADERSHIP

Some impressions of Korean political leadership that have emerged from this symposium are recorded. We realize that further research will confirm some of them, reject others, and raise entirely new questions.

Operational concepts of leadership by leaders themselves. A thorough inquiry into this subject needs to be made from the point of view of traditional rulers, the Japanese colonial controllers, and the leaders in North and South Korea since 1945. The essay by James Palais is a beginning for the Yi dynasty. We note the outlines of Yi rulership composed of (1) influence by moral example and of (2) neutral mediation or arbitration of factional disputes. We also need to inquire into the roots of the paternal idea of ruling on behalf of the people's welfare. Our study included no inquiry into concepts of rulership practiced by Japanese power figures or by the Korean resistance leaders. Eventually, we would hope to integrate ideas about rulership from the Yi and new elements introduced in the 1910–1945 period. Was there a weakening of traditional ideas of moral suasian in favor of granting the top ruler coercive power? Did the emerging counterconcepts allow more coercion than did the traditional competitive style of superior ideological purity? Or were ideas about legitimation and the uses of coercion left relatively undisturbed by the Japanese colonial interlude? And what happened to concepts of leadership at the village level, as compared with those in Yi conditions and in the divided state? Similarly we did not compare conceptions of leadership that have been held by Kim Il-sŏng in the North and various leaders in the South.

Personae. One impression gained from our study is that a century of historical development has tended to push the bases of Korean elite recruitment downward from higher to lower classes. This may be more pronounced in the North than in the South, although characteristic of both. The militarization of elites as a result of the anti-Japanese or pro-Japanese struggle and the Korean War is also probable. It was pointed out in chapter 4 that a large number of bureaucratic elite in South Korea, unlike their predecessors of the Yi dynasty, had military experience. It is likely that age levels are going down, a subject that requires investigation: are the core powerholding groups in both North and South less well "educated" as compared both with comparable Yi dynasty and Japanese groups? Do we have a situation in South Korea where the top political leaders do not possess attributes highly regarded by the population at large?

These are only a few of the questions that need to be asked about the personal characteristics of the individual men and women who have occupied or who may be recruited into political leadership roles.

Role. Both North and South Korea have seen the progressive revision of political leadership roles to legitimate exercise by the top executive. This has been more pronounced in Seoul than in P'yŏngyang. Temporarily, Pak Chŏng-hŭi has established the complete supremacy of the president over the legislature, a supremacy that was comparatively ineptly sought by Syngman Rhee. Except for the Chang Myŏn interlude, in which a brief experiment with a premiership based upon parliamentary democracy was attempted, the trend in the South has been toward making the South Korean president all-powerful. Although not couched in the same constitutional verbiage, a similar process has been occurring in the North, where the progressive veneration of Kim Il-sŏng has granted him extraordinary powers as president and general secretary of the party.

Organization. Four salient features of Korean organizational behavior are suggested by our discussions: (1) the importance of small group loyalty; (2) the widespread societal penetration of an organization that is an extension of the core inner group; (3) the consequent weakening of potentially competing organizations and institutions; and (4) the marked obedience of the populace at large.

The tendency for political leaders to surround themselves with a small group of intimate followers who have shared past hardships is common. Our essay on the Communist party leadership vividly documents the rise of the "partisan group" as the nucleus of power in P'yŏngyang. Although we lack comparable evidence for South Korea, our impression is that a similar core group has emerged from the military coup of 1961.

The power and influence of these inner groups are amplified and extended to the larger society by large-scale enforcement and surveillance organizations. Our impression is that the Central Intelligence Agency primarily performs this function in South Korea. We assume also that there is a fairly large amount of gratuitous informing, inspired by a variety of motives from monetary to emotional. The Inspection Committee of the Central Committee of the Workers' Party of Korea performs similar functions in North Korea, but we suspect that the actual mechanism of control that is linked to the partisan group and performs functions equivalent to the South Korean C.I.A. is smaller and more clandestine.

The organizational result of penetration by a single political intelligence organization has led to the weakening of other formal organizations, thereby mitigating their chances of making independent contributions to public policy. Neither press, legislature, courts, parties, or other groups are allowed to attain independence. They function rather as an arm of the core authoritative group within certain limits of tolerance. The successive declarations of martial law in South Korea and the overriding of "constitutional guarantees" for the operation of other institutions illustrates their fragility and vulnerability. The process is more subtle in North Korea, but the effect is the same: no organizations or institutions that exceed the tolerance limits imposed by Kim Il-sŏng and the partisan group can exist.

A characteristic of organizational behavior in Korea is the marked obedience of the Korean people as a whole. The political behavior of the Koreans has been to defer to superior force and authority.

By and large, Koreans seem to wait for authoritarian regimes to do themselves in as a result of their own extremes. Koreans seem to believe that their rulers are motivated by a self-defeating passion for power. When this exceeds the very wide tolerance levels of both individuals and groups close to power, as well as of broad public opinion, then a breakdown can be expected, which brings a temporary relief that may be more emotional than real; then the process of tightening up begins again.

Coupled with this deference to forceful authority is, of course, the potential, on the part of at least some segments of the populace, for dedicated loyalty to persons and, sometimes, causes. The revolutionary attachment of some Koreans to the cause of Korean independence is a case in point; it is likely that this same sentiment will motivate eventual Korean reintegration.

Paradoxically, the Korean people as individuals and groups display both obedience to authority and sometimes heroic resistance to authority. Such are the social psychological dynamics of leader-follower relations in Korean political culture. Both Korean regimes since 1945 have sought to exploit this dual nature of their followers.

Tasks. Certain tasks facing Korean political leaders require specification and analysis. Among those that require more detailed investigation are the following:

1. *The preservation of political identity and integrity.* The desire to preserve political identity has ancient roots, deep in traumatic historical events such as the Mongol and Japanese invasions; the collapse of the Yi dynasty and the loss of sovereignty to Japan; and the post-1945 dependence of the South upon the United States and Japan, and of the North upon the Soviet Union and China. One impression is that contemporary leaders of the North and South have approached this task with two different verbal strategies: militant rhetoric of autonomy in the North; emphasis upon external collaboration in the South. Leaders in both areas have shown skill in the ancient Chinese strategy of playing off barbarians one against the other: leaders in the North seem to have gained an advantage from Chinese and Russian antagonisms; leaders in the South seem to seek advantages by balancing American involvement against Japanese involvement. Additionally, each Korean regime hitherto has perceived the other as a threat to the autonomy and integrity of Korea, according to its own definition.

2. *Reunification: peace and war.* Each leadership group seeks to reintegrate the divided nation within at least the geographical

boundaries of the Yi dynasty. Favorable outcomes must be envisaged so that present actions may increase the probability of their occurrence in a ratchetlike progression. This unfinished task for both regimes has been employed to legitimate many less popular domestic and foreign policies, including the 1950–53 war and postwar militarization. The unfinished task of reunification is inextricably intertwined with preparations for war, fear of its occurrence, and search for peaceful techniques to gain advantages.

3. *The institutionalization or regularization of political processes.* By this is meant the creation and enactment of relatively stable ways of choosing political leaders, of making political decisions, and of carrying these decisions out, all of which have apparently been accomplished more successfully in the North than in the South. One reason for this is that the establishment of a single party control system in a society without a competitive tradition is relatively simple. Both Korean leadership groups, however, are faced with the unfinished task of establishing regularized procedures for ensuring leadership succession at the highest level.

4. *Economic planning and development.* Pioneered by the North in progressive one-, two-, three-, five-, seven-year plans, and lately emulated by the South in five-year plans, the task of gaining deliberate political control over the quality and quantity of economic development has become a major preoccupation of both contemporary leadership groups. More complex than under the Yi dynasty, more salient a task than it was for independence movement leaders, the problem of economic development has made both leadership groups more dependent upon technical economic advice and aware of economic conditions than ever before. A circular process is developing: the more Korea's political leaders engage themselves in directing complex, modern, economic processes, the greater the influence of economics upon their behavior. The problems of preserving the natural environment from industrial spoliation do not yet seem to be of great importance to Korea's leaders.

5. *The rural-urban problem complex.* Political leaders in both the North and South have found that they must reconcile the imbalances caused by rapid urban industrial development with lagging rural conditions. This problem was appreciated earlier in the North; Kim Il-sŏng recognized that rural conditions must be raised to levels comparable to those of cities. The urgent 1972 New Village Movement in the South seems devoted to the same task. Thus leaders in

both the North and South have had to provide urban amenities for burgeoning populations and have had to improve rural living conditions.

This survey of problems recalls only the most salient ones that have confronted Korean leaders. Many others need to be defined. Interrelations need to be shown and implications for leadership behavior need to be specified. It is helpful to recognize that some of the problems commonly confronting leaders of newly developing nations have *not* complicated the tasks of Korean political leaders: for example, Korean leaders have not had to solve major problems of communalism, linguistic diversity, religious tenacity, separatism, and extreme geographic dispersion. On the other hand, Koreans as a whole have both suffered and benefited more than *any other* small country in the world from a greater involvement of four of the world's greatest powers—the Soviet Union, the United States, China, and Japan.

Values. Korea is pervaded by certain values that can be grouped to provide a matrix for the contemporary analysis of Korean political leadership behavior at all levels in both parts of the country. These are (1) autonomy versus dependency, (2) authoritarianism versus permissiveness, (3) egalitarianism versus privilege, and (4) emotions versus technical rationality. Research on Korean political leadership behavior must specify precise measures for these values and explore how they function in relation to the way leaders perform, relate to others, and approach tasks. Relative emphasis upon these values may be one key to understanding both differences and similarities in North and South Korean developmental paths—as well as successes and failures of individual leaders and leadership groups at different levels and in different settings within each part of the country.

Using just two values, freedom and equality, the social psychologist Milton Rokeach has shown, through content analysis, that the writings of Fascist, Communist, conservative, and Socialist leaders contain them in distinctive combinations, as can be seen in figure 1. It is likely that research designs using these two values alone—and seeking to measure their intensity as well as frequency—would greatly illuminate the nature and direction of political leadership behavior at all levels and in both parts of Korea. The addition of two other value scales—autonomy versus dependency and human relations versus technical rationality—would create a valuable tool for value analysis specially appropriate for Korea.

Setting. The influence of setting upon Korean political leadership behavior requires more penetrating investigation. Korea's geo-graphical location necessitates that its leaders deal with China, Japan, and Russia but does not, of course, explain the quality and magnitude of those relationships. Nor does it explain fully the American engagements of leaders in the South. Similarly, other conditioning elements require exploration in terms of the oppor-tunities, limitations, and problems they present to Korean political leaders in both the North and South.

Fig. 1. Two-value differentiation of political leadership style.

Freedom

	High	Low
High	Socialist (Eric Fromm)	Communist (Lenin)
Low	Conservative (Goldwater)	Fascist (Hitler)

Equality (vertical axis label on left)

Adapted from Milton K. Rokeach, "A Theory of Organization and Change within Value-Attitude System," *Journal of Social Issues* 24, no. 1 (1968): 23.

Some technological aspects of the setting that deserve analysis are communication, transportation, and coercive technologies. An im-portant subject for research will be to trace how industrial effects upon Korea's natural environment generate demands for political leadership action. Salient social aspects of the setting that condition political behavior may be found by comparing this behavior in urban and rural contexts. Changes in the structure, cohesiveness, and socialization patterns of the Korean family also deserve investiga-tion, as they condition demands and opportunities for political lead-ership action. The size and composition of populations as condition-ers of leadership behavior merit inquiry. The implications for lead-ership of various systems of economic ownership and modes of production can also be investigated in Korea. One cultural element of interest worthy of investigation is whether the structure of the Korean language predisposes Koreans toward a certain pattern of leadership as well as follower responses. Leadership efforts to overcome this bias in a more egalitarian direction will be of special interest. The effects upon leadership behavior of marked discontinuities, imbalances, and contradictions arising out of rapid cultural change also need to be studied.

The combined study of personality, role, organizational, task, value, and setting determinants of political leadership behavior eventually will assist us in defining, explaining, and predicting behavior at all levels and in showing its relationship to the functioning of a political system in Korea. We need to study North and South Korea *separately* to ensure empirically sensitive understanding of each on its own terms; *comparatively* to identify similarities and differences that will aid appreciation of Korean political leadership; and *universally* to draw insights from Korean experience that will advance theories and methods for understanding political leadership anywhere.

APPENDIX

Toward a Political Leadership Profile for a Changing Society

GLENN D. PAIGE

INTRODUCTION

The intellectual task of creating a political leadership profile for a changing society presents an exciting challenge for pioneering inquiry into an immensely important but still surprisingly disordered subject. The basic outlines of what needs to be done are clear, but complicated. First, there must be concerted, alternative, and mutually reinforcing efforts to conceptualize political leadership as a subject for research, teaching, and service. Second, there must be explicit, cumulative, and mutually reinforcing efforts to link what is meant by political leadership to emerging, alternative ideas about the nature of a political system. And finally, both of the foregoing need to be traced over varying segments of the past, present, and future, so as to illuminate their relation to multidimensional societal development. Inquiries must be pursued at the microscopic and macroscopic levels; diverse research skills and approaches need to be brought to bear. The whole must constantly take into account a significant experience: *political leaders, as individuals and as aggregates, make significant contributions to societal development.* What needs to be done, in sum, is to show for any given society (1) who the political leaders have been, are, and will be; (2) what they have done, are doing, and will do; and (3) what reciprocal effects this has had, is having, and will have upon the political system and other aspects of society; this must be done in a way that allows focusing upon parts of political leadership behavior while maintaining a sense of the whole. The study of political leadership is not the study of the whole of political science, but it needs to become an important part of it.

An initial effort to be precise about the contribution of political leadership to total societal development is pioneering in at least the following ways: (1) political leadership has not been a special field of inquiry in political science;[1] (2) there is no specialized, theoretical monograph specifically linking political leadership in a comprehensive way with political or societal development;[2] (3) the scientific study of a total society is itself in its infancy, although probably on the threshold of a remarkable breakthrough as a result of linking multidisciplinary perspectives on development over long time frames with advances in computer capacities for processing large and complex bodies of information;[3] and (4) in many world societies, independent scientific inquiry into the nature of political leadership has not yet gained acceptance.[4] Important problems of conceptual focus, theoretical relevance, capacity, and interprofessional relationships gradually must be overcome. The problems of conceptual focus, methodological applications, field inquiry, and theoretical synthesis require pioneering efforts in order to create a developmental political leadership profile for a total society; there are many resources that deal with various aspects of political leadership studies that may be drawn upon.

In the following recently published examples, only a very few, mainly American in origin, are cited. This should not be taken to mean that only meager resources exist. If it were possible to inventory resources in all languages (including oral traditions), at least eleven relevant categories of political science literature could be identified: (1) *conceptualizing studies* that attempt to clarify ideas related to political leadership;[5] (2) *operational code studies* that seek to describe or prescribe leadership strategies for successful task accomplishment;[6] (3) *political biography studies* that seek insights into politics by studying, sometimes comparing, the careers of individual leaders;[7] (4) *role studies* that concentrate upon describing the problems and circumstances surrounding a given leadership position;[8] (5) *leadership institution studies* that focus upon aggregates of leaders who work together, such as legislatures and political parties;[9] (6) *elite studies* that emphasize changing socioeconomic and experiential backgrounds as a function of time plus the mobility of persons within, across, and beyond political roles and institutions;[10] (7) *follower studies* that probe the backgrounds, attitudes, and responses of persons to leadership initiatives;[11] (8) *community power studies* that inquire into the changing relationships within and among leadership groups in relation to historical community development;[12] (9) *value studies* that describe and compare the values held by political leaders and sometimes seek to relate them to developmental activities;[13] (10) *problem-solving studies* that show how leaders cope with certain problems;[14] and (11) *area surveys* that examine the political leadership of a given country or geographical area from a variety of viewpoints.[15]

In addition, many primary and secondary sources exist about historical and contemporary leaders, for the behavior of political leaders is probably more abundantly recorded than that of other men in history. Among such sources are oral traditions, official records, memoirs, letters, speeches, autobiographies, sound recordings, films, journalistic reports, poetry, plays, songs, public appearances, and so forth.

Despite the important studies already done, and despite the vast oral, written, and experiential legacy, the study of political leadership is still not accorded the intellectual focus and full-fledged scholarly specialization that it merits in political science. By contrast, studies and education in industrial and military leadership are more advanced. Among criticisms that may be directed to the existing literature as a whole are the following: there is insufficient attention to problems of conceptualizing political leadership within and across disciplines and cultures; there is a parochial emphasis upon American experience (although there are clear indications of a desire to escape from this limitation, especially via political elite studies); the theories and techniques necessary for cross-cultural comparisons of various political leadership roles is generally lacking; theoretical linkages between studies pertaining to leadership and concepts of a political system have generally been missing; there has been greater emphasis upon certain salient roles such as top, formal, and successful to the exclusion of a consideration of low-level, irregular, and unsuccessful ones; a comprehensive inventory of political leadership roles for a total society has not been worked out; studies already theoretically deficient have not been able to make the contribution to practical problem solving that good theory permits; and studies have generally been conducted on a short-time frame, which slight both historical depth[16] and future imagination.

What is needed for the advancement of political leadership studies is correspondingly clear: conceptual richness that seeks convergent and discriminant capability; more data as basis for understanding the total leadership behavior of any given political leader; more cross-role comparison; efforts to map a total political leadership system at various levels, including horizontal and vertical role relationships; greater efforts to make political leadership studies contribute to the development of general theories of a political system; corollary attention to problem solving; and expansion

of time consciousness to include both historical and future awareness.

It is suggested that a full-fledged field of political science (and
multidisciplinary) specialization in political leadership will be
characterized by mutually reinforcing advancement along four
main avenues of approach: construction of a theory, application of
knowledge, education, and critical evaluation of all the foregoing.
The outline of the first of these approaches is shown in table 1.

PROBLEMS OF CONCEPTUALIZATION

The practical importance of conceptualization in political leadership studies can be rather vividly illustrated. Havron and McGrath
report an experiment in the performance of twenty-four Army-
trained squads (emphasizing concentration of leadership functions
in the squad leader) compared with twenty-four specially trained
squads (emphasizing the sharing of leadership functions among all
squad members). Given a "mission" in which the formal squad
leader and his assistant squad leader were "killed," the results,
which were unexpected, were that *all* the specially trained squads
scored higher in mission accomplishment. The authors conclude:

> This is a dramatic illustration, we think, of one of the more important
> facets of leadership. A group can act effectively in a co-ordinated way
> even with a leader of indifferent ability or can reorganize quickly with-
> out leaders, if the *concept of leadership and how it is to be exercised
> operationally* is learned and appreciated by all members.[17]

This experiment on the problem of the concentration versus dispersal of leadership functions is reminiscent, of course, of political
struggles between executive and legislative, and between individual versus collective leadership.

Among other behavioral science controversies over conceptualization of leadership are the following: (1) *Trait versus situation.*
This has currently been "resolved" by Gibb's summary formulation: "The traits of leadership are any or all of those personality
traits which, *in any particular situation*, enable an individual to (1)
contribute significantly to group locomotion in the direction of a
recognized goal and (2) be perceived as doing so by fellow
members."[18] The literature on charisma should also be considered
in this context. (2) *Dominance versus voluntary compliance.* Some
researchers prefer to restrict the concept of leadership to situations
in which followers respond voluntarily to what they perceive as
legitimate leader initiatives; they would omit situations involving
coercion. Numerous writings on power, authority, and influence

TABLE 1

A Theory-Building Sequence in Political Leadership Studies

Conceptualization	Single Case	Comparison	Aggregation	Experimentation	Theoretical Integration
1. Natural and folk concepts	1. Biography	1. Biographies	1. Sample survey	1. Laboratory	1. Propositional inventories
2. Humanities	2. Case study	2. Cases	2. Co-acting aggregates	2. Field	2. Verbal theories
3. Behavioral sciences			3. Role-set analysis	3. Simulation	3. Mathematical models
4. Animal sciences			4. Mobility studies		

also merit attention in this context.[19] (3) *Group output versus group process*. This position argues that leadership should be measured in terms of the output or productivity of the group rather than in terms of the relationships among group members. Changes in productivity associated with the presence of different group leaders is taken to be the operational meeting of the concept of leadership.[20]

The conclusions that I have drawn from these conceptual controversies are that an adequate concept of political leadership should call attention to personality, organizational, and task variables, among others, and that it should encompass both coercive and consensual relationships.

Another conceptual problem revolves around methods for identifying leaders that include their formal positions, whether they provide a focus for emotions or information for group members, their reputation for influence attributed by others, their actual participation in decision making or other leadership behaviors, and sociometric choice-follower designation (for example, voting).[21] The conclusion that I have drawn from these controversies is that the study of political leadership in the first phase of its development should concentrate upon the incumbents of formal, culturally, and socially defined positions of manifest political authority, and upon the principal contenders, both overt or covert, for such positions. If it is found that incumbents and contenders for these positions are performing too few or too many of the functions considered necessary for a given formal structure within a political system, then attention should be extended to those outside the formal structure who could (or should not) perform such functions.

One possible solution to the problem of identifying leaders is to refer to certain roles, in the enactment of which behavior of interest to political leadership studies occurs. Among others, these would include monarchs, presidents, premiers, party leaders at all levels, legislators, chiefs, military governors, revolutionaries, and principal aspirants for all these positions.[22]

Further conceptual considerations involve questions of units of analysis. These are taken to be: (1) *individual leaders*, for example, a president or village chief; (2) *co-acting aggregates* (ad hoc or regular), for example, a faction, legislature, soviet, council, or party; (3) *dispersed aggregates*, for example, all governors, mayors, or village chiefs; (4) *combinations* of the foregoing, including a political leadership cluster for a total society, and (5) *aspirants* for the above, including both unsuccessful[23] and potential aspirants.

Another consideration involves the scope and level of analysis.

Where hierarchal structures prevail, we may wish to examine political leaders at different structural levels, defined often by relative authority and size of constituency; for example, high (national), middle (city, state, or province), and low (town, county, or village). Where hierarchy is not an important feature, emphasis may be placed upon relative scope of decisions over which a given leader exercises influence (for example, within a collegial decision-making body).

Before presenting a conceptual framework for the study of political leadership I would like to suggest that further progress toward more adequate conceptualization will be likely to result from the interaction between greater knowledge about how experienced political leaders in different cultures and levels think about what they do and greater sensibility among behavioral scientists about the implicit models of leadership that underly their own thought. Figure 1 gives some examples of different possible models: are there other cultural and subcultural variations?

Figure 1
Four Models of Leadership Relations

A. Hierarchial Model

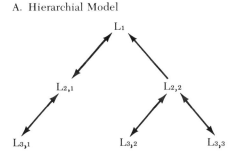

B. Centrality-Salience Model

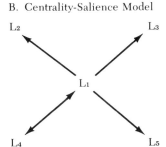

C. "Sump" Model: Leadership by "Default"

D. Egalitarian Model

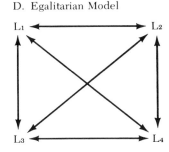

A CONCEPTUAL FRAMEWORK

In attempting to create a political leadership profile for a changing society there must be constant interplay between conceptualization, hypothesis formulation, perfection of research method-
ologies, empirical research, data analysis, and formal theoretical
integration. One starting point is to formulate a conceptual framework that focuses attention upon aspects of political leadership
behavior that seem to merit specialized inquiry if goals of adequate
theory are to be achieved. One such framework, which draws
upon concepts that cut across the sociobehavioral sciences and
permits their mutually supportive convergence, is the following: *political leadership consists in the interaction of six variables
(personality, role, organization, task, values, and setting) as expressed in the behavior of salient individuals who contribute to
variance in a political system (however defined) and to variance in
four dimensions of social behavior (power, affect, instrumentality, and association).*
   One way of thinking about this framework (only one way because
relationships may be reversed as a matter of analytic choice) is that
it is composed of six independent variables, a primary dependent
variable (leader behavior), a secondary dependent variable (the
political system), and a tertiary dependent variable (general dimensions of social behavior). These will be defined briefly below.

*Independent Variables: Personality, Role,
Organization, Task, Value, and Setting*

   By personality is meant all of the characteristics that identify the
unique human individual as well as attributes that may be shared
with other individuals. All the concepts, research tools, and other
resources of personality psychology, psychiatry, and social psychology need to be mobilized to illuminate the contribution of this
variable to leadership behavior. Attention needs to be given to the
development of the individual leader throughout life, not just at a
point in time.[24] Also, since efforts to find distinctive personality
traits in leaders seem to have been unsuccessful,[25] greater attention
must be given to discovering the effects of whatever personality
attributes they do have rather than in attempting to show they differ
from nonleaders.
   By role is meant the independent, analytical assessment of the
core behavioral requirements of a leadership position (president,
legislator, party secretary, governor, mayor, village chief, etc.) for a
given incumbent or, regardless of the specific incumbent, the be-

havior expected, based upon examination of reciprocal expectations concerning rights and obligations between the incumbent and others.[26]

Organization is used here in a different way than is usually intended. By organization is meant all forms of interpersonal behavior ranging from the dyad (leader-adviser relationship) through small groups (family, staff, council, faction), formal organizations (party, legislature, bureaucracy, military, police), and societal segments (class, sex, age, occupation, groups), ultimately to relations between a leader and all the members of a society.[27]

By task is meant the objective problems that a leader is expected to solve or decisions he is required to make. Task may be distinguished from role and organization by the following example. One of the decisions expected of a leader is when to use the police and military forces under his command. Since neither core expectations nor the organizational relationships between the leader and these coercive units is sufficient to describe the concrete requirements for their employment or restraint, specific requirements for action may be thought of as leader tasks. Other leader tasks include campaigning, deciding, planning, implementing, supervising, bargaining, and disengaging.[28]

By values, following Rokeach[29] and others, is meant ideas concerning desirable ends (terminal values) and desirable means (instrumental values). Studying the divided nations (China, Germany, Korea, and Vietnam) clarifies the values held by leaders (subnationally, nationally, and internationally) for developing politics, economics, society, and culture.

The concept of setting is intended to call attention to natural, man-made, and sociocultural aspects of the environment in which political leadership takes place. Factors like geography, technology, the economic system, the social system, and the cultural system are to be examined as sources of possible explanation for leadership behavior. One view is that such things constitute the theater in which the political actor performs, the stage and props that constrain and expand the possibilities of action, the physical arrangements that relate audience and actor, the socioeconomic system that influences who both audiences and actor might be, and the language culture that conditions communication.[30]

Primary Dependent Variable: Patterns of Leadership Behavior

The interaction of the six independent variables is hypothesized to result in both single acts and recurrent patterns of action by persons identified as political leaders. Both critical, single-event action and recurring patterns of individual and group behavior require attention. Here we focus inquiry exclusively upon just what it is that leaders do, and seek to discern those significant patterns in their behavior that are relevant for development.

Different ways of categorizing the patterns of leadership behavior should be sought for different analytical purposes, although some degree of overlap can be expected.[31] With special reference to leadership patterns related to developmental change, the following four kinds of behavior may be illustrative:

Resistance—opposition to changes in existing behavior.

Regression—changes in the direction of previously existing behavior.

Reform—marginal adjustments in existing behavior to make it more effective or acceptable.

Transformation—pursues fundamental changes in basic patterns of existing behavior.

Each of these four may be further differentiated by the degree of violent or nonviolent behavior associated with it and by other characteristics. Common language designations of leaders as radical, liberal, conservative, authoritarian, dictatorial, and reactionary need to be tested as potentially useful tools of analysis. The aversion by political leaders to simple labeling of their behavior suggests that adequate characterizations of styles of leadership will require multidimensional analysis. Since this aversion is based partly upon polemical overtones of conventional labels, scientific political leadership studies will benefit from efforts to create more adequate concepts, independent of common language terms.

Many interesting studies previously reported under the categories of personality and role orientations of political leaders may actually be viewed as pioneering analytical attempts to characterize political patterns of leadership behavior as a whole. Findings such as the following deserve continued attention: (1) Barber's categorization of legislators as lawmakers, spectators, advertisers, and reluctants depending upon their relations to two variables: activity and satisfaction;[32] (2) Barber's categorization of presidential personalities as stressing rhetoric, business, or interpersonal relations;[33] (3) Barber's categorization of committee chairmen as active or passive, and Hargrove's views on presidents of action or restraint;[34] (4) Eldersveld's classification of party workers as vote mobilizers, ideological mentors, or social welfare promotors;[35] (5) the classification by Wahlke et al. of legislators as trustees (emphasizing acting upon their own judgment), delegates (emphasizing acting in accordance with perceived wishes of constituents) or politicos (emphasizing acting both ways according to the situation); district-oriented, state-oriented, or district-state-oriented (depending upon conceptions of area representation); and facilitators, resistors, or neutrals (depending upon attitudes toward pressure groups);[36] (6) Clapp's view of congressmen as primarily legislation-oriented or constituency-oriented and Bass's categorization of leaders as task-oriented, interaction-oriented, or self-oriented;[37] and (7) Weber's conception of legal, traditional, and charismatic types of authority.[38]

These and other appropriate classifications, in various combinations, may gradually be developed into useful typologies of leadership behavior.

Secondary Dependent Variable: The Political System

Political leadership studies need to be related to conceptions of a political system and to ideas concerning the development of such a system. It is assumed that political leaders, singly, as competitors, and as aggregates make some contribution to the emergence, functioning, and change of a political system.

Among the leading contemporary ideas about a political system are that it is (1) the way a society makes decisions;[39] (2) the "interactions through which values are authoritatively allocated for society";[40] (3) the way society distributes power and responsibility;[41] (4) the relationship between structures and functions;[42] (5) the way dominant underlying economic interests are translated into compatible social control;[43] and (6) a cybernetic system of learning and innovation.[44]

The idea of decision making is so abstract that other concepts of a political system can be subsumed under it. One such formulation is that a *political system consists of the patterns by which a society makes its decisions concerning the distribution of power, the allocation of values, and other matters requiring authoritative choice.* Such a system is activated by demands for decisions and by the motivations of the decision makers themselves.

The study of political leadership faces the task of linking leadership behavior with ideas about a political system, whatever the preferred conception of it is. An illustration is provided by the definition offered by Lewis J. Edinger in connection with his plea for the study of political biography:

Political leadership is thus a position or—in the language of the cognitive approach to role analysis—the location of an actor or actors in a
group, characterized by the ability of the incumbent to guide the collective behavior of this group in the direction of a desired authoritative
allocation of values in a political community. . . . He perceives himself,
and may be perceived by other relevant actors, as playing one or more
roles oriented toward the exercise of decision making authority in a
political community by himself and/or other members of his particular
group.[45]

Whatever conception of a political system is adopted by individual researchers or by political science as a whole, two essential
questions must be asked constantly in order to achieve theoretically relevant political leadership studies: What contributions does
political leadership behavior make to the operation of such a system? and What objective requirements or opportunities for political
leadership behavior does such a system pose?

Considering developmental change in a political system adds
complications as it involves specifying (1) an initial state from
which change takes place, (2) a process of transition, and (3) an at
least temporarily stable outcome that differs significantly from the
initial conditions. An idea contributed by Riggs and others, which
has provided insights into this problem, is that the process of transition will be characterized by a mixture of forms of tradition and
modern behavior within and across persons and institutions.[46]

Again political science offers competitive ideas about what political development involves. Defined in terms of decision making, it
can be suggested that *political development consists in the making
of more decisions about more aspects of society, affecting more
people, involving more persons in the decisional process, and with
decreasing levels of violence.* It is possible for politics to be over-
developed as well as underdeveloped from this point of view; also
it is probable that a relatively wide variety of concrete political
institutions would satisfy the conditions of development, not just
one set.

There are other views of development, of course, and for
whichever one is adopted, the relation of political leadership behavior to development deserves examination. One of the clearest
specifications of developmental tasks (based on the assumption
that the developmental process consists of transition from lesser to
greater positions along these dimensions) is the specification of five
crises of political development by the Social Science Research
Council Committee on Comparative Politics: legitimacy, participation, distribution, integration, and regulation.[47] What contributions

has political leadership made at varying periods and levels to coping with these crises? What requirements for leadership action have these crises imposed?

An addition to the basic political system formulation of David A. Easton,[48] a framework for political system analysis, with which possibly fruitful linkages might be made, has been proposed by Gabriel A. Almond. Functional categories of a political system proposed by Almond include *generating inputs* (demands and supports); *processing inputs* (articulation, aggregation, rule conversion, rule application, political communication); *generating outputs* (extraction, regulation, allocation, symbolic production); and the exercise of performance capabilities (extractive, regulative, distributive, symbolic, and responsive).[49]

Tertiary Dependent Variables: Societal Dimensions

There are compelling reasons why the study of political leadership should be connected conceptually both to the idea of a political system and to a broader conception of society that encompasses explicitly political considerations. Contemporary concern with ecology is only one manifestation of the connection between man in society and in nature; our analytical abstractions are only partial insights into human society as a whole. And yet it is these same abstractions that make it possible for us to see common patterns that run from the microscopic to the macroscopic level.

It is proposed that the study of political leadership give attention to four dimensions of human behavior that seem to characterize the individual, the small group, the formal organization, the community, the society, the nation, the region, and the world. These are the dimensions of power, affect, instrumentality, and association. By power is meant differential capacities to reinforce behavior with rewards and punishments. By affect is meant the qualities of feelings and emotions. By instrumentality is meant objective task and problem-solving capabilities, processes, and technologies. Finally, by association is meant the structure of relationships by which the elements of a behavioral unit are combined.

The pervasive significance of these four dimensions can be appreciated by considering the striking convergences in contemporary approaches to the study of the individual personality, the small group, and the larger society. In psychology, for example, there are three principal approaches to personality studies: reinforcement or learning theory (power); theory of emotions (affect); and cognition (instrumentality). The fourth dimension (association) is often assumed by others, but is not taken for granted by the behavioral psychologist. In small groups, research has repeatedly revealed three dimensions of behavior concerning which group members have more influence or authority over others (power), which are best liked (affect), and which contribute most to solving the objective tasks facing the group (instrumentality).[50] The initial structure of the group is not usually made the object of explicit *theoretical* attention, since it is produced by the researcher (or selected as given from nature) in order to study the other things that interest him. Striking parallels have been discovered in sociology where Amitai Etzioni has analyzed institutions characterized by him as primarily coercive (power), expressive (affect), or utilitarian (instrumentality);[51] once more the structure of association, which underlies the emergence of these different types of institutions, is more assumed than made the subject of explicit concern. But the political scientist's concern for constitutional engineering, which does not allow assumption of the existence of a pattern of political association, provokes search for a concept such as association to call attention to the creative capacity for structural variability in human affairs.

In the present formulation, power, affect, instrumentality, and association are conceived of as being aspects of all the independent and dependent variables connected with political leadership. And it is suggested that political leadership behavior—and the political system itself—be examined in terms of its implications for the power, emotional, technical problem solving, and structural variability dimensions of a total society.

Through these four dimensions, the study of political leadership in relation to a political system can be connected to other key areas of human concern: to the power relationships of explicitly nonpolitical institutions; to religious, artistic, and other cultural modes of expressing feelings; to economic development, and other aspects of science and technology; and to social structural changes in such things as occupation, population distribution, mobility, and the ability to form groups and other forms of transpersonal relationships.

The conceptual framework that has been proposed for the study of political leadership is summarized in table 2.

TRACING DEVELOPMENTAL CHANGE

To construct a developmental political leadership profile it will be necessary to measure changes as a function of time in the various components of the conceptual framework. For each study it is de-

TABLE 2

Conceptual Framework for the Study of Political Leadership

Independent Variables	Primary Dependent Variables *Political Leadership Behavior*	Secondary Dependent Variables *Political System*	Tertiary Dependent Variables *Aspects of Social Behavior*
Personality	Leadership Styles Delegate Trustee Politico Etc.	Political System Decision Power Values Etc.	Power
Role			Affect
Organization	Change Orientations Resistance Regression Reform Transformation	Political Development Legitimacy Participation Distribution Integration Regulation Differentiation Etc.	Instrumentality
Task			Association
Values			
Setting			

sirable to show (1) the initial state of variables at Time One, (2) processes of change, and (3) outcomes at Time Two. The length of time upon which attention is concentrated should vary in accordance with theoretical concerns. Sometimes a century or more may be essential to appreciate fundamental change; at other times, several weeks or months may be sufficient.

Employing Cattell's categories of *population, structure,* and *group syntality,*[52] a study in developmental change should show changes in persons holding leadership positions, changes in their relationships with each other and with other members of society, and changes in the consequences of their behavior for total societal functioning. Or, in terms of the present concept, one would search for interacting changes in personalities, role prescriptions, organizational relationships, tasks, values, and setting as associated with different styles of leadership and with changes in the political system—further reflected in the power, affective, instrumental, and associational dimensions of societal behavior.

In the examination of political leadership aspects of developmental change, it will be necessary to create and test propositions that go beyond common static correlations of variables taken from a single time frame. In the sociobehavioral sciences there appear to be relatively fewer propositions that try to account for change than there are propositions that do not.[53] Four examples of the former kind of proposition with implications for the study of political leadership are the following.

Gregory Bateson's concept of *schismogenesis* (the origin of a schism) as "a process of differentiation in the norms of individual behavior that results from cumulative interaction between individuals,"[54] is one example. There are two forms: *symmetrical schismogenesis,* in which individuals may split apart in a cumulative process of competition and one-upmanship; and a *complementary schismogenesis,* in which two individuals may split apart because one becomes increasingly dominant while the other becomes increasingly submissive until the two have very little in common. These two processes can be observed, for example, in husband-wife relationships. Might they also not be observed in relationships among individuals and groups of political leaders? Could schismatic tendencies between conservative and revolutionary leaders, between competing factions, and between leadership groups and their followers, be examined in this fashion?

Joseph Geller's concept of four stages of development in newly formed groups of persons from different professional backgrounds in quasi-therapeutic group dynamics sessions meeting up to forty times with a group psychotherapist present also has implications for leadership over time.[55] The four stages are: *uncertainty*, characterized by anxiety, avoidance of involvement in the group, and overdependence on the group leader; *overaggressiveness*, marked by hostile and aggressive relations compulsively engaged in with "poorly controlled thoughts and presentations"; *regression*, characterized by unrealistic desires and demands, jealousies surrounding the leader, faction formation to pull down apparently confident and secure persons, massive feelings of anxiety by some group members, and obsessional defenses against emotional involvement; and *adaptation*, marked by greater feelings of group involvement, security, productivity, satisfaction, creativity, and tolerance.

Immanuel Wallerstein's application of Max Weber's concept of charisma to the process of political transition to a modernizing society is another example. According to Wallerstein, charismatic leadership is functionally useful in making the transition from traditional to rational legal authority.[56] The traditional leader says, "Do it because it has always been done this way." The charismatic leader says, "Do it because I, your leader, say so." The rational-legal leader says, "Do it because this is the rationally agreed-upon law."

Bae-ho Hahn's thesis that political development will be characterized by changes in the emphasis of political leadership factions from personalistic (person-centered) to utilitarian (patronage-centered), and finally to ideological (issue-centered) factions is another insight in which time is a significant variable.[57]

CYCLICAL VERSUS LINEAR CONCEPTIONS

Some propositions about leadership change over time will be predominantly cyclical in nature, such as analyses of the dynastic cycle in China or Hertzler's portrayal of the life cycle of dictatorships: (1) period of chaos, depression, and governmental breakdown, (2) the preparation for the rise to power by the nascent dictator, (3) the thrust at power, the *coup d'état*, (4) the conquest of "the revolution," (5) the entrenchment, (6) the decline, (7) the uprising and overthrow, (8) temporary restoration of the previous type of sociopolitical control, and (9) confusion and attempts to work out a new and more appropriate form.[58] Or leadership propositions may be linked to more linear theories of societal development such as (1) Marx's portrayal of human progression from primitive communism, feudalism, capitalism, and socialism to communism, (2)

Organski's portrayal of four stages of political development as "primitive unification, industrialization, national welfare, and abundance"[59] or (3) the ten projections of a group of Japanese futurists:

primitive society (1000 M.B.C.–12 M.B.C.)
collective society (12 M.B.C.–700 B.C.)
agricultural society (700 B.C.–1302)
handicraft society (1302–1765)
industrialization society (1765–1876)
mechanization society (1876–1945)
automation society (1945 – 1974)
cybernation society (1974–2005)
optimization society (2005–2025)
autonomous society (2025–2033)[60]

It is interesting to note that cyclical and linear theories of political leadership change are not necessarily unrelatable. Leadership cycles may occur within progressive stages of development. All that is needed is a linkage theory that explains how cycles become transformed into linear development or vice versa.

Social Learning and Political Leadership Development

One body of theory that deserves more attention in the study of political development—and which may serve as a link between cyclical and linear conceptions of political leadership change—is to be found in social psychological theories of social learning.[61] The basic idea of this approach is that individuals, groups, and societies learn in two ways: by emulating the behavior of others, and by innovation related to trial and error learning (table 3). Although usually associated with reinforcement theories of rewards and punishments (rewarded behavior persists; punished behavior is extinguished), there is no reason why such social learning theory cannot be supplemented by cognitive and emotional perspectives as well. That is, perception of punishment of others may motivate the rewarded self; emotions may be associated with the prolongation of behavior despite aversive reinforcement.

An early formulation[62] by Miller and Dollard may be especially appropriate for linking political leadership studies with developmental change. They advance four concepts: drive (hunger), cue (a bowl of rice), response (eating), reward (satiation).[63] The idea of models for behavior appears especially relevant as a cue. For example, leaders of an agricultural nation wish to industrialize (drive); there are different models of industrialization processes (cue); the leaders elect to follow one or more patterns (response); and they are either satisfied or frustrated (reward). Or, they seek independence, are colonized, revolt or collaborate, and experience states of autonomy or restraint that vary in levels of satisfaction.

TABLE 3

SOCIAL LEARNING AND THE INDIVIDUAL
POLITICAL LEADER

---

1. General Political Socialization.

   a. Father and other family members as leader models.
   b. Family as source of attitudes toward other leadership models.
   c. Leadership models as presented in educational curricula.
   d. Leadership models as influenced by peer group relationships.
   e. Leadership models as presented in the mass media.
   f. Major episodes of trial and error experience related to leadership.

2. Political Recruitment.

   a. Mode of engagement in political activity (inheritance, appointment, self-selection, election, coup, revolution).
   b. Effect of models on apprenticeship.
   c. Major episodes of trial and error learning.
   d. Mode of ascendance to first major political leadership position.

3. Leadership Role Performance.

   a. Pattern of role progressions (various combinations of executive, legislative, party cadre, administrative, military, police, revolutionary, and oppositional roles).
   b. Effect of models within and across roles.
   c. Major episodes of trial and error learning (prison, exile).
   d. Cumulative style of political leadership performance.
   e. Influence upon the political system.

4. Disengagement.

   a. Types of disengagement (voluntary withdrawal, electoral defeat, forced resignation, impeachment, violent displacement by coup or revolution, assassination, natural death).
   b. Effect of models on disengagement.
   c. Associated trial and error learning experience.
   d. Influences upon the political system.

5. Contribution to Future Social Learning by Other Leaders.

   a. Traces left upon sources of general political socialization.
   b. Self as a model for emulation or avoidance by other leaders.

Models of leadership behavior may exist within the society, may be emulated from abroad, or may be created partly by trial and error processes. They may diffuse partially or wholly, usually from higher to lower levels, from the more prestigious to the less prestigious, although it is possible for this sometimes to be reversed. Another key proposition of social learning theory is that past behavior that has been rewarded is usually projected into new and unfamiliar situations. Thus one could anticipate attempts by traditional leaders to cope with transitional problems in traditional ways, attempts by transitional leaders to cope with modernization problems from a transitional perspective, and attempts by developmental leaders to cope with uncertain futures on the basis of their own new learning experiences.

Social learning over time may be introduced into studies of political leadership and development in at least four ways: study of the life cycle of an individual leader; overlapping studies of clusters of political leaders; studies of groups working together in which a formal leadership organization or institution (party, legislature, etc.) is taken as a subject for emulating, innovating, recalling, generalizing, and transmitting experience; and holistic studies of a society's political leadership complex as a learning system.[64] Political leadership learning studies of both the past and the future may be accomplished. The scientist can formulate predictive hypotheses about the responses of present leaders to hypothetical future states of affairs based upon generalizations from past learning and can verify these hypotheses by a combination of simulation and the actual unfolding of the anticipated future events.

The combination of political leadership and social learning perspectives is illustrated by the following outline of the career progression of an individual political leader from early general political socialization through disengagement from political activity.

Individual careers may also be combined into overlapping generational clusters. The width of such clusters will vary according to political culture,[65] but for purposes of illustration they might be based upon twenty-year increments: 10-30 years; 30-50 years; 50-70 years; 70-90 years. Analysis would proceed to show how modeling and trial and error learning experiences vary both within and across these generational clusters.

Table 4 is designed to suggest how a social learning perspective might be brought to bear on the creation of a developmental political leadership profile for a total society. The terms traditional, transitional, industrializing, and alternative futures have been employed as heuristic devices to mark four stages, but other

TABLE 4

POLITICAL LEADERSHIP SOCIAL LEARNING IN A TOTAL SOCIETY

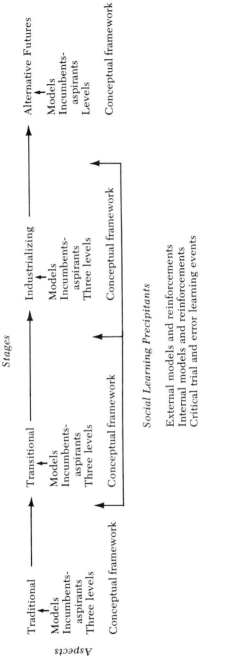

Stages

	Traditional	Transitional	Industrializing	Alternative Futures
	Models	Models	Models	Models
	Incumbents-aspirants	Incumbents-aspirants	Incumbents-aspirants	Incumbents-aspirants
	Three levels	Three levels	Three levels	Levels
	Conceptual framework	Conceptual framework	Conceptual framework	Conceptual framework

Aspects

Social Learning Precipitants

External models and reinforcements
Internal models and reinforcements
Critical trial and error learning events

designations, including more concrete (nineteenth century) and more abstract ones (Time One) might be employed as well.

Under aspects for each stage, attention is called briefly to certain features that merit special attention. By models is meant those conceptions of ideal, actual, and potential leadership that are characteristic and are both dominant and subdominant in the folk society and the great tradition. Reference to incumbents-aspirants focuses attention upon the implications of tensions among potentially alternative leaders. Three levels (high, middle, and low) serve as reminders not to overlook primary (village) and intermediate (provincial) leadership behavior when considering the more usual societal (national) leadership. By conceptual framework is meant the independent variables, and the primary, secondary, and tertiary dependent variables suggested earlier in this paper.

In addition, three precipitants of social learning shift from one stage to another are suggested: (1) the perception of external models of leadership, accompanied by external and/or internal rewards and punishments or demands and supports for attempts to emulate such models; (2) the internal creation of new models of leadership accompanied by external-internal reinforcements for implementation; and (3) the occurrence of major, sometimes traumatic events that provide occasions for developing new leadership responses (war, foreign conquest, uprisings, revolution, coups, and economic collapse). In addition, there may occur less episodic but nevertheless dramatic changes in setting variables that may precipitate new leadership learning (population growth, urbanization, rising levels of education, and improved transportation and communication).

TOWARD DEVELOPMENTAL POLITICAL LEADERSHIP PROPOSITIONS

As the study of political leadership progresses in general and in special relation to development or societal change, it will be important to accumulate a relevant set of hypotheses or propositions, which will grow out of a process of confrontation between logical, critical, and creative imagination[66] and rigorous comparative empirical tests. Each empirical study performed, however small or grandly conceived, from the study of the individual leader to the study of the societal aggregate, can aspire to contribute to the unfolding tapestry of knowledge in this field.

At least two related hypotheses are bound to receive recurrent attention: (1) are there individual and aggregate political leadership styles that are more or less functional for different phases of the developmental process; and (2) are we entering an era in which extant political leadership styles are no longer functional for the continuation of human society at the local, national, international, or world levels? To answer such questions we will have to focus attention upon those who follow as well as those who lead. Political "followership" studies are the natural complement[67] to the study of political leadership—until political leaders and followers as we know them now and have known them in the past blend into new forms of interpersonal political relationships.

NOTES

1. To cite American political science as an example, although it is only one segment of world political science experience, only 17 articles with titles mentioning leaders or leadership appeared in the *American Political Science Review* over a 57-year period from 1907 to 1963 out of a total of 2614. Only one title contained the word politicians. There were articles on roles specific to the American political system, such as president, senator, representative, and governor, but none on mayor. Five items referred to elites. Cross-level and cross-societal comparisons were not salient. Despite a noticeable increase in references to leadership appearing in books and articles in the period from 1963 to 1970, it is still possible to assert that political leadership is not yet a clearly differentiated political science specialty. Of course, all political scientists seem to recognize its relevance for their own work. Consult Kenneth F. Janda, *Cumulative Index to the American Political Science Review, Volumes 1-57: 1906-1963* (Evanston: Northwestern University Press, 1964). Five years later, in 1968, references to leaders or leadership had increased by 8 to 25 articles. Kenneth Janda, *Cumulative Index to the American Political Science Review, Volumes 1-62; 1906-1968* (Washington: American Political Science Association, XEROX/University Microfilms, 1969).

2. In American political science, for example, a volume on political leadership and political development was not a part of the pioneering Princeton University Press series on political development created under the leadership of the Social Science Research Council (SSRC) Committee on Comparative Politics. Volumes published thus far include those on political parties, education, bureaucracy, communications, political culture, and a comparison of Japanese and Turkish development. Although general theoretical focus upon leadership was not provided by the SSRC group (or even upon elites, which is a key concept in political sociological tradition), empirical studies of developing nations devoted to the analysis of political elites have appeared in increasing numbers; see Frank Bonilla, *The Failure of Elites* (Cambridge, Mass.: MIT Press, 1968), a historical-sociological study of political elites in Venezuela.

3. An intellectual landmark is Samuel Z. Klausner, ed. *The Study of Total Societies* (New York: Praeger, 1967).

4. But, following the acceptance of scientific inquiry into sexual and religious behavior, it is likely that scientific inquiry into a formerly taboo area of human experience such as political leadership will eventually gain world-wide acceptance as well. But even in societies where social scientists have gained acceptance, there is relatively little confidence between political leaders and political scientists.

5. For example, see Ann Ruth Willner, *Charismatic Political Leadership: A Theory* (Princeton: Center of International Studies, Princeton University, 1968); Kenneth F. Janda, "Towards the Explication of the Concept of Leadership in Terms of the Concept of Power," *Human Relations* 13, no. 4 (1960): 345–63; Jerzy J. Wiatr and Krzysztof Ostrowski, "Political Leadership: What Kind of Professionalism," in *Studies in Polish Political System*, ed. J. J. Wiatr (Wroclaw: Polish Academy of Sciences Press, 1967), pp. 140–55; Warren G. Bennis, "Post-Bureaucratic Leadership," *Trans-Action* 6, no. 9 (July-August 1969):44–51; and Donald D. Searing, "Models and Images of Man and Society in Leadership Theory," *Journal of Politics* 31, no. 1 (February 1969):3–31.

6. Aside from classics such as those of Machiavelli, Kautilya, Nizam al-Mulk, Sun Tzu, oral African traditions, and contemporary writings on strategy by leaders such as Hitler, Mao, and Che Guevára, this category includes recent political science writings such as Alexander L. George, *The 'Operational Code': A Neglected Approach to the Study of Political Leaders and Decision Making* (Santa Monica: The Rand Corporation, 1967); and W. Howard Wriggins, *The Ruler's Imperative: Strategies for Political Survival in Asia and Africa* (New York: Columbia University Press, 1969).

7. For example, see Lewis W. Edinger, "Political Science and Political Biography: Reflections on the Study of Leadership," *Journal of Politics* 26 (May 1964):423–39; Alexander L. and Juliette L. George, *Woodrow Wilson and Colonel House* (New York: Dover Publications, 1965); E. Victor Wolfenstein, *The Revolutionary Personality: Lenin, Trotsky, Gandhi* (Princeton: Princeton University Press, 1967); and Rodger Swearingen, ed., *Leaders of the Communist World* (New York: Free Press, 1970).

8. For example, see Richard E. Neustadt, *Presidential Power* (New York: John Wiley & Sons, 1960); Donald R. Matthews, ed., *U.S. Senators and Their World* (New York: Random House, 1960); Charles L. Clapp, *The Congressman* (Washington: Brookings Institution, 1964); Joseph A. Schlesinger, "The Politics of the Executive," in *Politics in the American States: A Comparative Analysis*, ed. Herbert Jacob and Kenneth Vines (Boston: Little, Brown, & Co., 1965); and Leonard D. Ruchelman, ed., *Big City Mayors* (Bloomington: Indiana University Press, 1969).

9. For example, see John C. Wahlke et al., *The Legislative System* (New York: John Wiley & Sons, 1962); and Samuel J. Eldersveld, *Political Parties: A Behavioral Analysis* (Chicago: Rand McNally & Co., 1964). Political leadership aspects of the study of other institutions such as the military and public administration are also relevant.

10. For example, see Harold D. Lasswell and Daniel Lerner, eds., *World Revolutionary Elites* (Cambridge, Mass.: M.I.T. Press, 1965); Carl Beck and J. Thomas McKechnie, *Political Elites: A Select Computerized Bibliography* (Cambridge, Mass.: M.I.T. Press, 1968); and Joseph A. Schlesinger, *Ambition and Politics* (Chicago: Rand McNally & Co., 1966).

11. For example, see public opinion surveys and voting studies such as Angus Campbell et al., *The American Voter* (New York: John Wiley & Sons, 1965).

12. See Robert A. Dahl, *Who Governs* (New Haven: Yale University Press, 1961); and Robert E. Agger, D. Goodrich, and E. Swanson, *The Rulers and the Ruled* (New York: John Wiley & Sons, 1964).

13. See Milton Rokeach, "A Theory of Organization and Change Within Value-Attitude Systems," *Journal of Social Issues* 24, no. 1 (1968):13–35; and Philip E.

Jacob, *Values and the Active Community: A Cross-National Study of the Influence of Local Leadership* (New York: Free Press, 1971).

14. See Elie Abel, *The Missile Crisis* (New York: Bantam Books, 1968); and Glenn D. Paige, *The Korean Decision: June 24–30, 1950* (New York: Free Press, 1968).

15. See Lewis E. Edinger, ed., *Political Leadership in Industrialized Societies* (New York: John Wiley & Sons, 1967); R. Barry Farrell, ed., *Political Leadership in Eastern Europe and the Soviet Union* (Chicago: Aldine, 1970); and John W. Lewis, ed., *Party Leadership and Revolutionary Power in China* (London and New York: Cambridge University Press, 1970).

16. Studies of the American presidency and of Chinese dynastic succession are outstanding exceptions to this.

17. M. Dean Havron and Joseph E. McGrath, "The Contribution of the Leader to the Effectiveness of Small Military Groups," in *Leadership and Interpersonal Behavior*, ed. Luigi Petrullo and Bernard M. Bass (New York: Holt, Rinehart & Winston, 1961). For another excellent conceptual discussion of dispersal versus concentration of leadership functions see Warren G. Bennis, "Post-Bureaucratic Leadership."

18. Cecil A. Gibb, "Leadership," in *Handbook of Social Psychology*, ed. Gardner Lindzey (Reading, Penna.: Addison-Wesley, 1968), p. 227.

19. For an overview of these issues consult Janda, "Towards the Explication of a Concept of Leadership Defined in Terms of the Concept of Power," pp. 345–63.

20. See Raymond B. Cattell, "A New Concept for Measuring Leadership in Terms of Group Syntality," *Human Relations* 4 (1951):161-84, and Fred E. Fiedler, *A Theory of Leadership Effectiveness* (New York: McGraw-Hill Book Co., 1967).

21. A good discussion of methodological problems is contained in Agger et al., *Rulers and the Ruled*, "Appendix A. Operational Definitions," pp. 688–759. See also Wendell Bell, Richard J. Hill, and Charles R. Wright, *Public Leadership* (San Francisco: Chandler Publishing Co., 1961); and Gibb, "Leadership," pp. 210–15.

22. Initially I am placing secondary emphasis upon other public administrators as a class on the grounds that (1) their powers are often derivative from a more basic political leadership authority, and (2) the subdiscipline and schools of public administration are giving them necessary attention. Where bureaucrats and ministers are actually more powerful than elected or revolutionary leaders, then attention may still be focused productively on the weaker roles. It may be asked why they are weak in one case but strong in another and how either may be changed.

23. A much overlooked but useful study of unsuccessful candidates for the American presidency is Irving Stone, *They Also Ran* (Garden City, N.Y.: Doubleday & Co., 1943).

24. See Theodore Lidz, *The Person: His Development Throughout the Life Cycle* (New York: Basic Books, 1968).

25. Ralph M. Stogdill, "Personal Factors Associated With Leadership: A Survey of the Literature," *Journal of Psychology* 25 (January 1948):35–71. For an excellent, much overlooked review of personality and conceptual efforts in political leadership studies, see also Elizabeth Hagen and Luverne Wolff, *Nursing Leadership Behavior in General Hospitals* (New York: Institute of Research and Service in Nursing Education, Teacher's College, Columbia University, 1961), chap. 1, "Leaders and Leadership."

26. The emphasis upon independent assessment attempts to depart from conceptions of role that are defined primarily with respect to the incumbent and in which

personality characteristics are inextricably confounded. The concept of *role*, like *personality*, is one of the most elusive concepts in the sociobehavioral sciences. Among recent contributions of great importance are: Neal C. Gross, Ward S. Mason, and Alexander W. McEachern, *Explorations in Role-Analysis* (New York: John Wiley & Sons, 1958), see especially chap. 2, "A Language for Role Analysis"; Wahlke et al., *Legislative System* and Michael P. Banton, *Roles: An Introduction to the Study of Social Relations* (London: Tavistock Publications, 1965).

27. A recent pioneering overview of organizational behavior that considers some, but not all, of these aspects is James G. March, ed., *Handbook of Organization* (Chicago: Rand McNally & Co., 1965).

28. I am not aware of any general treatise on the nature of human tasks in the sociobehavioral sciences. The burgeoning literature on problem solving and decision making is, of course, relevant. An important recent political science analysis of the leadership task requirement for aggregating power in developing countries has been presented by W. Howard Wriggins, *The Ruler's Imperative*. He cites eight of them: "Project the personality, build an organization, promote an ideology, reward the faithful and susceptible, intimidate the opponent and wavering ally, develop the economy, expand (or contract) political participation, and use foreign policy."

29. Milton Rokeach, *Beliefs, Attitudes, and Values* (San Francisco: Jossey-Bass, 1969).

30. A dramatical approach to setting might combine ideas such as those presented in Erving Goffman, *Presentation of the Self in Everyday Life* (London: Penguin Publishing Co., 1969), Roger G. Barker, *Ecological Psychology: Concepts and Methods for Studying the Environment of Behavior* (Stanford: Stanford University Press, 1968), and Christen T. Jonassen and H. Peres, *Interrelationships of Dimensions of Community Systems: A Factor Analysis of Eighty-Two Variables* (Columbus: Ohio State University Press, 1960).

31. Although many political scientists have been trained in the mutually exclusive operational differentiation of their concepts, biologists have accepted the idea of a certain degree of unavoidable overlapping of referents in their field. Behavior is in nature whole; analytical distinctions artificially fragment that wholeness. Hans Selye, *From Dream to Discovery; On Being a Scientist* (New York: McGraw-Hill Book Co., 1964).

32. James D. Barber, *The Lawmakers* (New Haven: Yale University Press, 1965).

33. James D. Barber, "Classifying and Predicting Presidential Leadership Styles: Two Weak Presidents," *Journal of Social Issues* 24, no. 3 (1968):51-80.

34. James D. Barber, *Power in Committees* (Chicago: Rand McNally & Co., 1966); and Erwin C. Hargrove, *Presidential Leadership: Personality and Political Style* (New York: The Macmillan Co., 1966).

35. Samuel J. Eldersveld, *Political Parties* (Chicago: Rand McNally & Co., 1964).

36. John C. Wahlke et al., *Legislative System*.

37. Charles L. Clapp, *The Congressman* (Washington: Brookings Institution, 1964), and Bernard M. Bass, *Leadership, Psychology, and Organizational Behavior* (New York: Harper & Row, 1960).

38. Talcott Parsons, ed., *Max Weber: The Theory of Social and Economic Organization* (Glencoe, Ill.: Free Press, 1947), especially, part 3, "The Types of Authority and Imperative Co-ordination."

39. See Richard C. Snyder, "Decision-Making, Approach to the Study of Political Phenomena," in *Approaches to the Study of Politics*, ed. Roland Young (Evanston, Ill.: Northwestern University Press, 1958), pp. 3–51.

40. David A. Easton, *A Systems Analysis of Political Life* (New York: John Wiley

& Sons, 1965). Lasswell cites eight values—"power, enlightenment, wealth, well-being, skill, affection, respect, and rectitude." Harold D. Lasswell, "A Note 'Types' of Personality: Nuclear Co-Relational, Developmental," *Journal of Social Issues* 24 (1968):83.

41. Marion J. Levy, *The Structure of Society* (Princeton, N.J.: Princeton University Press, 1952).

42. See Robert T. Holt, "A Proposed Structure-Functional Framework" in *Contemporary Political Analysis*, ed. James C. Charlesworth (New York: Free Press, 1967).

43. David B. Truman, *The Government Process* (New York: Alfred A. Knopf, 1951). Karl Marx and Frederick Engels, "The Communist Manifesto," in *Essential Works of Marxism*, ed. Arthur P. Mendel (New York: Bantam Books, 1961).

44. Karl Deutsch, *The Nerves of Government* (New York: Free Press, 1966).

45. Lewis W. Edinger, "Political Leadership and Political Biography (II)," *Journal of Politics* 26 (August 1964):653.

46. Fred W. Riggs, *Administration in Developing Countries: The Theory of Prismatic Society* (Boston: Houghton Mifflin Co., 1964).

47. A sixth category could be added—capacity for functional differentiation of institutions, for example, the differentiation of parties from fusion with monarchial, military, religious, or bureaucratic institutions.

48. Easton, *A Systems Analysis of Political Life*, p. 30.

49. Gabriel A. Almond, "A Developmental Approach to Political Systems," *World Politics* 17 (January 1965):183–214.

50. See Robert F. Bales, "Interaction Process Analysis," in *International Encyclopedia of the Social Sciences*, ed. David I. Sills (New York: The Macmillan Co., 1968), 7:465–71.

51. Amitai Etzioni, *A Comparative Analysis of Complex Organizations* (New York: Free Press, 1961).

52. Raymond B. Cattell, "New Concepts for Measuring Leadership in Terms of Group Syntality," *Human Relations* 4, no. 2 (1951):161–84.

53. One reason for this may be that they involve higher levels of abstract thought; i.e., the idea of change in a variable is logically more abstract than the idea of a steady state of that variable.

54. Gregory Bateson, *Naven* (Stanford: Stanford University Press, 1958), p. 175.

55. Joseph J. Geller, "Parataxic Distortions in the Initial Stages of Group Relationships," *International Journal of Group Psychotherapy* 12, no. 1 (January 1962):27–34.

56. Immanuel Wallerstein, *Africa: The Politics of Independence* (New York: Vintage Books, 1961), p. 99.

57. Bae-ho Hahn, "Factions in Contemporary Korean Competitive Politics" (Ph.D. diss., Princeton University, 1970), p. 262.

58. J. O. Hertzler, "The Life Cycle of Dictatorships," *Social Forces* 17 (March 1939):303–9.

59. A. F. K. Organski, *The Stages of Political Development* (New York: Alfred A. Knopf, 1965).

60. Kazuma Tateishi, Mititaka Yamamoto, and Isao Kon, "SINIC Theory—An Approach to the Future" (Paper presented at the International Future Research Conference, Kyoto, Japan, April 10–16, 1970).

61. See Neal E. Miller and John Dollard, *Social Learning and Personality Development* (New York: Holt, Rinehart & Winston, 1963).

62. As Richard C. Snyder has suggested, it may be beneficial for one science to

pursue ideas characteristic of another science at an earlier stage of its development in order to make progress rather than to concentrate solely upon borrowing directly from more advanced approaches.

63. Miller and Dollard, *Social Learning*, pp. 1-36.

64. Social learning perspectives can readily be combined with cybernetic models of a political system sketched by Karl Deutsch in *The Nerves of Government* (New York: Free Press, 1963) and with the decision-making perspective suggested by Wendell Bell and Ivan Oxaal, *Decisions of Nationhood: Political and Social Development in the British Caribbean* (Denver: The Social Science Foundation and Department of International Relations, University of Denver, monographs 3 and 4, 1963–64). Bell and Oxaal assume that new nations make such decisions as "(1) should we become a politically independent nation, (2) how much national sovereignty should the new nation have, (3) what should the geographical boundaries of the new nation be, (4) should the state and the nation be coterminous, (5) what should the form of government be, (6) what role should the government play in the affairs of the society and of the economy, (7) what type of social structure should the new nation have, (8) what should the national character of the people be, (9) what should the new nation's cultural transitions be, and (10) what should the new nation's global alignments be?"

65. It has been suggested that the accelerating rate of change in some societies may be so great that a gap of five years is sufficient to produce significantly different generational differences, at least in some aspects.

66. Suggested by Robert Jungk, "Three Modes of Futures Thinking," keynote address, International Future Research Conference, Kyoto, Japan, April 10-16, 1970.

67. Furthermore, to guard against elitist bias that may unconsciously come to pervade the scientific study of political leadership, researchers in this field may direct their attention often to the study of the most disadvantaged members of a society.

Index

Accountability, 54–56, 59–61
Adaptability, 53–54, 56, 62, 84
Adaptive role, 81–85
Administrative Council, 195, 212–14, 217
Administrative experience, xiii, 93–111, 128
Administrative role, 125–27
Affect, 246, 251–52, 254
Alienation, xiv, 135, 137–39, 142, 152, 229
Allegiance, 134–35, 137
Almond, Gabriel A., 91, 136, 138, 251
Andong Kim, 11, 20, 26
Apter, David, 41
Aristocracy, 3, 6–7, 11, 28–29
Association, 246, 251–52, 254
Auditing Committee, 161, 182–83
Autonomy, 49, 84, 234

Banfield, Edward, 118
Barber, James D., 248
Bass, Bernard M., 249
Bateson, Gregory, 254
Braibanti, Ralph, 98
Buddhism, 28, 31, 96, 117
Bureaucracy, 3, 8, 42, 47, 91–92, 102, 109, 153, 186, 189
Bureaucrat, xiv, 4, 5, 7, 9, 11, 62–63, 93, 100, 125–26, 129, 188, 228
Bureaucratic elite, 91–133, 193, 230
Bureaucratic leader, xii, 21–28, 34, 118, 120. *See also* Bureaucrat
Bylaws, 161, 182

Campbell, Angus, 138
Candidate member, 168–70, 179, 204–5
Career civil servant, 93, 103, 127, 130
Cattell, Raymond B., 254
Censorate, 4, 8–9, 17
Central Committee, xii, xiv, xv, 159–62, 164, 182, 186, 198, 204, 206, 208, 211–13, 216–18, 231

Central Intelligence Agency, 70–71, 77–78, 231
Central People's Committee, xv, 195–98, 204, 207–12, 214, 217–18
Central Procurator's Office, 197
Chang, Myǒn, 45, 230
Change, pattern of, 160, 162–86
Charisma, 159, 242, 255
Charismatic leadership, xii, 4, 6–7, 63
Chinbohoe, 23, 32
Cho, Kwang-jo, 9, 17–19
Ch'oe, Chae-u, 200, 203–4, 208, 212
Ch'oe, Che-u, 31–32
Ch'oe, Ch'ang-ik, 166, 174, 177, 180, 216
Ch'oe, Hyǒn, 166, 176, 180, 199, 202, 206, 211, 214–15, 218
Ch'oe, Ik-hyǒn, 27
Ch'oe, Kwang, 165, 181, 215
Ch'oe, Si-hyǒng, 31–32
Ch'oe, Wǒn-t'aek, 166
Ch'oe, Yong-gǒn, 162, 166, 172–73, 175–76, 180, 195–96, 199, 201–2, 205–6, 211–12, 214–15
Ch'oe, Yong-jin, 199, 202, 207, 211
Ch'ǒljong, 20
Ch'ǒndogyo, 23, 32
Chǒn, Ch'ang-ch'ǒl, 199, 202, 215
Chǒn, Pong-jun, 32
Ch'ǒn, Se-bong, 200, 203, 216
Chǒng, Chun-gi, 200, 203, 215–16
Chǒng, Chun-t'aek, 166, 180, 199, 202, 212
Chǒng, Il-yong, 166, 172, 175–76, 178, 180
Chǒng, Kyǒng-hǔi, 199, 202
Chǒng, Tu-hwan, 200, 203
Chǒng, Yǒ-rip, 30
Chǒngjo, 11, 20
Chǒngmu wǒn, 195, 212–14
Chu, Yǒng-ha, 171, 173–74, 180
Chungjong, 9
Citizen perception, 135–36
Civil liberty, xiv, 120–23, 130

267

CONTRIBUTORS

DONG-SUH BARK is Professor of Public Administration and Dean of the Graduate School of Public Administration, Seoul National University. He is President of the Korean Association of Public Administration. His major works include *Public Personnel Administration* (1971) and *Korean Public Administration* (1972).

BAE-HO HAHN is Professor of Political Science and Head of Japan Study Division of Asiatic Research Center, Korea University. His major works include *Theoretical Political Science* (1965) and *Comparative Politics* (1971).

SUNG-CHICK HONG is Professor of Sociology and Chairman of the Department of Sociology, Korea University. He is Head of Social Survey Research Division of Asiatic Research Center, Korea University. He is the author of *The Intellectual and Modernization* (1967) and *A Study of Korean Values* (1969).

CHONG LIM KIM is Associate Professor of Political Science and Associate Director of the Comparative Legislative Research Center at the University of Iowa. He is a co-author of *Patterns of Recruitment* (forthcoming). His articles have appeared in the *American Political Science Review, Comparative Politics,* and other scholarly journals.

HA-RYONG KIM is Professor of Political Science, Chairman of the Department of Political Science, and Head of Communist Bloc Studies Division of Asiatic Research Center, Korea University. He is a contributor of articles to *Journal of Asiatic Studies, Social Science Research Review,* and other scholarly journals.

CHAE-JIN LEE is Associate Professor of Political Science and member of the East Asian Studies Center at the University of Kansas. He has published a number of articles in *Midwest Journal of Political Science, Asian Survey,* and other scholarly journals.

CHONG-SIK LEE is Professor of Political Science at the University of Pennsylvania. He is Chairman of the SSRC-ACLS Joint Committee on Korean Studies. He is the author of *The Politics of Korean Nationalism* (California, 1963), and co-author of *Communism in Korea* (California, 1972).

YOUNG HO LEE is Director of the Policy Research Institute, Seoul. Dr. Lee has contributed articles to *Midwest Journal of Political Science, Journal of Comparative Administration,* and other scholarly journals.

GLENN D. PAIGE is Professor of Political Science and member of the Social Science Research Institute at the University of Hawaii. He is the author of *The Korean Decision* (Free Press, 1968) and editor of *Political Leadership* (Free Press, 1972).

JAMES B. PALAIS is Associate Professor of History and a member of the Institute for Comparative and Foreign Area Studies at the University of Washington. He is the author of *Policy and Politics in Traditional Korea, 1864-76* (forthcoming) and articles in *Journal of Asian Studies* and other scholarly journals.

DAE-SOOK SUH is Professor of Political Science and Director of the Center for Korean Studies at the University of Hawaii. He is the author of *The Korean Communist Movement, 1918-48* (Princeton, 1967) and *Documents of Korean Communism* (Princeton, 1970).

BYUNG-KYU WOO is Senior Staff member of the National Assembly, Republic of Korea, and Lecturer of Political Science at Chungang University. His articles appear in *Midwest Journal of Political Science, Asian Survey,* and other scholarly journals.

PUBLICATIONS ON ASIA OF THE INSTITUTE
FOR COMPARATIVE AND FOREIGN AREA STUDIES

1. Compton, Boyd (trans. and ed.). *Mao's China: Party Reform Documents, 1942–44.* 1952. Reissued 1966. Washington Paperback-4, 1966. 330 pp., map.
2. Chiang, Siang-tseh. *The Nien Rebellion.* 1954. 177 pp., bibiliog., index, maps.
3. Chang, Chung-li. *The Chinese Gentry: Studies on Their Role in Nineteenth-Century Chinese Society.* Introduction by Franz Michael. 1955. Reiussed 1967. Washington Paperback on Russia and Asia-4. 277 pp., bibliog., index, tables.
4. *Guide to the Memorials of Seven Leading Officials of Nineteenth-Century China.* Summaries and indexes of memorials to Hu Lin-i, Tseng Kuo-fan, Tso Tsung-tang, Kuo Sung-tao, Tseng Kuo-ch'üan, Li Hung-chang, Chang Chih-tung, 1955. 457 pp., mimeographed. Out of print.
5. Raeff, Marc. *Siberia and the Reforms of 1822.* 1956. 228 pp., maps, bibliog., index. Out of print.
6. Li Chi. *The Beginnings of Chinese Civilization: Three Lectures Illustrated with Finds at Anyang.* 1957. Reissued 1968. Washington Paperback on Russia and Asia-6. 141 pp., illus., bibliog., index.
7. Carrasco, Pedro. *Land and Polity in Tibet.* 1959. 318 pp., maps, bibliog., index.
8. Hsiao, Kung-chuan. *Rural China: Imperial Control in the Nineteenth Century.* 1960. Reissued 1967. Washington Paperback on Russia and Asia-3. 797 pp., illus., bibliog., index.
9. Hsiao, Tso-liang. *Power Relations within the Chinese Communist Movement, 1930–34.* Vol. I: *A Study of Documents.* 1961. 416 pp., bibliog., index, glossary. Vol. II: *The Chinese Documents.* 1967. 856 pp.
10. Chang, Chung-li. *The Income of the Chinese Gentry.* Introduction by Franz Michael. 1962. 387 pp., tables, bibliog., index.
11. Maki, John M. *Court and Constitution in Japan: Selected Supreme Court Decisions, 1948–60.* 1964. 491 pp., bibliog., index.
12. Poppe, Nicholas, Leon Hurvitz, and Hidehiro Okada. *Catalogue of the Manchu-Mongol Section of the Toyo Bunko.* 1964. 391 pp., index.
13. Spector, Stanley. *Li Hung-chang and the Huai Army: A Study in Nineteenth-Century Chinese Regionalism.* Introduction by Franz Michael. 1964. 399 pp., maps, tables, bibliog., glossary, index.
14. Michael, Franz and Chung-li Chang. *The Taiping Rebellion: History and Documents.* Vol. I: *History.* 1966. 256 pp., maps, index. Vols. II and III: *Documents and Comments.* 1971. 756, 1,107 pp.
15. Shih, Vincent Y. C. *The Taiping Ideology: Its Sources, Interpretations, and Influences.* 1967. 576 pp., bibliog., index.
16. Poppe, Nicholas. *The Twelve Deeds of Buddha: A Mongolian Version of the Lalitavistara; Mongolian Text, Notes, and English Translation.* 1967. 241 pp., illus. Paper.
17. Hsia, Tsi-an. *The Gate of Darkness: Studies on the Leftist Literary Movement in China.* Preface by Franz Michael. Introduction by C. T. Hsia. 1968. 298 pp., index.
18. Hsiao, Tso-liang. *The Land Revolution in China, 1930-1934: A Study of Documents.* 1969. 374 pp., tables, glossary, bibliog., index.

19. Gasster, Michael. *Chinese Intellectuals and the Revolution of 1911: The Birth of Modern Chinese Radicalism.* 1969. 320 pp., glossary, bibliog., index.
20. Thornton, Richard C. *The Comintern and the Chinese Communists, 1928-31.* 1969. 266 pp., index.
21. Lin, Julia C. *Modern Chinese Poetry: An Introduction.* 1972. 278 pp.
22. Huang, Philip C. *Liang Ch'i-ch'ao and Modern Chinese Liberalism.* 1972. 200 pp., illus., index.
23. Gerow, Edwin and Margery Lang, eds. *Studies in the Language and Culture of South Asia.* 1974. 174 pp.
24. Morrison, Barrie M. *Lalmai, A Cultural Center of Early Bengal.* 1974. 190 pp., maps, drawings, tables.
25. Hsiao, Kung-chuan. *A Modern China and a New World. K'ang Yu-Wei, Reformer and Utopian, 1858-1927.* 1975. 669 pp., transliteration table, bibliog., index.
26. Ryan, Marleigh Grayer. *The Development of Realism in the Fiction of Tsubouchi Shōyō.* 1975. 133 pp., index.
27. Suh, Dae-Sook and Chae-Jin Lee, eds. *Political Leadership in Korea.* 1975. Tables, figures, index.